WHAT YOUR COLLEAGUES ARE SAYING . . .

"*Essential Connection Skills* is a practical, specific, inspirational, and must-have resource for any teacher, coach, school leader, or parent who aims for a more empowered and successful student."

Julie O'Connell Alholm, Instructional Coach and EL Teacher, IL

"*Essential Connections, K–6* is a call to action. In this crucial resource for educators, Paonessa and Zwiers identify the greatest challenge facing our schools today—the loss of connection and community—and provide an effective and intuitive framework to address it. By leveraging the power of schools to help students develop meaningful connections (to themselves, to others, to their community, to their own learning, and to other learners), students will develop the skills they need to navigate school and realize the basic promise of education: to be fully engaged as members of an interconnected society. This, very simply, is the right book at the right time."

Doug Bolton, Educator, Clinical Psychologist, Author of *Untethered: Creating Connected Families, Schools, and Communities to Raise a Resilient Generation*

"*Essential Connection Skills, K–6* is a powerful and insightful guide for educators seeking to transform their classrooms. With a focus on fostering meaningful conversations, this book highlights the profound impact of teaching students how to connect with each other and themselves. By cultivating these essential relationships, teachers can unlock a deeper level of engagement and learning, making this a must-read for anyone dedicated to creating a more inclusive and interactive elementary learning environment and helping students be successful in life outside of the classroom."

Gina Greenwald, Principal, Hoover-Wood Elementary School, Batavia, IL

"Anne Paonessa and Jeff Zwiers make a compelling case for academic and social-emotional learning to be integrated every day, in every content area, and in every possible way. This must-read book creates a roadmap for building much-needed connections to ensure that SEL is not merely a designated period but an integral daily practice. I urge all K–6 educators to explore this volume, which is rich in practical references and jampacked with lots of carefully crafted, ready-to-implement lesson ideas."

Andrea Honigsfeld, Professor, Molloy University, NY

"The goal of *Essential Connection Skills, K–6* is to foster student success. It is a well-crafted resource for all educators and partners. It provides educators with the skills needed to empower their students and give them the tools required to be lifelong learners and critical thinkers."

Eileen Matos, K–3 Bilingual and K–12 EL Educator, IL

"*Essential Connection Skills, K–6* is an invaluable resource for educators navigating the challenges of reintegrating social connections into the learning environment after the pandemic. With practical strategies and real-world examples, this book provides effective ways to foster collaboration, empathy, and community, making instruction more engaging and responsive for students in today's world."

Melissa Payne, Former Elementary School Principal, IL

"*Essential Connection Skills, K–6* is a must-read for any teacher—whether you're already focused on social skills or looking to include them more in your teaching. The suggestions in each chapter are practical for novice to veteran teachers."

Amber Quirk, Regional Superintendent,
DuPage County Regional Office of Education, IL

"This is an inspiring and timely book that reminds us of the power of human connection. It offers practical tools and illustrates how teaching SEL competencies in schools transforms students' lives, fostering social emotional intelligence, resilience, and empathy."

Ellen Swanson, PhD, Associate Director of Strategic Initiatives,
CAREI (Center for Applied Research and Educational Improvement),
University of Minnesota, Twin Cities

"*Essential Connection Skills, K–6* is a game changer for new or veteran educators. As technology becomes more present in our classrooms, we are forgetting that early learning is a social endeavor. When students have the confidence and skills necessary to interact with one another in a supportive learning community, academic gains will follow. This book clearly presents the research explaining why connection skills are so important and provides ready-to-use activities, tips, and tricks to build those skills in students."

Kevin Skomer, EdD, Retired Elementary Principal, IL

"This book reminds us of an important truth—when we intentionally teach connection skills, we don't just improve classroom culture; we prepare students for life. Paonessa and Zwiers offer a roadmap for educators to help students develop social and emotional competencies while excelling academically. *Essential Connection Skills, K–6* equips educators with practical strategies that can be applied across all content areas."

Todd Whitaker, Professor/Educational Consultant,
University of Missouri

Essential Connection Skills, K–6

Essential Connection Skills, K–6

First Edition

Strategies for Integrating Social Connections Into Core Content

Anne Paonessa
Jeff Zwiers

CORWIN

FOR INFORMATION:

Corwin
A SAGE Company
2455 Teller Road
Thousand Oaks, California 91320
(800) 233-9936
www.corwin.com

SAGE Publications Ltd.
1 Oliver's Yard
55 City Road
London EC1Y 1SP
United Kingdom

SAGE Publications India Pvt. Ltd.
Unit No 323-333, Third Floor, F-Block
International Trade Tower Nehru Place
New Delhi 110 019
India

SAGE Publications Asia-Pacific Pte. Ltd.
18 Cross Street #10-10/11/12
China Square Central
Singapore 048423

Vice President and Editorial Director: Monica Eckman
Senior Publisher: Jessica Allan
Senior Content Development Editor: Lucas Schleicher
Associate Content Development Editor: Mia Rodriguez
Senior Editorial Assistant: Natalie Delpino
Production Editor: Nicole Burns-Ascue
Copy Editor: Shannon Kelly
Typesetter: C&M Digitals (P) Ltd.
Proofreader: Sarah J. Duffy
Cover Designer: Rose Storey
Marketing Manager: Olivia Bartlett

Printed and bound by CPI Group (UK) Ltd, Croydon, CR0 4YY

ISBN 978-1-0719-6182-7

This book is printed on acid-free paper.

26 27 28 29 30 10 9 8 7 6 5 4 3 2 1

Contents

Acknowledgments

I am thankful to the countless students I have had the privilege of teaching! You have inspired me with your questions, insights, and the learning we have shared together along the way. This book would not be possible without you!

I am also grateful to those teachers who took the time to connect with us as students; they got to know us as individuals, helped us find our strengths, and held a genuine belief that we could learn and succeed.

And, my sincere appreciation for the support from my family and friends while writing this book; those that read for feedback or early reviews, my daughter Lauren for her encouragement, and my husband Sean who would optimistically ask, “What are we doing this weekend?” just in case I would say something other than, “I am working on the book.”

This world is filled with so many remarkable people- and you must be one of them since you are here reading this book! I hope it inspires some new ideas, sparks conversations, and helps you to create and share meaningful connections!

PUBLISHER’S ACKNOWLEDGMENTS

Corwin gratefully acknowledges the contributions of the following reviewers:

Jennifer French
Elementary School Principal
Clark County School District
Las Vegas, Nevada

Katie Grisham
Professional Learning Coach
Jeffco Public Schools
Golden, Colorado

Shari Taylor
Assistant Principal
Alpine School District
Lehi, Utah

About the Authors

Dr. Anne Paonessa holds a PhD in curriculum and instruction leadership. She is currently an assistant superintendent and a speaker/consultant. She has served as both an elementary and middle school principal/teacher. She also served as a director of multilingual learners in pre-K through high school. Dr. Paonessa has designed and taught graduate-level college courses related to innovation within instruction and meeting the needs of culturally and linguistically diverse learners. Her research focus is enhancing instructional outcomes through the integration of social structures.

Dr. Jeff Zwiers was previously a senior researcher in the Stanford University Graduate School of Education and is now an educational consultant. He has taught all subjects bilingually in secondary and elementary settings. His research and work focus on collaborating with teachers to enhance instruction and assessment for multilingual students, with an emphasis on improving student–student interactions. Jeff has also written books and articles on literacy, conversation, and language development, along with children's books and curriculums.

Introduction

Essential Connections Within Instruction

As a district-level administrator/consultant (Anne) and a provider of professional development (Jeff), we understand the pressure that today's teachers are experiencing. Teachers are working hard to address behavioral disruptions, tailor their instruction to accommodate a diverse range of skill levels, help students catch up on missed lessons due to increased absences, and effectively respond to the current English language development levels of their multilingual students. Many districts have adopted web-based adaptive programs for math and literacy. These programs are followed by small-group instruction and independent practice to help bridge students' learning gaps. However, despite these efforts, academic progress can be slow, leaving our teachers feeling overwhelmed as they strive to juggle multiple demands while also teaching grade-level content. This overall sense of pressure often trickles down to our students as well.

With the best of intentions, we have swung the pendulum too far toward singularly focusing on computerized and small-group, teacher-led instruction. While this approach certainly holds value and is necessary in teaching today, we must strive for a balance by incorporating well-planned and purposeful social interactions within our classrooms. It is important to recognize that not all students are motivated solely by earning stickers or advancing in computer-generated lessons. Many students continue to lack the skills and confidence to effectively collaborate with others in social and academic settings. Even though we have returned to in-person instruction, many of our classrooms are missing out on the joy of being together, forming connections, and learning through meaningful interactions with one another!

WHAT ARE WE STILL MISSING?

Outside of our schools and classrooms, a general decline has also occurred in spoken conversation, which directly impacts our students. At a restaurant, it is common to see a family with parents on their phones and children of all ages on either phones or tablets. This phenomenon of being physically present with others but having devices potentially disrupting interactions and conversations is known as *technoference* (McDaniel & Radesky, 2018). While some families have successfully managed to limit screen times and set aside time for family conversations, there are countless others who spend less time engaged in speaking with each other. The general decrease in face-to-face interactions often results in students who have difficulty engaging in conversations with their peers and teachers within our classrooms.

During remote or hybrid instruction, students missed out on having social interactions during key developmental stages in school. As a result, many of today's students are lacking in social skills and struggle to initiate and sustain conversations with others, including their peers. The reduced opportunities for socialization have left an impact on many learners. This includes not learning social cues or being able to read body language, or not acquiring both the skills and confidence needed to engage in sustained conversations. The impact from the downturn in communication and in-person social interactions already present before the pandemic became amplified during the sustained periods of isolation and continues to be an issue.

As a result, many of our students have varying levels of social anxiety. According to the National Institutes of Health (Fortuna et al., 2023), about 20 percent of eighty thousand youths surveyed across the globe have experienced increased anxiety. Some students struggle to identify their own emotions after missing out on in-person learning, making emotional regulation more challenging. When asked to cue into their own emotions, many students are lacking in the ability to pick up on and then label their feelings. They also struggle to read the emotions or responses of others, which provides additional obstacles to sustaining positive interactions. With reduced social exposure, some students may find it challenging to recognize and understand the perspectives of others or even to imagine themselves in another person's shoes and feel empathy for them.

Students today not only are limited in engaging in direct conversations but also have reduced experience in navigating group dynamics. This includes developing skills for effective collaboration and managing conflicts by finding common ground, learning how to compromise, or creating a new solution with others. Some of the other symptoms of social anxiety include being worried about being embarrassed in front of others, fear of offending someone, and fear of being judged by others. With our well-intended focus on filling in the academic achievement gaps through the use of devices and small-group instruction directed by the teacher, we are failing to address important life skills and competencies our students need to build the social capital necessary to be successful in life.

IT SOUNDS LIKE WE SHOULD PRIORITIZE SOCIAL-EMOTIONAL LEARNING CLASSES!

Well, not so fast. Let's put it this way, if you had never played tennis before but you had a stand-alone lesson every week where the teacher taught you one tennis skill and then you talked about it as a class or with a partner, do you think you would internalize it and start to "know" tennis? Maybe when you actually had the chance to pick up a racquet and try to hit a ball, you would remember some of what was taught and do somewhat better than you would have without the text-based tennis class. Or maybe there would be a disconnect from what you had heard and discussed in the class and the moment when you actually try to apply that knowledge.

We acknowledge that our tennis analogy has limitations, but research shows that stand-alone social-emotional learning (SEL) classes have limitations in their effectiveness and lasting impact for students (Taylor et al., 2017). Integrating SEL instruction into core classroom instruction has several advantages, including the opportunity for students to apply what they have learned. Through integration within academic content, there is consistency and continuity toward developing core competencies. Modeling of skills by core-content teachers and the intentional and explicit integration of social-emotional skills in meaningful ways also help to create closer student–teacher relationships and helps to create classrooms where all students feel accepted, valued, seen, and heard.

BUT WAIT, THERE'S MORE!

When we started this conversation, we were focusing on the need to help our students achieve better academic outcomes and make up for any academic ground that was lost through interrupted learning. If we do add in these social-emotional skills during our instruction, won't we be losing valuable instructional time? There is only so much time in the school day, and many students are already so far behind. If we take time away from our core instruction to add in lessons on social skills, they will never catch up academically, right? Wait for it . . .

Research shows us that by integrating SEL instruction centered around essential connection skills (ECS) into our core instruction, we can improve our students' academic outcomes (Durlak et al., 2011). Please go back and read that last sentence one more time—it's that good! Not only will you be helping your students to develop important life skills and develop key competencies but also time spent building these skills into your core instruction will positively impact their academic learning. By focusing on the development of ECS, you are providing a pathway for equity ensuring that all voices are included, valued, and accepted. This is the power of an integrated learning approach.

When there is a holistic approach to teaching and layering social and emotional skills and competencies within core instruction, it leads to improved student engagement. Students tend to take on more ownership of their learning and better understand the value of what they are learning. It also creates an improved classroom setting where students develop empathy and an understanding of others within a community of learners, which creates a safe place for students to take risks in their learning.

Many of the tasks that students engage in also require higher-order thinking, problem-solving, and collaboration to achieve a shared outcome. All of this requires a deeper interaction with the content, which results in a better understanding and improved retention of the learning standards. For this to happen, students are required to communicate effectively with each other in meaningful ways and to navigate a range of social interactions. They are growing their academic knowledge and understanding while also building their interpersonal skills.

Including this focus within your instruction also helps students to become more aware of their emotions and how they respond to them. Students see how their words and actions impact others, which results in fewer distractions within the learning environment. Students working together, learning academic content while acquiring social and emotional skills, provides an enhanced experience that results in improved academic outcomes and nurtures students' overall well-being. Our students need far more from us than a narrow focus on improving their scores on standardized assessments.

This book is a call to action! It is time that we swing the pendulum back from the majority of the school day being spent on individual and small-group or computerized instruction to including the use of strategies that intentionally have our students working together. While using data is one important aspect of effective instruction, this needs to be balanced with providing integrated learning opportunities. Our students benefit from time to learn together. Opportunities to practice and strengthen the important skills that will prepare them to be successful across settings and circumstances as they go through life should also be a top priority in our schools.

I'M READY TO TRY IT, BUT HOW DO I EVEN BEGIN TO GET STARTED?

You're in the right place! This book will provide you with an overview of the foundational skills needed by students along with practical strategies to enhance your core instruction. The book is built around four key domains of ECS: connections to self, connections to others, connections to learning, and connections to community. Within each domain, there are four key areas essential for students to develop the skills and competencies necessary for successful connections in that domain.

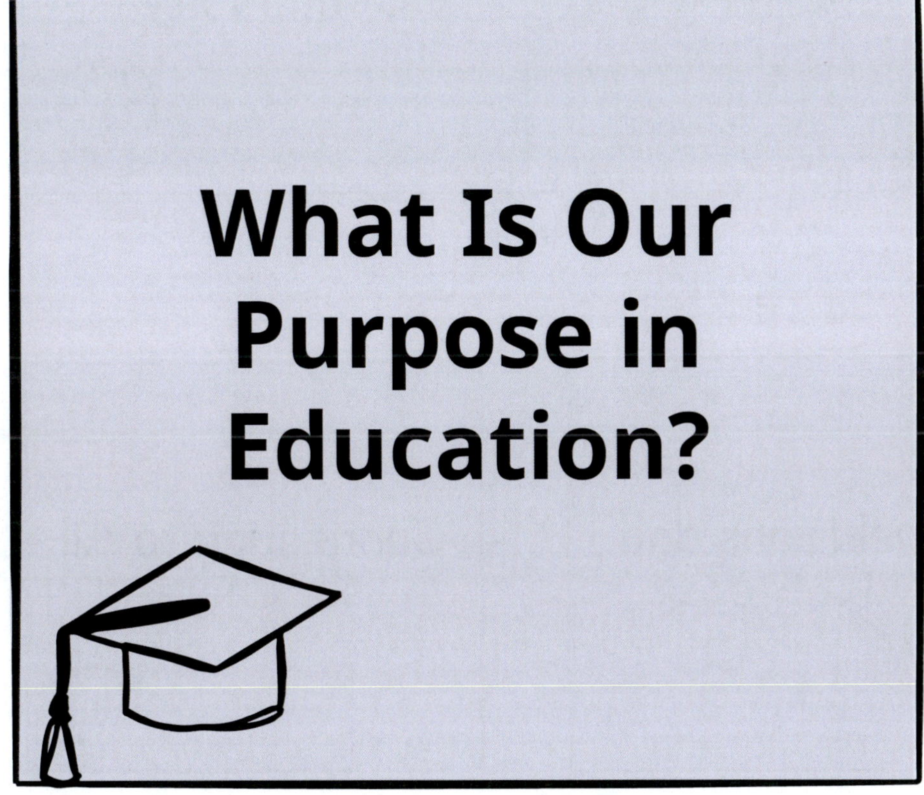

Essential Connection Skills

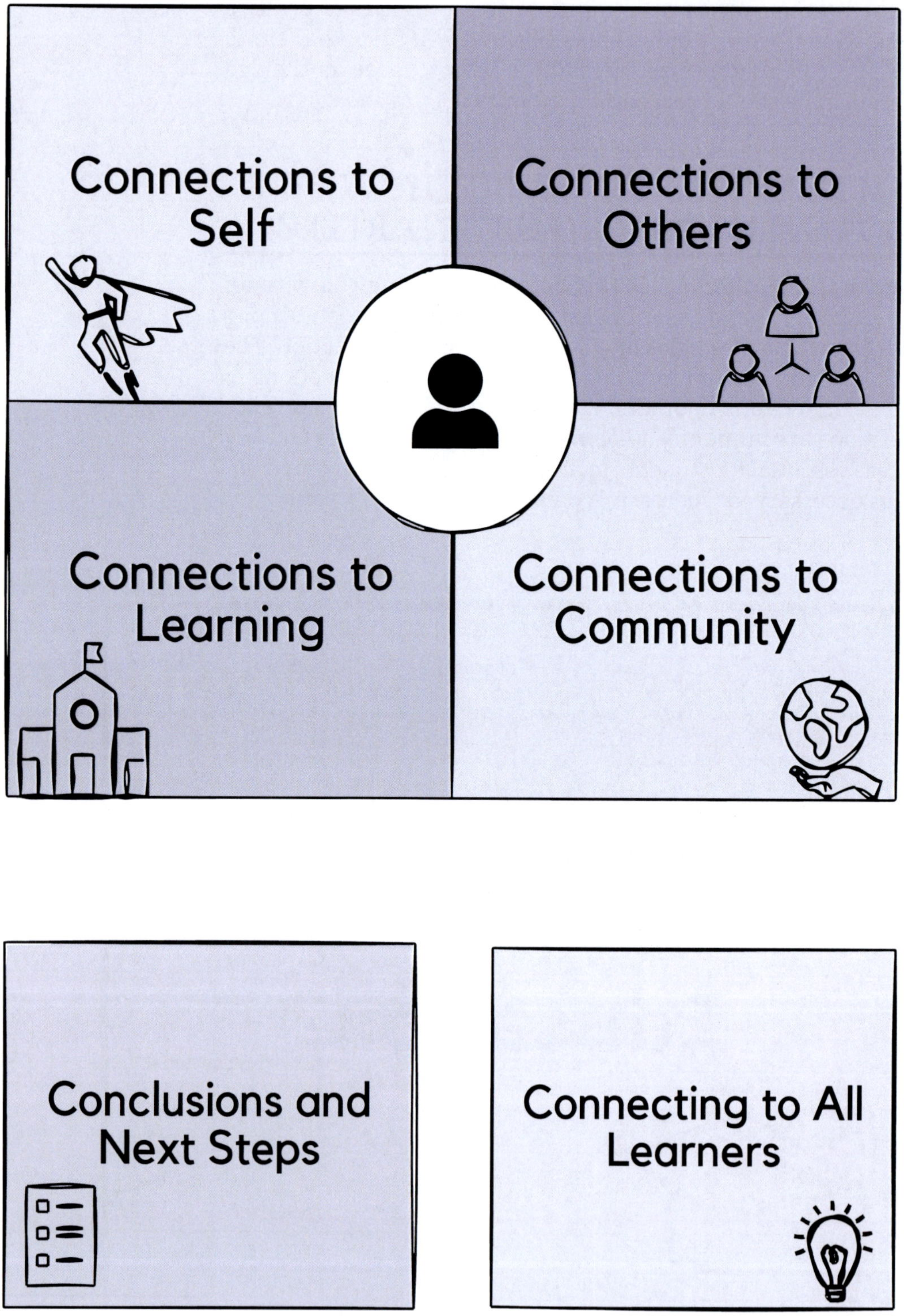

Connections to Self

Connections to Others

Connections to Learning

Connections to Community

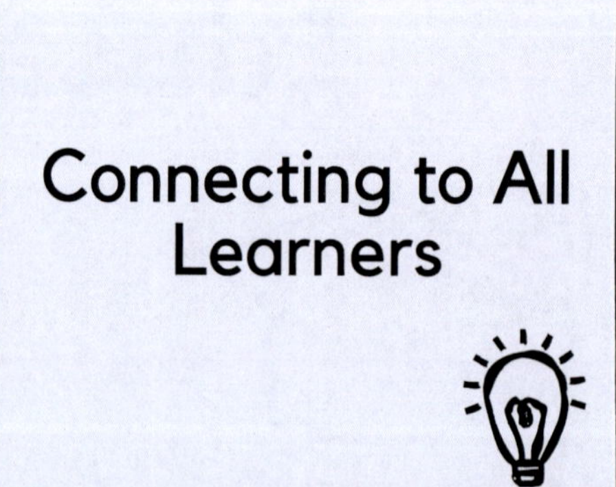

AN OVERVIEW OF THE BOOK

The content of this book is focused on supporting teachers of kindergarten through sixth grade in enhancing their instruction through the addition of ECS. A chapter is dedicated to each of the four connection domains. You will find an explanation of those components necessary for a student to be successful within each connection area. It will include the *what*, the *why*, and the the all-important *how*. You will also find examples of strategies that teachers have tried with their students and additional methods that you can use to help your students build these connection skills within your content. The goal is to help provide you with the information you need so that you can start to visualize how you can build ECS opportunities within your own instruction. While many of the techniques are to be directly layered into your existing instruction, you will also find some minilessons that will set the foundation for the ECS strategies and promote the development of these important life skills.

Chapter 1, "What Is Our Purpose in Education?," provides you with information and reflection concerning trends we're observing in today's classrooms. Chapter 2, "Connections to Self," focuses on connections that are needed to help students develop a growth mindset, to see themselves as capable learners, to celebrate their strengths, and to have an appreciation of self that lays the foundation for positive interaction with others. Chapter 3, "Connections to Others," centers around connections where students have multiple opportunities to become effective communicators and collaborators, all while learning with and from each other, their teachers, and the community. Chapter 4, "Connections to Learning," highlights connections where students gain competencies that will fuel their interest in learning, increase engagement in content, and help them to take on a larger role in their own education. Chapter 5, "Connections to Community," involves connections where there is a focus on belonging, inclusivity, and developing agency.

In Chapter 6, "Connecting to All Learners," you are provided with tools and strategies to make adaptations or use additional strategies to reach a wide range of students, including culturally and linguistically diverse students, those who are shy or hesitant to participate, those who are natural leaders, and those with learning differences. Chapter 7, "Conclusion and Next Steps," provides information to help you balance your educational approach and better meet the needs of your students and also supplies useful resources. Now let's get started!

What Is Our Purpose in Education?

CHAPTER 1

> ***"Educating the mind without educating the heart is no education at all."***
>
> **—Aristotle**

WHAT IS THE PURPOSE OF EDUCATION?

When you think about that question, what is the first answer that comes to your mind? We are guessing that most of you didn't answer, "To help prepare students to get amazing scores on standardized assessments" or "Making sure that students are prepared to do well on any tests that may come their way in the future." We couldn't agree more. However, if you look at how our education system is set up, the vast majority of our time, energy, and focus is spent on just that—helping our students make gains on that next benchmark assessment or standardized test.

While we can all recognize the need for accountability and some measures to ensure that all students are receiving a quality education, we should also be able to see that the ability to do well on these tests will only go so far toward our students' futures. Right now there is more pressure than ever to make those academic gains. This tension to produce better scores is being felt by students, teachers, and administrators. But if you think back to how you answered the question about the purpose of education, or to the reason you decided to go into education in the first place, it most likely goes far beyond scores and extends past academic gains. The vast majority of educators go into the field to make a difference in the lives of their students.

This motivation to become an educator typically centers on the desire to cultivate both the minds and the hearts of students. As John F. Kennedy said back in 1963, "Children are the world's most valuable resource and its best hope for the future" (Kennedy, 1963). What type of future will we have if we maintain our current path of narrowly focusing most of our time and attention on only the minds of our students? Is that a smart investment in our collective future? Academic test scores are only one factor within education. We are calling for a shift from a test-centric education to an approach that takes into account both the mind and the heart. Our collective purpose includes teaching our students to succeed beyond tests—to provide them with an education that allows them to reach their full human potential. This includes a vast array of skills and competencies that never show up on a test.

Nancy Astor (2018) once stated, "Real education should educate us out of self into something far finer; into a selflessness which links us with all humanity" (p. 75). Education that provides for both the mind and the heart has the potential to help every student have the skills and confidence they need to successfully navigate their way through life and also to develop the critical thinking skills, interpersonal skills, and compassion that will empower them to make a difference in the world. In order to create a society where each person is valued for who they are, where everyone has equal rights and opportunities, we need to stop and reflect on the educational experience we are providing. Having solid test scores does not equate to an individual who can communicate effectively, who is open to taking on and valuing the perspectives of others, and who is ready to act on their beliefs.

WHAT IS INTEGRATED LEARNING?

The quote at the start of this chapter, which is attributed to the Greek philosopher Aristotle, captures the essence of integrated learning. His words speak to the importance of education in developing an individual's intellectual and physical well-being along with developing their character. It highlights the importance of not only growing one's academic knowledge but also the need to balance this with a holistic education that nurtures the development of ethics, empathy, resilience, and overall well-being. Integrated learning provides intellectual instruction combined with personal development. This approach to education is what is needed to prepare our students to be successful in both school and life.

Learning that is one-dimensional and only addresses the requirement to learn grade-level academic content does not comprehensively give our students what they need. An integrated learning approach works to develop both the mind and the heart, helping students to become well-rounded individuals who are prepared to thrive in an ever-changing world, to make thoughtful decisions, and to communicate effectively for a range of purposes. This level of integration also prepares our students to consider others in the world with acceptance and empathy. It builds the confidence and skills our students will need in order to take action, to become advocates for themselves and others, and to help lead the changes necessary to improve the world around us.

Research shows us that providing integrated learning, which simultaneously addresses both intellectual and personal dimensions of a student's growth, has several advantages. According to Kaspar and Massey (2022), those students who were provided integrated learning had higher levels of academic achievement, greater levels of emotional intelligence (EQ), and better interpersonal skills than their peers who experienced traditional curriculum. This built on the earlier study of Schaps et al. (2001), who also found that those students who were provided integrated learning showed notable gains on standardized achievement tests, had fewer attendance concerns, and exhibited improved behavior in the classroom as compared to control groups.

Additional studies reveal the overall improved outcomes for students when their personal development is layered into content instruction. A study by Shoshani and Steinmetz (2013) showed that students provided with this integrated approach to learning had better academic growth and better interpersonal skills and overall emotional well-being than those peers in a control group. An article by Langreo (2023), specific to integrated learning within math and coding, showed that students with an integrated approach had greater achievement in math content and also developed higher levels of perseverance, self-efficacy, and growth mindset than those who were taught with a more standard approach.

WHAT ARE ESSENTIAL CONNECTION SKILLS?

The foundational skills to be integrated into core content instruction in order to educate both the mind and the heart have been grouped into four key domains of essential connection skills (ECS): connections to self, connections to others, connections to learning, and connections to community. Each of the domains includes four key areas for teachers to focus on with their students. Helping students to grow in these skills and competencies will help them to develop ECS in each domain. The strategies provided within each chapter of this book will help you to plan content lessons with integrated learning opportunities. Your students will benefit in so many ways, including increased engagement in academic content, improved academic learning outcomes through opportunities to reflect and set goals, opportunities for collaboration to complete authentic tasks, increased frequency and quality of communication within the classroom, and discovering more relevance in their learning.

- Self-Awareness
- Self-Reflection
- Resilience
- Cultural Competence

Connections to Others

- Communication Skills
- Teamwork
- Problem-Solving
- Responsibility

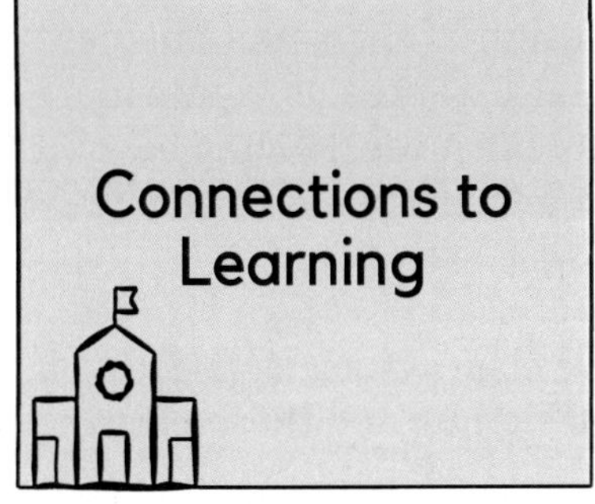

- Curiosity and Inquiry
- Perseverance
- Goal Setting
- Relevant Learning

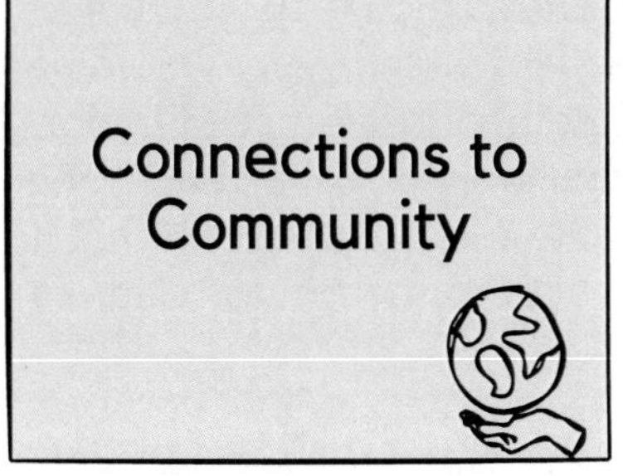

- Belonging
- Advocacy
- Global Community
- Social Responsibility

LET'S TAKE A MOMENT TO TRAVEL BACK IN TIME

Think back to your own time in school. What are some of your happiest memories? Few of you probably thought back to a time when you got a "Great job!" at the top of a worksheet or when you worked by yourself on a computer program and completed an advanced level. For most of us, those best memories from school center around a favorite teacher who inspired you to try your best, or a special project completed with your friends. Some of us remember being involved in a project that reached into our community and made a positive difference in the lives of others.

One of the memories that comes to mind for me (Anne) took place in junior high. Mrs. Watts shared that she would be placing us into groups to form our own companies. This was a huge departure from the typical round-robin reading of our social studies book followed by note taking, quizzes, and an end-of-unit test. We suddenly found ourselves running our own cookie businesses. We were so focused on the task at hand and excited for the opportunity to work together that we were not aware of the many additional layers of learning and skills being developed through this project. At the time, I did not understand the intentional planning behind the design of the small business project. Looking back, Mrs. Watts clearly wanted us to gain more than a basic understanding of small business. Moving beyond the typical read, discuss, and quiz model helped us to gain real-life skills and competencies.

We were working together with our classmates, negotiating a wide range of decisions including designing and then selecting a logo, scripting a commercial to be broadcast over the intercom, and using math to determine our product costs and how much we would need to charge for our cookies to make a profit. We made the cookies, sold them to other students and teachers at lunch, and then donated our profits to a charity. There was a bit of friendly competition to see which company would be the most profitable. I can easily remember the sense of importance I felt at the time, knowing that we would be generating actual profits that would be donated to a local cause. Not that it matters, but I am pleased to report that Granny Annie's Chunky Chippies took the lead.

What I wasn't aware of at the time were the skills I was developing. During this project we were forced out of our comfort zones with the need to interact with others we typically didn't speak to. I gained insights from those classmates and learned from their perspectives. We also needed to navigate dividing and assigning tasks and then bringing them back to the full team to complete the project. While quite a few years have passed, I can easily remember having to explain my ideas to the others in our company in different ways until I had clarified and supported my thinking for them. I also remember feeling genuinely excited when someone shared an idea that I would have never thought of to make our approach even better. Initially I was nervous about the idea of speaking over the intercom for everyone to hear, but I felt more comfortable knowing that I would be doing it with others on the team. Once we were done with our live on-air commercial, I found that I had enjoyed it and my confidence grew.

Fast-forward to fifteen years later when I experienced opening an actual small business. I owned and operated a martial arts school for over twelve years. It was such a rewarding and, at times, challenging experience. I had taught first grade, stayed home with my own children, and then decided to stay involved in education in a different form by teaching martial arts. Looking back, I know that the brief experience my teacher provided us in junior high planted the seed that owning and running a business was not out of the realm of possibility. I went from speaking over the intercom to sharing information in several live segments on the Chicago area news. Actually "experiencing" a small business with my classmates had a lasting impact on me, far more than reading a chapter in a textbook. I eventually sold that martial arts school and returned to the traditional classroom, bringing with me several lessons that I learned through my time as a small business owner.

Based on my own experiences and seeing the needs of my students, I taught in a similar way to Mrs. Watts. As a teacher at the elementary and middle school levels, it was always a priority to use integrated learning experiences that would increase engagement, promote the development of social skills, strengthen communication, and be centered around a shared purpose. These strategies were focused on learning academic standards while developing social-emotional learning (SEL) competencies, all while having fun! When I think back to other teachers and my overall schooling experience, I have the strongest memories of the integrated learning experiences provided by those special teachers, and I can recall how they made me feel as a learner. The experiences with those teachers were far different than those with teachers who relied only on teaching through a workbook.

During my own research in this area, which included interviewing former students twelve years after I had been their teacher, the lasting benefits of providing integrated instruction came through loud and clear (Paonessa, 2023). Over a decade after having these opportunities, the students spoke about the motivation they felt and how they remembered putting far more effort into integrated learning projects than they did in other classes that relied solely on traditional instruction. The former students shared that they gained confidence in both their learning and their ability to interact with a wide range of people through the ECS-driven projects. For those students identified as culturally and linguistically diverse learners, these experiences provided meaningful reasons to use English while being focused on completing a task rather than being focused on language demands.

The former students also spoke directly about the learning community we were able to form through getting to know each other better as individuals as we navigated the projects together. Many shared that they felt supported and that they internalized the belief they were capable as learners through successfully navigating work together. Several of the former students that were interviewed also shared that these learning experiences had a direct impact on who they are today. If we pause to think about the experience of today's students, some are missing out on these shared learning experiences that are shown to not only improve their academic outcomes but also help them to grow in ways that will stay with them long after their time with us.

As students in our classrooms now sit and work on their computers and participate in small- or whole-group instruction with the occasional turn-and-talk thrown in, they are missing out on the potential of developing ECS. Many are silently comparing themselves to their peers to try to determine their own ability level. Most of us can easily remember figuring out pretty quickly that you had arrived if you were able to become a part of the Blue Birds reading group. Our students make observations about student groupings and try to figure out where they fit in. Some students are internalizing beliefs that they are "less than" others and are simply "not capable, so why try?" With connected learning, every learner is seen and heard and has something of value to contribute. Students discover their unique strengths and more readily develop a growth mindset.

VYGOTSKY'S INSIGHTS

Lev Vygotsky (1896–1934) was a teacher and psychologist who developed the sociocultural theory of cognitive learning, which highlights the role of social interactions in learning. This theory asserts that learners continue to construct knowledge and grow their understanding of the world through engaging with others (Vygotsky, 1978). This includes interactions with both peers and teachers, providing individuals with opportunities to negotiate meaning and to give their perspectives through discussions and sharing of ideas. This constructivist viewpoint holds a sharp contrast to students passively receiving information and processing it independently or spending hours throughout their school day on a computer.

Vygotsky's theory asserts that individuals benefit from learning at the next level from knowledgeable others that are beyond their own independent level, or the zone of proximal development. Students construct their learning and understanding through these interactions, which they internalize and make their own, helping their own knowledge base to grow (Vygotsky, 1978). These social learning interactions allow students to build on each other's ideas, help them to fill their gaps in understanding, and provide them with the opportunity to collectively build new knowledge together. All of these active learning interactions help to strengthen student engagement and build a more increased depth of knowledge than does passive or independent content.

As teachers, administrators, researchers, and consultants, we have witnessed students' increased motivation when they have the opportunity to learn with and from each other. According to Braren (2024), as humans, we have evolved with a need for social connection because it has become necessary for our survival. Over time, we have become hardwired to interact with others and to form relationships. Teachers that leverage this drive to interact with others have students who become far more engaged in the learning process. There is also a level of instant accountability knowing that you will be sharing your work or ideas with your peers rather than having them in a Google Doc or web-based program, or written down on a paper that only your teacher will eventually read.

Students enjoy interacting with each other during instruction infused with ECS. While having students turn and talk or share with a partner is a step in the right direction, it is not enough to provide them with the interactions necessary for meaningful conversations or to navigate decisions together through collaborative structures. When teachers intentionally provide these opportunities within their classrooms, students learn at a deeper level and they gain valuable ECS they will use throughout their lives. Turning to share a response with a partner and listening to that partner's ideas adds to instruction, but it does not provide the length or types of interactions needed to learn effective conversation skills. In ECS-integrated instruction, interactions often require active listening skills, being open to the perspectives of others, and, at times, learning negotiation skills as the individuals interact to move the group's ideas or project forward.

WHAT DOES A TYPICAL SCHOOL DAY LOOK LIKE NOW?

Teachers are working with students who have a wider range of abilities than ever before, and they are expected to teach grade-level content while simultaneously filling gaps for some and providing extensions for those students who are already secure in the content. We have all observed stressed teachers and administrators working to address the impact of interrupted learning that is a lingering result of the pandemic. Everyone is looking for ways to help our impacted students not only catch up but thrive within their school experience. Everyone is analyzing academic outcome data to determine if we are making the gains needed to be back on track or, preferably, performing even better than before.

Enter adaptive technology. There are technology tools that will assess students' needs in both math and reading, identify where the gaps are, and then provide lessons to help meet their individual needs. With many districts having one-to-one devices, it is not uncommon to see these tools being used across grade levels. While students still have time with their teachers leading instruction, for some students, a good portion of their day is being spent on a device.

A typical day for a student may go something like the daily schedule below.

Morning Meeting	An initial start to the day, typically used to build classroom community and include SEL skills or topics. Students may go around in a circle answering a prompt provided by the teacher or share ideas with their elbow partner.
Literacy Block	The teacher starts with a whole-group lesson or by reading aloud to the class. The teacher then takes a small group to work with her or him at the guided reading table while other students spend time on a laptop interacting with an adaptive technology program, reading on their own and responding in a journal, or traveling through centers until it is their time to work with the teacher in a small group.

Specials Block	The class spends time engaged in art; music; physical education; science, technology, engineering, and mathematics (STEM); or a stand-alone SEL class. While this provides students with variety and balance in their day, this time is typically structured to meet the teacher's learning objectives.
Lunch/Recess	Students have time to eat their lunch and talk with those around them. Depending on their grade level, they will most likely have recess and will spend time navigating the social gauntlet of the playground.
Math Block	The lesson may launch with a Number Talk where students attempt to answer a math problem on their dry erase boards and then either take turns listening to how their classmates tried to solve the problem or share their method with a neighbor. Back to the computer for time on adaptive math programs to help address skill loss and then structured time with the teacher in a small group.
Science/Social Studies/SEL Class	This time is spent with the teacher sharing information, followed by some independent or small-group work on the content. The subjects might rotate on a unit-by-unit basis or have one day each week dedicated to a stand-alone SEL lesson.

While this is just one sample schedule, it does reflect the typical day in many of today's classrooms. There is, understandably, a heavy data-driven focus to get students "caught up." And there is, of course, much value in using the technology-driven assessment tools that we have available today. The more targeted instruction that we can deliver, the better off we are in responsively meeting students' needs. However, we need to ask ourselves if, by following these models of instruction, we are truly meeting all of our students' needs. And are students growing academically at the rate we had hoped? Are we providing them with a well-rounded education that is setting them up to be successful across *all* areas of life? In many cases, our students are missing out on opportunities to engage in integrated learning with their peers. Even those who are making academic gains may be missing needed practice in developing ECS. We need to ask ourselves what type of memories from school they will have to look back on and what impact today's school experiences will have on their enduring ideas, beliefs, and character traits.

WE NEED EQUITY OF THE MIND AND HEART!

With the best of intentions, many school systems have shifted to an instructional approach that relies on a blend of adaptive technology and small-group instruction provided by a teacher. We understand the benefits of using available technology to help identify gaps in students' learning and then providing lessons and learning activities to help fill those gaps. For those who have access, adaptive technology tools have been shown to be effective in helping to increase students' learning. Navab (2022) highlights the use of adaptive learning in math, showing that the students who used an adaptive online tool showed better gains than their classmates who did not use the tool. Some of the reasons for this impact included immediate and personalized feedback, learning activities tailored to meet individual needs, and progress-tracking tools.

It is clear that the adaptive technology tools that many schools now have available to them can have a positive impact on students' learning outcomes. These tools allow students to grow in core content areas by providing individualized lessons, progress monitoring data for the teacher, immediate feedback for the students, and continued targeted lessons based on the students' performance. Several of these programs are designed with gaming elements that can be very appealing to students. We understand there is value to the judicious use of these technology tools to help maximize student learning outcomes.

While there are many advantages to the integration of technology into our instruction, there are also several dangerous pitfalls. In some cases, students are learning in such isolation that their language skills and interpersonal skills are suffering. I (Anne) have walked into many classrooms where I observed every student working on a laptop while the teacher sat at their desk engaged in their own work. To be clear, these classroom visits were taking place during a "typical" instruction block and not during a standardized online assessment. Every student was on their own device, the same as their teacher. There was not one human interaction taking place within those classrooms. Several of the students were wearing headphones and were not even aware that anyone had entered their classroom.

An article by Alhumaid (2019) found that when there is an excessive use of technology within classrooms, it results in fewer face-to-face interactions, which is detrimental to the development of communication skills. Further, due to limited interactions, students have impaired social skills. While we all want our students to make academic gains, it should not be at the expense of acquiring ECS that they will need to be successful throughout their lives. If students only acquire skills and knowledge in math, literacy, science, or social science, this will have limited value if they struggle to communicate effectively or if they fail to develop the social skills needed in school, in the workplace, and in life. If they are unable to understand how to work collaboratively or develop an appreciation for the perspectives of others, we are limiting their potential. We need to give consideration to skills beyond academic outcomes.

It is our responsibility as educators to provide a well-rounded education that will prepare our students to thrive and make contributions within our ever-changing world. In today's headlines, there is no shortage of news stories related to troubled individuals who end up harming themselves or others. As a society, we have the potential to prevent some of the challenges we face through providing an education that not only values academic growth and intelligence quotient (IQ) but is equally as committed to helping our students develop the skills they need to have a strong sense of well-being and emotional intelligence. When individuals have a high EQ they develop empathy and caring, and they have the skills needed to form positive, healthy relationships.

This book is a call to action. We need to ensure that we are balancing the instructional experiences that we are providing for our students. If the majority of their school day is spent working independently on technology tools or in small-group instruction led by their teacher, we are falling short of what they deserve and what we need collectively as a society. To fully prepare our students for what they will need when they leave us, we need to balance our instruction with experiences that enable them, with repeated opportunities, to develop ECS. The strategies within this book will help you to do just that! And, keep in mind, the integration of strategies that develop ECS also helps students to make academic gains—it's a win-win! As students work together, their interactions help them to grow in their understanding and retention of the content while they develop integral life skills.

WHY ARE ESSENTIAL CONNECTION SKILLS SO IMPORTANT?

A study completed by Pearson (2022) of labor markets in the United States, United Kingdom, Australia, and Canada looked to identify the most sought-after skills in today's ever-evolving workplace. All of the skills identified are human skills, not technical skills. These "power skills" have been recognized as the capabilities that are most needed to continue economic productivity. The skills that were identified in this global study are those that are developed when ECS are included within our classrooms. The chart below highlights the top five power skills.

PEARSON SKILLS OUTLOOK: POWER SKILLS IN THE MODERN WORKPLACE (2022)	
	**Communication** The most in-demand power skill across the board.
	**Customer Service** The ability to actively listen to a wide range of customers and respond to their needs.
	**Leadership** The skills needed to successfully motivate, guide, and organize others to achieve a common goal.
	**Attention to Detail** The ability to be accurate in your work and to pay attention to even the smallest of details.
	**Collaboration** The ability to work effectively with others including active participation in reaching a shared goal.

Image Source: Istock.com/StudioU

The National Association of Colleges and Employers (2023) identified several of the same qualities in their 2024 job outlook survey. When asked what qualities they sought in potential hires to fill their job openings, 90 percent of responders indicated that they look for individuals who are capable of solving problems, and 80 percent look for those that possess strong teamwork skills. If we hold the course with a large portion of our students' days being spent working alone on adaptive computer programs, completing work independently, or working in a small group directed by the teacher, future employers may have challenges in finding candidates with strong communication skills and the ability to work effectively with others in completing collaborative tasks. The table below represents the top attributes employers are seeking on a resume and the percentage of businesses that listed them as a skill set they are looking for in new employees, as reported by the same study.

TOP ATTRIBUTES EMPLOYERS SEEK ON A RESUME	
Problem-Solving Skills	88.7%
Ability to Work in a Team	78.9%
Communication Skills (Written)	72.7%
Strong Work Ethic	71.6%
Flexibility/Adaptability	70.1%
Communication Skills (Verbal)	67.5%
Technical Skills	67.0%
Analytic/Quantitative Skills	66.0%
Initiative	65.6%
Detail-Oriented	61.3%

Source: National Association of Colleges and Employers (2023).

Beyond the need and desire for individuals with these skills and abilities in the modern workplace, there are a number of other benefits for those who develop ECS. An individual who has a strong sense of who they are and can engage in self-reflection will have enhanced emotional well-being. When you have a strong sense of who you are and understand your strengths, values, goals, and purpose, you are more likely to have high self-esteem and self-acceptance. If you have the ability to reflect on your own emotions and needs, to advocate for yourself, and to identify areas for growth, then you can build a solid foundation to have a satisfying and fulfilling life. This same foundation helps you to establish and sustain positive relationships with others, develop empathy, and cultivate consideration of multiple perspectives.

If they have a strong sense of self and the ability to reflect, individuals are more likely to develop a growth mindset and resilience. Those with emotional and mental well-being are better prepared to successfully navigate life's challenges and obstacles. When faced with adversity, these individuals tend to have more coping skills and are better able to maintain a positive outlook, recognizing that their challenges are temporary and may even hold some benefits that they are unable to see. These same individuals are better equipped to support those around them, which aids in forming and strengthening communities. Helping students to develop ECS equips them with skills and competencies that have elasticity and can be stretched and applied across a wide range of future circumstances.

Within our public schools, we have students coming to us from an incredibly wide range of backgrounds, experiences, and family lives. While some students come from families that are able to foster a sense of safety and security and can help them to build a positive self-image, other students have a far different experience. In our classrooms we have the opportunity to provide learning experiences that will help *all* of our students to be seen, heard, and valued for who they are. Intentionally planning for instruction that includes essential connection skills and competencies our students need in life will allow us to help their overall development, both in mind and in heart, in a way that a thirty-minute stand-alone SEL class cannot match.

WE ONLY HAVE SO MUCH TIME IN THE SCHOOL DAY

The one resource that we never seem to have enough of in education is time, so, regardless of the school or district you work in, you must make the most of the time that you *do* have with your students. If you have ever been inside a Jamba Juice, you can probably picture the wide range of vitamin and protein boosts that you can add to your smoothie. While your Caribbean Passion or Orange Dream Machine smoothie might look the same as others from the outside, it may have any number of boosts, such as a soy protein or nonfat Greek yogurt, that add value and benefits to it. The strategies within this book, which add ECS to your instruction, provide you with a way to boost your instruction, layering benefits into the time you have with your students.

One of the keys to keep in mind is that infusing these strategies into your classroom will not only help your students develop skills and competencies that will help them succeed in life and the workplace, it will also help them to learn at a deeper level and will positively impact academic outcomes as well. Beyond that, many educators today report feeling increased levels of stress and pressure. In a K–12 Dive brief, Merod (2024) reported that, according to the Pew Research Center, more than 77 percent of the 2,531 teachers surveyed said their job is frequently stressful, with 68 percent calling it overwhelming. The study also showed that 58 percent of teachers reported the need to address behavioral issues on a daily basis. Research shows us that when students are engaged and motivated in the classroom, there are fewer behavioral disruptions, which provides positive benefits for both the students and the teachers. Teachers often share that implementing ECS into lessons has helped them to remember why they chose teaching as their profession.

When ECS are integrated into instruction, it helps to build relationships both between classmates and between students and their teachers. These strategies help to shift ownership of the learning to the students, who become far more engaged in the work and report having fun while working with their classmates. Teachers who use these strategies with their students have shared with us that they enjoy seeing the creativity and growth of their students and that it has helped to reinvigorate their passion for teaching. The closer relationships created within the classroom result in fewer behavior issues and are a compelling factor in having the students invest their resources, time, energy, and attention toward their learning. As novelist Taylor Caldwell (2016) wrote, "Learning should be a joy and full of excitement" (p. 187). Teachers and students are finding joy in the classroom again when ECS are included!

MOVING FORWARD

Hopefully by now you are ready to try out some of these strategies in your schools or in your classroom. In the next four chapters, we will be sharing a closer look at each of the ECS domains, and then we will give you the tools you need to integrate them into your lesson planning. Each chapter will include strategies that you can use and adapt across grade levels and content areas. We will provide you with examples, planning tips, and assessment tools. In Chapter 6, "Connecting to All Learners," you will find additional resources that will help you meet the differing needs of the students within your classroom. We are excited for you and your students and the elevation of their learning that you are about to provide!

Reflection Questions

1. Why are you reading this book? What do you hope to gain?
2. What is the primary purpose of education according to this chapter, and how does this differ from the current emphasis on standardized testing?
3. What are the ECS that students in your setting need the most? How can you tell? What additional information might you gather to answer this?
4. Why is there a need to integrate ECS into classroom experiences?
5. What challenges might educators face when implementing ECS strategies in a school environment focused on technology and data-driven instruction? How can those schools overcome these challenges?

CHAPTER 2

> ***"When you know yourself you are empowered.***
>
> ***When you accept yourself you are invincible."***
>
> **—Tina Lifford**

Your Snapshot Guide

Connections to Self

WHAT?	Having a strong sense of self greatly contributes to individuals' overall well-being. Students who possess a positive self-image are able to build healthy relationships with others and foster a growth mindset. Such students understand and embrace their strengths, perceiving themselves as capable of learning and in approaching social interactions.
WHY?	Helping our students develop strong connections to self is too important to be left to chance. Students with a low sense of self-esteem are more likely to give up easily and withdraw. These individuals can feel a sense of hopelessness and struggle to get along with others, and they are more likely to develop depression or social anxiety.
HOW?	Integrating strategies into your instruction that provide students with opportunities for self-reflection and assist them in discovering their strengths and identifying their beliefs and values can help them to connect to self and to develop a positive self-image.
BONUS	A classroom environment where students have a strong sense of self and respect for others creates a positive and accepting learning space. Within this environment, students feel safe to take risks with their learning, and the classroom is inclusive of all learners.

Four Key Areas Within the ECS Domain of Self-Connection	
Self-Awareness	Resilience
Self-Security	Cultural Championship

Image Sources: Istock.com/MicrovOne; Istock.com/BRO Vector; Istock.com/lineartestpilot; Istock.com/bananajazz; Istock.com/Enis Aksoy

ESSENTIAL CONNECTION SKILL: CONNECTIONS TO SELF

What does it mean for students to develop a connection *with themselves*? When an individual truly knows themself, they possess an understanding of their strengths and weaknesses, their values and beliefs, and their emotions, and they are aware of their hopes and dreams for the future. When our students establish a strong bond with themselves, it becomes a solid foundation for their overall well-being. The more secure they are in their own identity, the more open they become to acknowledging and appreciating the perspectives of others as well as embracing their differences. Students with a strong connection to self display heightened confidence, a willingness to explore new opportunities, and an increased motivation to actively participate in the learning process.

According to the *Merriam-Webster Dictionary* (Merriam-Webster, n.d.-c), self-esteem is defined as "confidence and satisfaction in oneself." Having a strong sense of self-esteem and a positive opinion of oneself deeply impacts all aspects of life. We acknowledge that our students come from diverse family backgrounds. While some families are able to encourage a positive self-perception in their children, others may not possess the necessary tools to do so, or they may even contribute to a negative self-image due to neglect or abuse. Many of our students have experienced different levels of trauma and are solely focused on surviving each day. If we restrict the support of developing self-connections to a stand-alone SEL class (often six weeks or so in duration) or course within the weekly grade level, we miss countless opportunities throughout the day to strengthen this foundational ECS domain through four key areas: self-awareness, self-security, resilience, and cultural championship.

THE IMPORTANCE OF STRONG SELF-CONNECTION

Multiple studies highlight the importance of strong self-esteem in elementary-age children. Research by Lin and Guo (2024) confirmed that higher levels of self-esteem serve as a protective factor against conditions such as depression and anxiety. A study focused on the impact of self-esteem on academic achievement showed that students with higher levels of esteem were more motivated to learn and more likely to develop perseverance when faced with challenges (Moyano et al., 2020). A longitudinal study (Trzesniewski et al., 2003) found that those individuals with higher self-esteem throughout their elementary school years were also more likely to continue to have higher academic achievement as they carried through their schooling.

Having a strong sense of self makes it easier to form and maintain friendships. When students have a positive self-view, they become more approachable and enjoyable to be around. Those with high self-esteem tend to be more confident, making it more likely for them to reach out to others. Research has shown that individuals with strong self-esteem have lower levels of social anxiety. Additionally, this higher self-esteem helps them to navigate and resolve conflicts with others. They feel more comfortable expressing their opinions and often exhibit higher levels of empathy and compassion, which helps in maintaining their friendships.

According to a study conducted by Juvonen and her colleagues (2019) at UCLA, students without friends tend to receive lower grades and are less academically engaged compared to those who have at least one friend. Further research indicates that having a friend present helps to reduce stress and enhances self-worth, thereby minimizing the impact of social or academic missteps. Even with just one friendship, students are able to bounce back from mistakes more quickly, unlike those without friends, who may become trapped in a negative thought cycle, questioning their self-worth. Students are more engaged and resilient in a learning environment when they have friends.

As students develop a stronger sense of self, including an appreciation for their cultural background and values, it provides a basis for them to acknowledge and appreciate cultures that differ from their own. By understanding their own unique background and culture, it better equips them to engage with others and to be open to learning about other ways of life and experiences that are different than their own. As they place importance on their own beliefs and customs, it assists them in understanding the value that others attach to *their* backgrounds. Consequently, this fosters curiosity and admiration for diversity, promoting respect and acceptance of others.

BUILDING CONNECTIONS TO SELF INTO CONTENT INSTRUCTION

The following strategies and protocols can be adapted across grade levels and content areas to integrate opportunities into your instruction for students to develop within the four key areas of the ECS domain of self-connection: self-reflection, self-security, resilience, and cultural championship. An ECS tool or strategy will be introduced and we will explain how to frame it for successful implementation within your classroom. This will be followed by examples to help you visualize possibilities with your own students. Please keep in mind that Chapter 6, "Connecting to All Learners," will provide you with additional strategies and scaffolds to meet the needs of those students that may require extensions or extra help to access the strategies.

THE GEORGES SEURAT EFFECT

If you have had the chance to visit the Art Institute of Chicago or have watched the iconic 1980s film *Ferris Bueller's Day Off*, you can probably visualize Georges Seurat's famous painting, *A Sunday Afternoon on the Island of La Grande Jatte*, which is the painting that Cameron, Ferris, and Sloane pause to view. This painting is renowned not only for its depiction of life in the 1880s but also for the painting technique known as pointillism. Pointillism entails the artist creating a comprehensive image by layering small, distinct dots. From a distance, the viewer perceives the larger image; however, upon approaching the painting and spending time observing it, the smaller dots eventually become visible.

How does a painting technique relate to connections to self? Often people only view a painting created with pointillism from a distance where the larger image remains in focus. However, it is only when you take the time to get closer to the painting, to pause and spend time with it, that you discover the many small, distinct elements that come together to create the whole. Similarly, unless we purposefully examine ourselves, pausing and reflecting, we may overlook the multitude of qualities and talents that make each of us a unique individual. Through creating intentional opportunities for your students to pause and reflect, you can empower them to gain new levels of self-awareness, which promotes the development of a positive self-view.

Without the support of these techniques, some of our students may automatically focus on any negative feedback they receive and then internalize it. Others may compare themselves to their peers and decide that they are less competent than their classmates. Without these supported, intentional pauses, it is too easy to only glance at the surface level. Just like the Seurat painting, it is only when you approach the canvas and take the time to look closer that you can see the many intricate details that work together to create the whole. We can empower our students by helping them to see the many unique characteristics, strengths, values, and talents that make each one of them so special.

There are multiple ways for you to incorporate reflection opportunities into your teaching, which can help all of your learners connect with themselves. You can provide your students with the necessary time and tools they need to look closer and discover their unique identities. It is through these reflective pauses that they can also gain insight into themselves as learners. Our students will also learn how to reflect on their own, which is a skill that will continue to serve them in all aspects of life. Every student should discover and believe in their own unique abilities! For some of our students, the moments of reflection we offer, which focus on identifying strengths and goals, may be the only means for them to begin to see themselves as competent and valuable individuals.

KEY AREA 1: SELF-AWARENESS

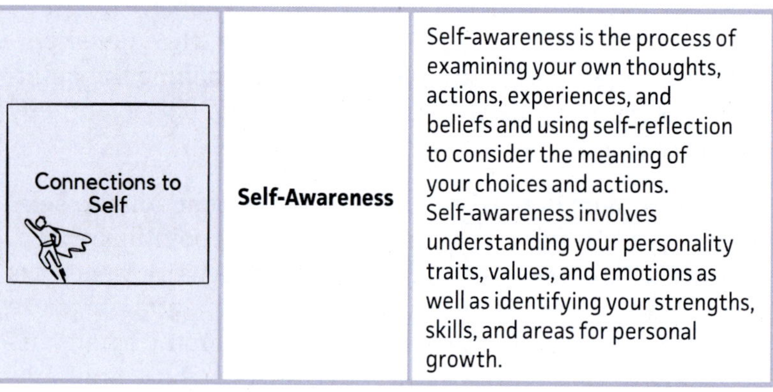

Connections to Self	**Self-Awareness**	Self-awareness is the process of examining your own thoughts, actions, experiences, and beliefs and using self-reflection to consider the meaning of your choices and actions. Self-awareness involves understanding your personality traits, values, and emotions as well as identifying your strengths, skills, and areas for personal growth.

Across hundreds of hours of classroom observations, many times we have watched teachers ask their students to share something they like or a favorite within a category. While some students can quickly share a preference and then go right into the reasons they made that choice, some students sit and look back at the teacher blankly, and others simply shrug their shoulders and say, "I don't know." There are many possible reasons why some students may struggle to identify a preference or that others may not even try. Think of your students: Can you name at least one who rarely offers their opinion or preference?

One possible concern for students being unable to state something they like is a lack of engagement in the lesson or a disinterest in trying to think about their own preferences. Others may struggle with self-expression; they may not have confidence or may lack certainty about their choices. Some may rarely be asked at home to share what their likes or preferences are, and they haven't thought about it on their own. Those who struggle in this area may face challenges in developing friendships and connecting with others, which often happens through finding common interests. It may also be an indicator of low confidence, which can negatively impact a student's academic learning potential, may make them more vulnerable to bullying, and may impede their overall well-being.

Self-awareness—knowing one's preferences, hopes, strengths, and growth areas—is foundational to orienting yourself within your learning and your interactions with others.

STRATEGIES FOR INTEGRATING SELF-AWARENESS INTO CONTENT INSTRUCTION

And the Award Goes to . . . Evaluation and Communication Skills

STRATEGY **And the Award Goes to . . .** 	**What:** This strategy provides each of your students with an opportunity to grant an award. **Build an understanding:** Spend time discussing the concept of an award with your students. Some of your students may be familiar with awards in sports, and others may quickly recognize the round Caldecott award symbol on some of their favorite books. Some families may watch kids' baking shows where someone wins after several rounds of competition.
Step 1: **Award Criteria** 	**Developing an award rubric:** While sports typically have a game or competition with a clear winner, other awards use specific standards to determine the winner. **Caldecott award example:** You can share with your students the five criteria used when awarding a picture book with a Caldecott award: artistic technique (medium used), pictorial interpretation (represents the words/characters), style (concept/mood), delineation (shows plot/theme), and audience (motivation to pick up the book). **Model rubric development:** Staying with the book example, work with your students to develop your own class award. You can come up with a name and determine the criteria students will use when identifying a winner.
Step 2: **Award Design** 	**Physical or digital awards:** Once the criteria are set, each student or the class as a whole can decide the design of the award. You may use stickers, ribbons, paper, or certificates for the award. Another option is to have a digital Wall of Fame, such as a Google Slide, where students can record their awards.

(Continued)

(Continued)

Step 3: **Award Topics** 	**Determine topic:** Please see the "Amazon Review" table below this one for sample topics to help get you started. **Class or individual award:** Once your students understand how to create an award and develop a rubric, you can decide whether to have the class collaborate on one topic or have each individual student design a unique award.
Step 4: **Awards Showcase** 	**Award selection:** Once your students have created and given their awards, set aside time when they can share the results with other classmates, younger students, or invited guests. This is an opportunity for your students to explain the criteria they used when they made their selection. **Follow-up questions:** Model for students possible follow-up questions they can ask when someone shares information about their award. Possibilities include the following: • Can you tell me more about the process you went through in deciding how you wanted to give out your award? • Can you share any specifics about what stood out to you about the winner? • What do you think the next award you would like to give out will be and why? • Were there similarities in the awards given out? How were the awards different from each other?

Image Source: Istock.com/da-vooda

The Amazon Review: Critical Thinking and Communication

STRATEGY **The Amazon Review**	**What:** Students will be writing their own Amazon-style review. This will include awarding stars based on a scale of 1–5. They will identify what they like most about the item (the pros) as well as any concerns or limitations (the cons). **Build an understanding:** Build a common understanding of an Amazon-style review by previewing and selecting one or two reviews to share with your students.
Step 1: **Create an Example**  	**Model:** Create an example of an Amazon-style review for your students. You can include them in the writing process. Using a simple graphic organizer, include a headline that provides a hook into the review, a space for drawings/pictures of the item, five stars that can be colored in based on the item's pros/cons, a pros section, a cons section, and a brief summary highlighting if the student would recommend this item to others. Younger students can select the number of stars they would give an item and then draw or write what they liked and did not like about the object of their review.

<table>
<tr><td>Step 2:
Topic Selection
</td><td>Once your students understand how to write a review and they know that by completing one they will be growing in both their critical thinking and communication skills, you then provide your students with the guidelines for what they are to review.

Please see the list of potential topics below. It is suggested that you start with something tangible and concrete that students are directly familiar with, such as a book, park, or playground, or something they have experienced, such as a field trip.

Once the students become familiar with the process, you can move on to more abstract items or concepts, such as reviewing a mathematical practice, varying mediums in art, or instructional technology programs.</td></tr>
<tr><td>Step 3:
Publish the Reviews
</td><td>When their writing will be made public, even if that just means being shared with peers, students are motivated to do their best. If a piece of writing is viewed only by the teacher, some students may give minimal effort to meet the expectations of the assignment.

You may choose to print the review or make copies and put them into a physical book that students can check out of your classroom library. You may create a free web page using a tool such as Google Sites or Jamboard where you can post the students' reviews. In this way they can be shared with families through a web link that can even be extended to friends and family that live in other areas.</td></tr>
<tr><td>Step 4:
Review the Review!
</td><td>As a class you can collaboratively develop a rubric for the Amazon-style reviews based on grade level. Students can reflect on their writing and identify any celebrations as well as set a goal for improving their next review.

With practice and guidance, students can provide meaningful feedback to each other to continue to grow and improve in the process.</td></tr>
</table>

Image Sources: Istock.com/Dimitris66; Istock.com/da-vooda; Istock.com/StudioU

Potential Topics for Awards or Amazon-Style Reviews

<table>
<tr><td rowspan="4">Potential Topics for Awards or Amazon-Style Reviews
</td><td colspan="2">Start with the personal: Starting the awards or reviews in areas that students can easily relate to will help them get started. If you are creating a class award or writing a review together, you can determine the topic/item together. If an individual award is being given or an individual review is being written, you can provide students with a bank of possible topics or options.</td></tr>
<tr><td colspan="2">Personal Topic Examples

Give consideration to food, movies, TV shows, animals, hobbies, sports, video games, places to visit in your community, or seasons of the year.</td></tr>
<tr><td colspan="2">Content-Related Topic Examples</td></tr>
<tr><td>Science
</td><td>Give consideration to areas of science (environmental, earth, chemistry). Provide an award for a favorite scientist, inventor, experiment, job within the field of science, or strongest hypothesis for an experiment. Students can write reviews related to the previous options. Provide an award or review for video clips related to a science topic.</td></tr>
</table>

(Continued)

(Continued)

	Social Science	Students can give an award to the person they would most like to meet from those they have studied in history. Create an award or write a review for time periods within history, geographic locations, or community leaders. Provide an award to someone making a positive difference in the world. Write a review for a social science book, article, or technology tool.
	Math	Give consideration to mathematical practices and strategies. Give an award to a favorite strategy or write a review that features the pros/cons related to a potential strategy. Provide an award for a favorite mathematician from history. Identify and write reviews for jobs that use math.
	English Language Arts	Give consideration to book genres. Give an award to your favorite book, author, or illustrator. Write a review for a book that you have read. Provide multiple selections of persuasive writing on the same topic and give an award to the most convincing one. Take the book you are reading at the moment and create an award for your favorite sentence that supports careful examination of word choice and sentence structure. Write a review of a poem or article that you have read.
	Specials	**PE:** Which is your favorite sport or athlete? Do you have a "go-to" strategy or technique that improves your performance? Create a review for a game played in PE class. **Music:** Provide an award for your favorite type of music or instrument. Do you have a favorite singer or band? **Art:** Review works of art within the same category and provide an award for the one you like the best. Select a favorite color or medium. Give an award to your favorite artist. **STEM:** Give an award for your favorite invention or inventor that you have learned about. Provide an award for your favorite technology tool. Give an award to your favorite class project.

Image Sources: Istock.com/da-vooda; stock.com/Turac Novruzova; stock.com/ozcan yalaz; stock.com/Pavlo Stavnichuk; stock.com/bounward; stock.com/Kharom Pleedee; stock.com/rashadashurov

Everyday Heroes: Identifying Character Traits

<table>
<tr><td>STRATEGY
Everyday Heroes
</td><td>What: Students will have the opportunity to reflect and consider what makes someone an “everyday hero.” This is an opportunity for students to identify some of the values and beliefs that are important to them.

Build an understanding: There are multiple options for grade-level books, including picture books for all ages, that feature a character with heroic qualities. This may include someone who has befriended a new student at school or stood up for someone who was being picked on. Use any of these books or video clips as a springboard for a discussion on what makes an everyday hero.</td></tr>
<tr><td>Step 1:
Class List of Traits or Characteristics
</td><td>Classroom list: Collaborate with the students to create a list of possible traits and characteristics of everyday heroes. Here are some options to get you and your students started.

Kindness | Respectful | Responsible
Compassion | Generous | Trustworthy
Bravery | Honest | Empathy</td></tr>
<tr><td>Step 2:
Dig Into the Traits/ Characteristics
</td><td>Through discussions and examples of heroes in books, textbooks, or video clips, continue to build your students’ understanding of the traits that you have identified and add new ones to your list.

Students can have their own journals, either paper or digital, where they can create their own lists. This can include having them circle or highlight the traits they feel are most important to them.</td></tr>
<tr><td>Step 3:
Build a Friend
</td><td>Create opportunities for reflection.

Build a friend: What traits and characteristics do you appreciate in your friends? Why do you enjoy spending time with them? If you could create your own new friend, which traits would you give them?

Be a friend: Which traits and qualities do you have that make you a good friend? Are there areas that you would like to grow in to become an even better friend or classroom community member?</td></tr>
<tr><td>Resource
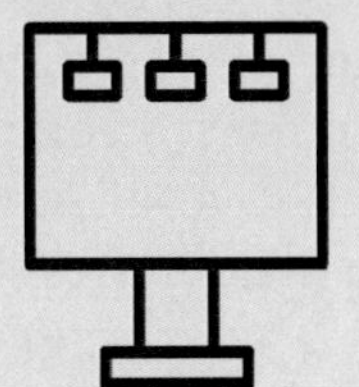
PassItOn.com
The Foundation for a Better Life</td><td>Resource: PassItOn.com is a free resource that contains a number of quotes, inspiring videos, and billboards that feature everyday heroes.

These resources can continue to help your students learn about human values and traits, which will help them to build their own lists. Reflecting on these characteristics and evaluating which are important to them helps students to develop a foundation for making decisions and setting goals.

Create: Your students can collaborate to create their own “Pass It On” videos or design billboards. The students can give acknowledgments to the everyday heroes in their lives by creating billboards or quotes posters about them. These can be shared throughout the school or on your classroom website.</td></tr>
</table>

(Continued)

(Continued)

Content Integration **Content-Area Heroes** 	**Which heroes can you highlight?** Within and across content areas, you can search for: • **Biographies:** Showcase individuals that have contributed to a subject area. Many may have been pioneers in their field and used perseverance to blaze a trail or set a goal. • **Current events:** You can share and feature those that are making contributions in areas such as science, the local or global community, environmental causes, writing, music, arts, or sports. You may find student-friendly articles or videos to make these individuals come to life for students. • **Award winners:** You can highlight those within content areas who have received an award in their field, sharing some of the reasons for their selection. Possible awards are the Nobel Peace Prize, the Pulitzer Prize, the Fields Medal in math, and locally given awards by area police and fire departments or local governments.

Image Sources: Istock.com/da-vooda; Istock.com/ozalp; Istock.com/Nobelus; Istock.com/appleuzr; Istock.com/DStarky

KEY AREA 2: SELF-SECURITY

	**Self-Security**	Self-security is based on an individual having a strong sense of identity and self-worth. This includes being comfortable with who they are and not relying on the approval of others. Individuals who are self-secure have a deep belief in themselves and have unwavering confidence.

STRATEGIES FOR BECOMING MORE SELF-SECURE

The American Psychological Association (n.d.) highlights the importance of supporting students in developing an understanding of who they are as individuals. Their research has found that those students who are self-secure have stronger social skills, better academic outcomes, and more overall emotional well-being. Teachers are able to foster students' self-security by helping them to identify their many strengths and helping them see themselves as capable. When students have higher levels of self-security it contributes to their ability to take risks in their learning and to advocate for themselves, and it helps them to gain confidence in their own capabilities.

Students should be made aware of the reasons that you are presenting opportunities for them to build a sense of self-security. While integrating these strategies into your instruction will help to build that foundation, the strategies become even more powerful when your students understand *why* you are including reasons for them to think about their strengths and abilities. When we take time to think about who we are, including reflecting on what makes us unique and recognizing our strengths, it gives us a chance for self-discovery. This knowledge equips us to have the foundation and confidence we need to believe in ourselves and our abilities. Individuals who are self-secure often experience greater happiness and are not dependent on the approval or validation of others.

You can help your students to see that connecting to their personal strengths has other benefits, including boosting their self-confidence and self-esteem. When you integrate discussion and awareness of the importance of being self-secure, you set the stage for your students to grow in this foundational area. Developing these attributes will greatly assist students in various aspects of their lives. By being able to step back and model how to reflect upon your own self-worth and many unique strengths, you will help students to view themselves from an assets-based perspective rather than a deficits-based viewpoint.

Using Reflective Pauses Within Your Instruction: Three Key Areas

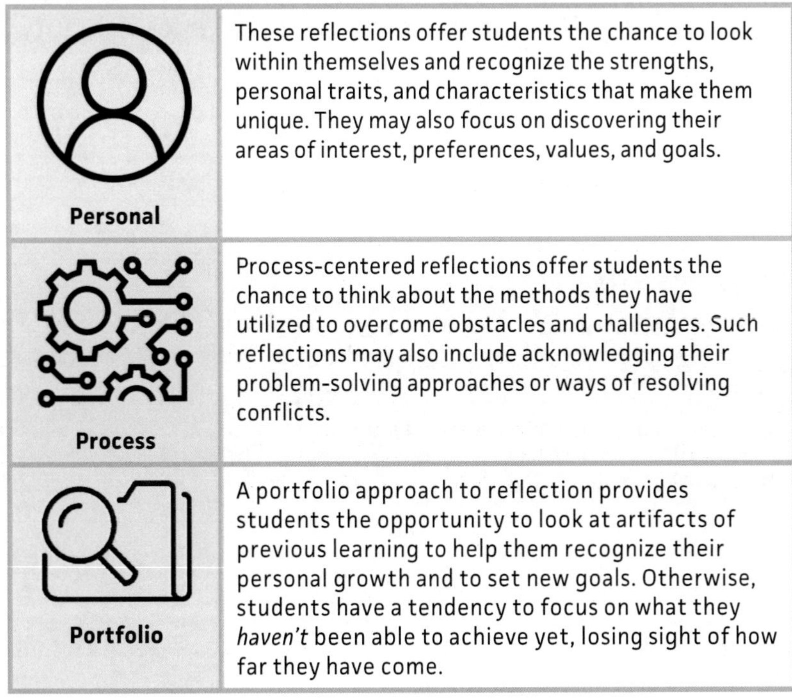

Personal	These reflections offer students the chance to look within themselves and recognize the strengths, personal traits, and characteristics that make them unique. They may also focus on discovering their areas of interest, preferences, values, and goals.
Process	Process-centered reflections offer students the chance to think about the methods they have utilized to overcome obstacles and challenges. Such reflections may also include acknowledging their problem-solving approaches or ways of resolving conflicts.
Portfolio	A portfolio approach to reflection provides students the opportunity to look at artifacts of previous learning to help them recognize their personal growth and to set new goals. Otherwise, students have a tendency to focus on what they *haven't* been able to achieve yet, losing sight of how far they have come.

Image Sources: Istock.com,/Ville Heikkinen; Istock.com/kadirkaba; Istock.com/fonikum

FRAMING A REFLECTIVE PAUSE

It is important to clearly communicate the purpose of the reflection to help all students understand why it is important and how it can help them to better understand themselves both as individuals and as learners. All students should know that there are no wrong answers; this is a time to think through the questions you will provide them with to discover more about themselves. Modeling self-reflection for them with a think-aloud, which can help them to better understand the process, will set them up to better engage in using the strategy. You will need to provide your students with enough time to pause, reflect, and process their thoughts. We know that teachers are incredibly resourceful and imaginative; please consider the examples provided below and consider how you can adapt them for your grade or content area.

Once the class has completed the reflection activity, there will be time for students to share with each other. Depending on your topic and your class, you can include opportunities for the students to add peer feedback. This provides students with the opportunity to validate what their classmates observed about themselves and to potentially add another strength or characteristic that stands out for them about that individual. As the teacher, you will continue to reinforce the idea that each of us has our own strengths and special abilities and that every person adds value to the classroom community. When students pause to reflect on their own strengths, they start to identify the strengths and attributes that they appreciate in others.

INTEGRATING A REFLECTIVE PAUSE TO BUILD SELF-CONNECTION

Identify Content Standard
Identify Reflective Pause: Personal, Process, or Portfolio
Pre-assessment: Baseline Data
Instruction Integration of Reflective Pause
Post-assessment: Formative Data

Classroom Example: Personal Reflective Pause

<table>
<tr><td>Content Standard</td><td colspan="2">CCSS.ELA-LITERACY.RL.K.3
With prompting and support, identify characters, settings, and major events in a story.
Book: The Recess Queen by Alexis O'Neill/Laura Huliska-Beith</td></tr>
<tr><td>Reflective Pause</td><td>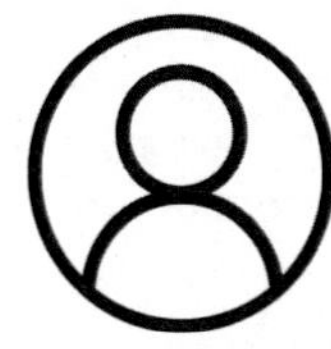
Personal</td><td>"Today we will pause in our lesson to think about the special traits of the characters in our book and then to think about what makes each one of us special. Taking time to pause and think is important because it is one way that we can learn more about ourselves and others. All of us have strengths and special abilities, but if we don't take the time to think about them it can be easy to forget they are there."</td></tr>
<tr><td>Pre-assessment:
Ask and Observe
</td><td colspan="2">During a read-aloud, ask the students to think about the characters in the story and their traits. Ask the students to write or draw the characters and add their traits.
Ask students to draw or write about what makes the characters special.
Observe:
• Which students are able to generate traits and explain why they selected them?
• Which students struggle to identify traits or explain their choices?</td></tr>
<tr><td>Instruction Integration</td><td colspan="2">Model identifying the strengths of a character from a book read-aloud to the class. Provide a trait with supporting evidence.
Example:
"Today while I read the story I am going to stop and think about any superpowers that the characters in our story have. All of us have special traits and abilities inside of us that are like our very own superpowers! In this story I think that one of Katie Sue's superpowers is being friendly because she asked Mean Jean to play with her even when Jean wasn't being nice to her. Draw Katie Sue on chart paper, then write 'friendly' on a name tag and place it on her picture."
Collaborate with the students to identify more superpowers of characters from the book and add more superpower tags.
"I know that I have some superpowers too! One of my traits is being patient. When I am trying to learn something new, like a harder pose in yoga, I know it will take me some time and practice before I can do it. I am patient with myself and keep trying until I get it. I am going to write 'patient' on a tag and draw a yoga pose on it too!"
Students then write and/or draw three of their own superpowers on name tags and wear them throughout the day. Build in time for them to meet with other students and share about their powers. Provide students with prompts and model for them: "I agree that you are __________ because __________" or "I think you also have this superpower, __________, because __________" to get them started.</td></tr>
</table>

(Continued)

(Continued)

Post-assessment: **Ask and Observe** 	In your next read-aloud, ask the students to identify the superpowers of the characters in the story and to support their claims with evidence. Ask the students to think through and identify more of their own superpowers and give examples for their choices. Observe: • Which students are now able to generate traits and explain why they selected them? Continue to extend their reflection to include traits they would like to develop; for example, which traits do they like in a friend that they can work on growing? • Which students continue to struggle to identify traits or explain their choices? Continue to pause when you see an opportunity to support them in identifying one of their traits with an example of that trait you observed.
Additional Possibilities	• Identifying strengths and preferences as a learner • Reflecting on individual abilities within content areas, such as math, science, music, PE, foreign language, or English language development • Drawing connections between traits and strengths of characters in books or individuals from history with themselves

Image Sources: Istock.com,/Ville Heikkinen and Istock.com/Oksana Sazhnieva

Classroom Example: Process Reflective Pause

Content Standard	**CCSS.MATH.CONTENT.3.NF.A.3** Explain equivalence of fractions in special cases and compare fractions by reasoning about their size.	
Reflective Pause	 **Process**	"In today's math class we will continue to work with fractions. As you work through the practice problems after our review lesson, I am going to ask you to pause and reflect on the steps you took to work out the answer. When we stop to think about the process we used to solve the problem, it helps us to build an even better understanding of fractions and to think more about our thinking (metacognition), which helps us to grow as learners."
Pre-assessment: 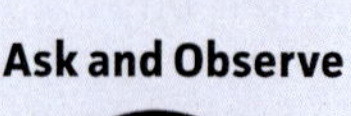 **Ask and Observe** 	While teaching a lesson related to fractions, ask the students to pause and reflect on the thinking they used to solve the problem. Observe: • Which students were able to identify and communicate the steps they took to solve the problem? • Which students had difficulty trying to break down the process they followed or included some but not all of their steps? • Were any of the students able to explain why they took the steps that they took?	

Instruction Integration	During your fraction lesson, model identifying the steps in a think-aloud and share why you decided to try the steps that you did. You may want to include modeling a mistake, reflecting on why the step didn't work, then sharing the new step you will take as you work to solve the problem. In the think-aloud, include any emotions that might occur during the steps; for example, "I am frustrated because ________," "I feel stuck, but what I do know is ________, so I will try ________," "I am not sure but I think this step is right because ________," or "Now that makes sense—I think that might be right because ________, and I am proud that I didn't give up." You can complete the process reflection with a simple two-column table that has the steps on the left side, your reasoning on the right side, and a learner takeaway at the bottom. **STEP** | **REASON** Something I better understand about myself as a learner is ________ because ________.
Post-assessment: Ask and Observe	Once you have modeled this for your students, ask them to complete a process reflection using the same organizer when they solve the next problem. Observe: • Which students were able to share both the steps and their reasoning when solving the problem? You can extend their thinking by having them map out more than one process. • Which students were able to get all or most of the steps? Were they able to explain their thinking? Provide additional practice/support to help them reflect and capture their reasoning. • For those students who struggle to capture their steps, continue process reflections together when working through problems.
Additional Possibilities	• Reflect on the process and steps used to resolve a conflict with peers. • Use this tool to reflect on the process that can be used to get better at a skill or task. • Use the process reflection to break down the steps to write and revise a paper, to improve a soccer kick, to make a prediction when reading a book, or to make a hypothesis in science.

Image Sources: Istock.com/kadirkaba and Istock.com/Oksana Sazhnieva

Classroom Example: Portfolio Pause

<table>
<tr><td>Content Standard</td><td colspan="2">CCSS.ELA-LITERACY.W.6.2
Write informative/explanatory texts to examine a topic and convey ideas, concepts, and information through the selection, organization, and analysis of relevant content.</td></tr>
<tr><td>Reflective Pause</td><td>
Portfolio</td><td>"In today's ELA class we will take time for you to pause and reflect on some of your earlier informational writing and then compare it to your most recent piece. Reflecting through comparing samples of your own writing that have been completed over time will help you see how much you have grown, help you identify areas that you would still like to work on, and identify your overall strengths as a writer. It can be easy to forget where you were before, and it helps us to continue to grow when we intentionally pause and reflect."</td></tr>
<tr><td>Pre-assessment:
Ask and Observe
</td><td colspan="2">Ask your students to compare two pieces of their own writing. One should be an earlier piece and the other more recent.
Observe:<ul><li>Were students able to accurately reflect and make relevant observations?</li><li>To what extent were your students able to identify and articulate the differences between the two pieces of writing?</li><li>Were some students challenged to identify any changes?</li></ul></td></tr>
<tr><td>Instruction Integration</td><td colspan="2">Use two samples of writing to model a portfolio reflection for your students. This can be from anonymous student work samples that you have saved over time or examples that you have created as if you were a student to highlight key developmental differences.
You can guide the reflection by using a rubric that is aligned to the piece of writing. A portfolio reflection organizer can help you model the process with a think-aloud for your students.
<table>
<tr><th>ELEMENT OF FOCUS</th><th>IN COMPARISON</th><th>CELEBRATIONS AND GOALS</th></tr>
<tr><td>Introduction</td><td>In my first piece of writing, my introduction was overall clear and straightforward. In my recent writing, my introduction was stronger because it included a hook to catch the reader's attention, and I had more descriptive wording.</td><td>In comparing both of my introductions, I can see that I am growing as a writer. The first introduction seems a bit plain compared to the one with a hook and the use of some words that are not as common.
I will continue to focus on changing my sentence structures next for more variety.</td></tr>
<tr><td colspan="3">What I have learned about myself and my growth:</td></tr>
</table></td></tr>
</table>

Post-assessment: Ask and Observe 	Have students save samples of their writing in portfolios, either physical or digital, to be able to observe their growth and development over time. For each observation made, specific evidence should be provided. Ask your students to compare two pieces of their writing using the aligned rubric as a guide, along with a portfolio reflective pause tool. Observe: • Which students were able to accurately reflect on the writing samples and make relevant observations? You can help them to extend their thinking by setting specific goals for continued growth. • Were the students able to identify and articulate the differences between the two pieces of writing? For those that were challenged to articulate the differences, help them by having them explain their thinking during peer or teacher conferences. • Were there some students that struggled to identify any changes? Work with them through guided reflection, which will help them gain practice and support in learning the process.
Additional Possibilities	• In science or social science, save a portfolio of written projects or test responses for students to analyze and then reflect on their growth. • In music, band, or reading fluency, use recordings of the students for them to observe and compare their progress and growth. • In math, students can consider their growth as mathematicians by reflecting on the number of tools and strategies they have to solve problems through observing examples of their problem-solving over time. • For those working to acquire English, portfolios across all four domains of language and WIDA rubrics can help students to observe growth over time.

Image Sources: Istock.com/fonikum and Istock.com/Oksana Sazhnieva

KEY AREA 3: RESILIENCE

	**Resilience**	Resilience involves knowing how to cope when things do not go as planned and having the ability to bounce back from hard times or challenges. You acknowledge your feelings and then actively move forward toward continued growth.

BUILDING RESILIENCE AND A PERSONAL GROWTH MINDSET

As an educator you have multiple opportunities throughout the school day to help students build resilience and a personal growth mindset. The *Merriam-Webster Dictionary*

(Merriam-Webster, n.d.-b) defines resilience as "an ability to recover from or adjust easily to misfortune or change." This ability is key to empowering students to overcome both obstacles within their learning and also those challenges they will inevitably face in life as well. Understanding and developing resilience should start from the youngest ages and it should be intentionally integrated into classroom instruction, not relegated to be taught as a stand-alone unit within an SEL class.

When we hear the term *growth mindset*, most of us in education automatically think of the work of Dweck (2006) that centers around the belief that one can learn and grow versus operating from the concept of a fixed level of intelligence. This definitely has merit as it relates to learning, but it is also reflective of the education system's obsession with standardized testing (the mind) over personal human growth (the heart). According to University of Wisconsin-Madison professor Ryff (2013), one component to psychological well-being is personal growth, which is centered around valuing new experiences that challenge us to think about ourselves and what we know about the world. Ryff's view focuses more on supporting individuals in discovering who they are, reflecting on their growth over time, and remaining open to, and even embracing, change.

Strategies and protocols that integrate both building resilience and supporting a personal growth mindset within our instruction will help our students to develop as a whole person (heart) without a singular focus on growing intelligence for higher test scores (mind). Both of these promote increased engagement in instruction and higher levels of learning; however, the personal growth emphasis will encourage our students to be open to seeking out and growing as a person through challenging activities. As teachers you can empower your students to develop the confidence and the tools they need to expand and grow overall as a person through continually seeking growth opportunities. The impact of this will last and extend far beyond any test scores. We want every child to be able to successfully unlock and pursue their dreams, to continually reflect and grow, and to be prepared to move past obstacles or challenges along the way.

STRATEGIES FOR INTEGRATING RESILIENCE INTO CONTENT INSTRUCTION

The Feelings Factor: Include Emotional Literacy

<table>
<tr><td>STRATEGY
The Feelings Factor
</td><td colspan="3">What: Learning does not occur in isolation. The feelings and emotions of students, whether they are positive or negative, interact with and impact their learning. It is essential that we enhance our students' emotional literacy as it enables them to both express and process their emotions as well as identify and carefully consider their responses to emotional triggers. Without this understanding, students can shut down when they become frustrated.
Build an understanding. Try the following:
• Initiate a conversation about emotions with your students by reviewing some common emojis of faces representing different emotions.
• Share pictures, pause in a read-aloud, or create a scenario relevant to students' age group and ask them to draw or hold up the emoji of how they would feel. Ask them to share with a partner what they would be feeling and why.
• Revisit some of the teaching moments you used in the step above and ask students what they would do or how they might respond in those situations.</td></tr>
<tr><td rowspan="5">Step 1:
Identify Common Emotions
</td><td>Happy</td><td>Sad</td><td>Angry</td></tr>
<tr><td>Excited</td><td>Scared</td><td>Proud</td></tr>
<tr><td>Surprised</td><td>Jealous</td><td>Calm</td></tr>
<tr><td>Frustrated</td><td>Hopeful</td><td>Curious</td></tr>
<tr><td>Bored</td><td>Nervous</td><td>Serious</td></tr>
<tr><td>Step 2:
Emotional Responses
</td><td colspan="3">What: When a trigger occurs, such as an experience, event, or object, we often feel an emotion and we may respond to it without thinking. A big emotion, like anger, can have us responding quickly before we even think about it or may have us responding to a situation when we only have a portion of the information or facts.
Share the domino effect: The actions you take may cause other actions to take place around you. If you are kind and helpful toward someone, they may stop to help someone else. If you are angry and raise your voice to someone, they may be upset and end up hurting someone else's feelings. Your actions, good or bad, can impact others.
Discuss the potential impact for social interactions and learning: Helping our students to see that their responses impact others and the way others will interact with them is important. If you become angry easily as a member of a group and do not listen to the ideas of others, people will be reluctant to have you on their team. If you become frustrated and stop trying, you may miss out on new experiences.</td></tr>
</table>

(Continued)

(Continued)

Step 3: Pause, Name, and Think It Through 	**Build emotional literacy:** Model for students and guide them through the process of pausing and identifying their emotions. • **Pause:** Stop to think about how you are feeling. • **Name:** Name the emotion that you are experiencing. • **Think it through:** Now that you are aware of the emotion that you are feeling, how will you respond?
Step 4: Emotional Response Tools 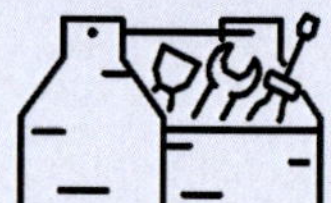	**Building a toolbox of responses to your emotions.** Students may try the following: • **Deep breathing:** Taking a deep breath is linked to attention and awareness. Breathing in and out for a set count or a deep exhale, like blowing out birthday candles, can help an individual to become calm when feeling a big emotion such as anger or frustration. • **Squeeze a ball:** Pretend you are holding a ball, squeeze your hands into fists, hold for a count of three, and then release. • **Count it down:** Have students count down from or up to ten slowly. This helps to refocus their mind on the task of counting while building in a pause from an immediate response to their emotions. • **Movement break:** When possible, get up and step out of the situation. Get a drink of water or do some stretches before returning. • **Positive self-talk:** Once you have named the emotion, tell yourself things such as "I can handle this," "I am not going to give up," "I can find a different way to do it," or "I can be calm."
Step 5: Emotions and Learning 	Students can experience a wide range of emotions during the learning process: • **Positive emotions:** Curiosity, fun, and excitement are all positive emotional states that can positively impact learning outcomes. As the teacher, intentionally leverage strategies that will elicit these emotions to help better engage students and set the stage for a positive learning experience. • **Negative emotions:** When students experience frustration, stress, or a feeling of being overwhelmed while learning, they may shut down or struggle to concentrate and focus, which can cause additional stress. • **Include emotions in your teaching:** As a student, if no one tells me that I may become frustrated when I am trying something new, or that I may become nervous before reading or answering in front of the class, I may feel like I am the only one and I may be unsure of how to respond.

	• **Normalize emotions in learning:** Examples of including emotional responses in your instruction include the following: ○ "How are you feeling? For those of you that may be feeling stressed about this, remember, it is okay to make a mistake—just focus on trying your best." ○ "I know that some of you do not like to answer in front of the class and you may be feeling nervous. Remember, we are all in this together, and in this classroom we support each other. The more you have a chance to share, the easier it may become." ○ "It can be frustrating when you are trying to learn something new, like a new skill in math. When you feel stressed or frustrated, you may feel like you will never get it or that you do not even know where to start. Take a deep breath and focus on what you *do* know, pause to think about any resources you have to help you, and embrace mistakes because they help us learn."

Image Sources: Istock.com/Ksenia Omelchenko; Istock.com/Drypsiak; Istock.com/bsd studio; Istock.com/Richard Chambers; Istock.com/matsabe; Istock.com/Andrii Moroziuk

An Itchy Sweater in the Woods: Embracing Some Discomfort

STRATEGY **An Itchy Sweater in the Woods** 	**What:** When we are learning and trying to make sense of new information and figuring out how it fits with what we already know, we may feel discomfort or cognitive dissonance. As our brains receive and process new information, new pathways, or synapses, are developed. With repeated exposure and practice, these connections become stronger, and, with repetition, the brain becomes aware that the information or skill is important and the information should be remembered. Over time we "get it," or it becomes easier. **Build an understanding:** As educators, if we do not make our students aware of the discomfort that can occur when learning something new, they may believe they are the only ones feeling that way. They may stop at the first sign of struggle or discomfort, taking it as a sign that they just won't be able to "get it." The more that students know that this is an expected part of the learning process and that it means their brain is working through the new information to build up their knowledge, the better chance we have of them staying the course and not giving up. In time, they might even embrace that discomfort as a sign that they are learning. **Analogies:** You can help your students build an understanding of these concepts through the use of analogy: • When you get a new sweater, even one that looks nice, it may feel a bit rough against your skin or even feel itchy. The more it is washed, the softer it becomes. Over time, it feels even more comfortable. What was once itchy and distracting is now worn without a second thought. • If you are hiking in the woods in an area without a trail, you may have to move sticks or other obstacles out of your way. The more you take this same path, the clearer and easier to follow the trail will become each time. When we practice new skills and review information, we are making new pathways in our brains. We are connecting the information to what we have already learned until it becomes easier. Picture the sweater becoming softer or the pathway being made in a forest and stick with it—in time it will become easier!

(Continued)

(Continued)

<table>
<tr><td>CONCEPT BUILDING
Metacognition:
"Thinking About Thinking"
</td><td>Metacognition: Integrating metacognition—helping students to think about their thinking—into content instruction will help them to be reflective and aware of how they learn the best:
• When students have a basic understanding about the learning process, it helps them to become active participants rather than passively taking in information.
• Focusing on the strategies they can use for the task at hand and the resources they can use when they get stuck empowers students to move past hurdles.
• Helping students to monitor their learning, to see which strategies and techniques work best for them, gives them more control over their learning.</td></tr>
<tr><td>Step 1:
Use Analogy
</td><td>Analogies: You can help build your students' resilience through the use of analogy.
• Introduce the analogy of "The Itchy Sweater in the Woods" just before introducing a new lesson, especially one that you anticipate may be especially challenging or rigorous for your students.
• You may consider having the students draw their own pictures to represent the analogy. This visual can serve as a reminder that feeling unsure or occasionally overwhelmed is a natural part of the learning process. Their artwork can encourage them to keep going, use their resources, and remember that, with time, it will become easier!
• You might want to create a poster to be displayed in the classroom as a collective reminder of the "Itchy Sweater in the Woods" analogy. Every student, along with you as the teacher, can sign it to symboloze your commitment to persevering, even when learning becomes challenging.</td></tr>
<tr><td>Step 2:
Not So Sure . . .
</td><td>"I'm stuck!": Normalize the feeling of being stuck with your students. Discuss what it can feel like and share that all people, even adults, can feel stuck and unsure of what to do. This can happen when you are trying to learn something new—it is a sign that you are growing and learning!
Take action: A lack of action can make you feel more unsure and less confident, and you can begin to feel small. Take a deep breath, then try a step toward becoming "unstuck." Taking action helps you to take control and explore what might work.
Where to start? Have students talk through the problem. What is it they do know about the task? Where do they think they are getting stuck? What resources do they have to turn to? Can they try to map out a plan or attempt to solve the problem? If they end up being wrong, they will learn from their mistake.
Share: Provide your students with examples of times you felt stuck and how you moved past it. Look for examples in your classroom and have students share how they moved past being stuck.</td></tr>
<tr><td>Step 3:
Way to Grow!
</td><td>Learning is growing: The more we can help our students understand that learning is a process that helps them grow, the better. If they give up and stop trying, they will stay stuck. When something is challenging and you stay with it, you will gain a sense of accomplishment and you will continue to grow.
Share: Continue to look for opportunities within your instruction to remind students of times when they were stuck and how they worked past it. Remind them of how difficult or challenging something seemed at first and how it became easier. These reminders reinforce the concept with tangible examples.</td></tr>
</table>

Step 4: Looking Back 	**Reflection:** It is so easy for us to stay focused on what we can't do yet and to forget about how far we have come. Provide continuing opportunities for your students to pause and reflect on their growth and progress. What are they proud of? What used to be really hard but has become much easier? It is important to stop and recognize even small victories.
Step 5: Looking Forward 	**Reflection:** While we want our students to pause to reflect on their growth or journey as a learner, we also want them to look ahead and set new goals. These goals can be related to academics, to making new friends, or to learning a new skill or trying out a new hobby. Helping students to set a goal, plan out the steps they will take to get there, and monitor their progress along the way will set them up with a valuable lifelong skill.

Image Sources: Istock.com/Maria Milovanova; Istock.com/bgblue; Istock.com/AbdulHayue; Istock.com/muhammad sukron makmun; Istock.com/Penti-Stock; Istock.com/Stakes; Istock.com/Genestro

How You See the Glass: The Power of Perspective

STRATEGY The Power of Perspective 	**How do you see it?** Sharing the idea of seeing the same glass as either half full or half empty is a concrete, visual way of helping students to understand perspective. It is a clear example of how different people can view the same object or situation and both "see" it differently. **No right or wrong:** When helping our students understand multiple perspectives, we will want to emphasize that there can be several viewpoints without any one "right way." We should step back and give consideration to the views of others. **Go positive:** Talking through situations where individuals can take a negative or positive perspective has value. These talk-through exercises can support students' understanding that they can make the choice of taking a positive view. A positive mindset will help them through challenges or negative situations.
Tool: Gratitude Journal 	**Positive focus:** Research shows us that regularly practicing gratitude can help to build resilience and develop optimism. This practice has been linked to improving overall well-being, increasing happiness, and developing a mindset that can move past setbacks. Here are some tips: • Start a weekly practice of you and your students writing down three things that you are grateful for. To get them started, you can share examples that include "nonthings" such as hearing birds singing, spending time with a friend, or doing well on a test. • Journals can be a simple notebook or a digital format. • Consider a dedicated day of the week to start your class, such as having "Gratitude Wednesdays"; this will help to solidify the practice within your schedule.

(Continued)

(Continued)

<table>
<tr><td>Tool:
Agency—You Choose!
</td><td>Empower: As an educator you have the ability to empower your students by helping them to develop a sense of agency. When students recognize that their decisions and choices influence events, they can gain a sense of control over their own lives. When students see that even small choices lead to real outcomes, they begin developing a sense of agency. This realization empowers them to take more ownership of their learning and will transfer to other areas of their lives. Here are some ideas for helping students develop agency:
• Share examples or look for opportunities in books to highlight individuals exercising agency in their lives through the choices or actions that they take.
• Examples of agency can come from interactions with peers or adults. Other examples can be directly connected to learning, such as taking time to study, asking for help when needed, or giving their best effort.
• Finding a Plan B: When something doesn't go as planned or a mistake is made, help students to see they can take some agency over what will happen next.</td></tr>
</table>

Image Sources: Istock.com/designer29; Istock.com/Muhammad khaleeq; Istock.com/Anastasia Usenko

KEY AREA 4: CULTURAL CHAMPIONSHIP

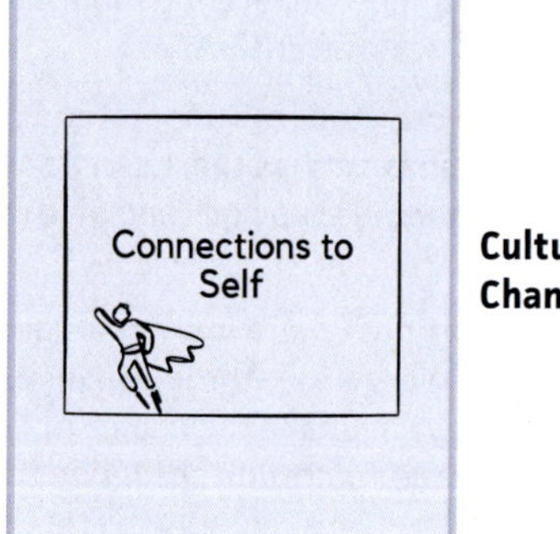	**Cultural Championship**	Cultural championship starts with comprehending your own culture and values while also being able to understand, respect, and appreciate the diverse backgrounds and differences of others. It includes an ability to communicate and interact with those from diverse cultural backgrounds.

INTEGRATING CULTURAL COMPETENCE INTO INSTRUCTION

As you may recall from Chapter 1, one of the top qualities that employers are looking for is cultural competence. With today's diverse world and workplace, we need individuals who are able to effectively interact and collaborate with people from culturally and linguistically diverse backgrounds. Beyond comfortably navigating conversations and tasks with people who have a different background than your own, it is important to be able to seek and value the diverse experiences, backgrounds, and perspectives of others. When cultural championship is a value and a priority within an environment, it creates an atmosphere of inclusivity and belonging for everyone there. Culturally responsive instruction helps students from backgrounds outside the mainstream develop a strong sense of identity and provides them with pathways to use their knowledge base within their learning, thus making it relevant to them.

When you take a moment to pause and visualize an entryway to a school, we are fairly confident that many of you pictured "Welcome" on a poster or sign written in multiple languages. Unfortunately, we cannot "Etsy" our way to create an inclusive school environment. Placing a sign on the wall or having an annual Cultural Celebration Night does not necessarily create a place where cultural awareness is fostered within classrooms and across locations throughout the school on a daily basis. We must shift our mindset away from the idea that dedicating just one night a year to showcase customs or posting signs in multiple languages is enough to consider schools culturally competent.

We have interviewed former students who now have the maturity and experience to reflect back on their time in school. Several reported that having time to ask each other questions and to find out about the backgrounds and experiences of others helped them to learn about their peers as well as learn more about themselves. Many felt that including conversations where students were able to share information from their unique backgrounds or incorporate their heritage language helped everyone to see beyond themselves and gain insights from others, and it enabled everyone to be seen, valued, and heard. Students in classes where connections are continually made to diverse backgrounds, cultures, and experiences come to see themselves as a part of a broader shared human experience and a multicultural community.

We need our schools to prioritize cultural championship as a cornerstone component within and across our educational system. Schools should view culture as entailing more than certain foods or traditional clothing; culture includes knowledge, experiences, values, and beliefs. According to Bartlett (2022), *culture* can reference race, ethnicity, gender, sexual orientation, ability, age, religion, income level, or geographical location. As shared by the National Education Association (2022), "Students have a right to a safe, welcoming, and affirming learning environment in a school that respects and values them and is free of bias." This statement calls for us as educators to be intentional and relentless about creating and sustaining a learning space that acknowledges and values diversity on a daily basis.

STRATEGIES FOR INTEGRATING CULTURAL COMPETENCE INTO CONTENT INSTRUCTION

Take a Closer Look: Similarities and Differences

<table>
<tr>
<td>STRATEGY
Take a Closer Look
</td>
<td>What: In guiding your students to take a closer look at the ways they are similar to and different from their diverse peers, you can support them in building cultural competence. Raising this awareness promotes a deeper appreciation for the multicultural world that we live in.

Build an understanding: You can support your students in understanding the meaning of cultural competence. Cultural competence can include the following:

• Understanding and appreciating individuals from diverse backgrounds
• Showing respect for different backgrounds, experiences, and languages
• Seeking out and valuing the perspectives of others
• Listening to understand others, not to judge them
• Treating everyone with kindness and respect
• Going out of your way to make sure everyone is included and welcomed</td>
</tr>
<tr>
<td>Tool:
Same and Different
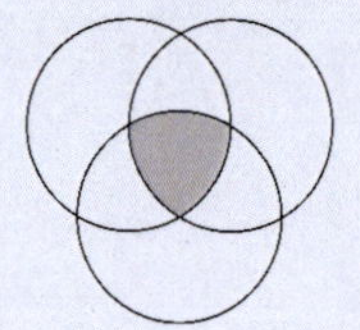</td>
<td>Compare and contrast: Students of all grade levels benefit from time spent identifying similarities and differences in multiple contexts. This can include the following:

• Identify what is the same and different about students in a class; this can include finding out where they were born, which languages they speak, their ages, their favorite foods or holidays, and their favorite sports or hobbies.
• Compare characters in a book and determine how they are alike and how they are different. How do they learn from each other?
• Choose individuals from history, sports, or the arts. What do they have in common? What is unique to them? How did their experiences impact their lives?
• Take a glimpse across the globe using a free tool such as Dollar Street (gapminder.org), which is designed to help people see similarities and differences around the world by introducing families from other countries through pictures and videos.</td>
</tr>
<tr>
<td>Tool:
In the Same Boat
</td>
<td>In this together: Students have shared that they felt supported and connected when they were able to talk with others in their classes who were going through similar experiences. These challenges can also be shared through text or video clips from others. These challenges may include the following:

• Academic challenges: Help students to realize they are not the only ones who are struggling with new content or finding a learning task to be difficult.</td>
</tr>
</table>

	• **Transition challenges:** These might include moving to a new grade level or school, moving from a new country, or trying a new club or team for the first time. • **Emotional challenges:** These challenges include becoming easily frustrated, feeling shy, or experiencing the loss of a loved one or pet. • **Social challenges:** This may mean finding it challenging to make friends, having a friend shift away to others, feeling excluded, or feeling judged for their appearance, food, or clothing choices.
Tool: **Learning From Others** 	**What have you tried?** Students can support each other with strategies or by hearing about the experiences of others. Everyone faces challenges, but it is easy to feel alone in trying to handle them. Normalizing the challenges we face by integrating them into instruction helps students. • **Modeling:** You can share some experiences that you have had and share with students how you or your friends met different challenges. • **Conversations:** Provide your students with opportunities to learn from each other through facilitating discussions where they can share their unique experiences. • **Examples:** Within every content area there are examples of individuals who faced struggles and overcame them to go on to be successful. Some used a negative situation as an opportunity to help others or they demonstrated perseverance to achieve a goal.
Tool: **Multicultural World** 	**Embracing diversity:** Intentional, ongoing effort is required to create learning spaces that are welcoming and inclusive of all. Fostering cultural understanding and dialogue to dissolve common stereotypes and break down barriers is important. Celebrating and integrating diverse cultures, ethnicities, and backgrounds builds welcoming classrooms. • **Culturally inclusive curriculum:** Ensure that instructional materials reflect diverse perspectives, cultures, and histories. Include instructional resources that offer multiple perspectives. • **Inclusive environment:** Create a classroom community where all students feel seen, heard, and valued. Promote a sense of belonging for all students and provide opportunities for students to share their diverse backgrounds. • **Literature and books:** Provide your students with multiple books that celebrate diversity and feature characters from many diverse backgrounds. Students should be able to see themselves reflected in book options and to learn about others. • **Celebrating contributions:** Highlight the contributions made by individuals and groups from diverse cultural backgrounds. Incorporate stories and biographies of those from diverse backgrounds and celebrate their achievements in science, literature, art, history, and other subjects.

Image Sources: Istock.com/Turac Novruzova; Istock.com/Ekaterina Grebeshkova; Istock.com/Anzela Alikina; Istock.com/Blankstock; Istock.com/DESKCUBE

The Power of Words: Building Kindness and Empathy

The Power of Words 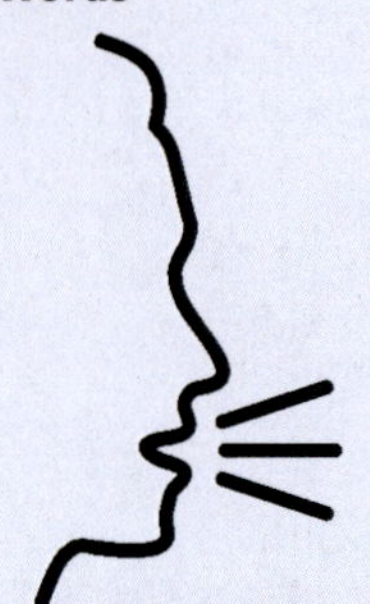	**What:** As educators we have an opportunity to help our students understand the power of the words that they use. Building this awareness promotes kindness, empathy, and effective communication skills. If we do not address the power of words, students may repeat hurtful things they have heard or not think through their words carefully. **Build an understanding:** You can help your students understand the consequences of the words that they use. Sharing examples of positive, respectful language as opposed to words that can hurt or minimize others builds an awareness of their impact on others. Collaborating on expectations for word choice and active listening within your classroom creates the foundation for a safe, supportive environment.
Tool: **Word Choice** 	**The weight of words:** Help students to evaluate words and the power that they hold. Work together to create lists of words and the emotions or reactions that may be connected to them. • **Words related to learning:** Explore positive and negative words that can be used in learning, such as *growth, failure, curiosity, confusion, improvement, difficult, challenging, impossible, discovery*, or *struggle*. How can these words impact the outlook on learning? • **Words in conversation:** Raise students' awareness of how the words they use with others may impact them. Create lists together of kind, respectful language and words or those that may be insulting, exclusionary, or hurtful.
Tool: **Active Listening** 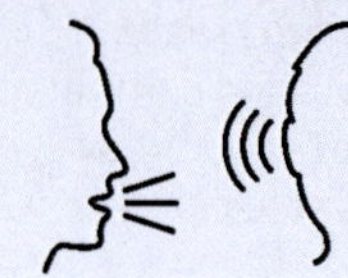	**Listen to understand:** Help students to develop active listening skills that allow them to be fully present and seek information from others rather than waiting to respond. • **Show:** Demonstrate that you are ready to listen with eye contact, smiling, and showing that you care about what the other person is saying. • **Ask questions:** Teach your students to ask clarifying questions or questions that seek more information related to what the person has shared as a way of showing engagement and interest. • **Summarize:** Have students practice summarizing or paraphrasing what others have said. They can repeat some of the key points to check if they heard the intended message.
Tool: **Pause and Think** 	**You can't take it back:** Work with students to understand the value of the pause. Speaking before thinking, especially when you are feeling strong emotions, may lead you to say something you wish you could take back and then you may need need to apologize for some harm that has been done. • **Pause:** Help students to think through their words by asking how they would feel if someone said those words to them. • **Reframe:** How can you say or ask something in a way that will feel safe and nonjudgmental to the person you are speaking with? • **Model:** Collaborate with your students on ways that other words or phrases could be used. Create examples of reframing, such as changing "What are you eating? That smells gross" to "I have never seen that kind of food before. Can you tell me about it? What do you like about it?"

Tool: **Role-Play Scenarios** 	**Act it out:** The more that students can visualize the power of their words, the better prepared they will be to make better choices when speaking with others. Helping students see multiple ways to reframe what they are saying can help to create a kinder, more empathetic learning space. • **Teacher-provided examples:** You can provide examples for your students to act out. These can include teaching points you want to cover or you can branch out from a text you have recently read with your class. • **Student-created examples:** Once students understand role-plays, they can work in groups to create and present their own scenarios. The group can lead the class in a discussion afterward.

Image Sources: Istock.com/Pavlo Stavnichuk; Istock.com/Pavlo Stavnichuk; Istock.com/Blankstock; Istock.com/Janis Abolins

In Their Shoes: Tableau for Multiple Perspectives

In Their Shoes 	**What:** Use the strategy of tableau to provide students with opportunities to consider the perspectives of others. This strategy involves students creating a frozen picture using their bodies to represent and explore a specific scene, emotion, idea, or perspective. **Build an understanding:** Help students to understand the concept of a tableau: They will be creating a "picture" or scene using themselves and props. When they receive a tap on their shoulder, they will be asked to share what the person they are representing in the scene might be thinking. There are multiple videos of this strategy being used in school settings; you may choose to preview and share some of these examples to help students gain a better idea of the strategy.
Step 1: **Picture of a Scene** 	**Select a scene or scenario:** Collaborate with your students to select a scene from a book or a scenario related to your content area. • **Plan:** Plan out the scene, including how many people will be needed to recreate it and if any props will be used. Remind students that no one will be moving—they are creating a still snapshot. • **Review:** Make sure that everyone is clear on their role within the tableau. Ask them to think about how their character is feeling or what they may be thinking during that specific scene. • **Shoulder tap:** When a student is tapped on the shoulder, they unfreeze and share what their character is thinking and feeling during the scene. • **Multiple perspectives:** This strategy is helpful to show students that even those in the same scene or experiencing the same event from history may have very different viewpoints on the occurrence.
Step 2: **Explorer Perspective** 	**Perspective:** Further students' understanding that perspective is the way that someone understands or sees a situation based on their own unique background, previous experiences, feelings, and beliefs. • **Explore:** Use tableau experiences to place different characters into the same scene in order to hear how individuals may have different perspectives even when faced with the same situation or circumstance. These snapshots can come from historic events or books, or even from current events.

(Continued)

(Continued)

	• **Academic outlook:** You may create a snapshot of an academic challenge and then have differing characters, such as a person that becomes frustrated and gives up, one that is okay with making mistakes and trying things a number of ways, and one that seeks resources to solve a problem.
Step 3: **Create Your Own** 	**Topic possibilities:** Provide students with a range of topics, emotions, social situations, or outlooks that you would like for them to explore. Options include social anxiety, making friends, peer pressure, or specific topics or scenes related to content areas. • **Groups or individuals:** Have students collaborate on creating these scenarios, or have individual "directors" create the scenes and work with students to play roles.
Step 4: **Reflect and Analyze** 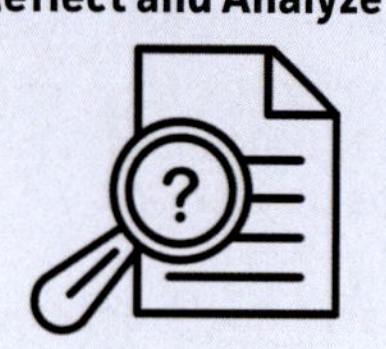	**What is your takeaway?** Guide students or have them lead reflections after the tableau. • What was your takeaway from what you just saw? • Do you think there are other perspectives that could be represented? • Share something you have learned from this tableau.

Image Sources: Istock.com/SAM Designs; Istock.com/appleuzr; Istock.com/Miray Celebi Kaba; Istock.com/Urfan Dadashov;

CHAPTER SUMMARY

Having a strong sense of self is the foundation for learning and interacting with others. Every child should recognize and understand their strengths, talents, and interests, and see themselves as capable of achieving their dreams. We invite you to reflect on ways to apply the ideas and strategies in this chapter, which focuses on the essential connection skill of connection to self. Consider ways in which you can weave the key areas (self-awareness, self-security, resilience, and cultural championship) that make up this skill into your curriculum, instructional practices, assessments, and relationships with students.

Reflection Questions

1. What are you already doing in classrooms to foster the essential skill of connecting to self?
2. Which of the four key areas (self-awareness, self-security, resilience, and cultural championship) need to be developed in your setting?
3. How can educators support students in developing a positive self-image and a strong sense of identity, especially for those who may have experienced trauma or low self-esteem?
4. What role does cultural competence play in building students' connections to self? How can schools ensure they are fostering a culturally inclusive environment?
5. Which of the strategies suggested in this chapter will you enact in your setting, and how will you gather data on its effectiveness?

Connections to Others

CHAPTER 3

"The business of business is relationships; the business of life is human connection."

—Robin Sharma

Your Snapshot Guide:

Connections to Others

	The ability to connect with others not only enhances learning but is also a valuable lifelong skill. When students develop effective communication skills, it paves the way for collaboration. As students work together on projects, they expand their problem-solving abilities. By participating in team activities, students learn to take responsibility for their own contributions and also provide support to ensure the success of their fellow team members.
	Individuals that have the ability to form strong connections with others develop strong social and emotional skills, thus enhancing their overall well-being. At school, students who have connections with their teachers and peers have been shown to have higher levels of engagement in their learning. These connections also help students to gain exposure to diverse perspectives, which helps to foster empathy and appreciation for differences.
	Integrating strategies into your instruction that provide students with opportunities to develop connections with others supports both deeper learning of content (mind) and enhanced personal growth (heart). These strategies incorporate increased levels of meaningful communication, critical thinking, teamwork, and ownership of learning.
	A classroom environment that incorporates learning through connections with others not only has increased academic outcomes but is also preparing students to thrive in the workplace and life. These connections increase a sense of belonging and acceptance, which allows students to take risks in their learning and motivates them to try their best.

Four Key Areas Within the ECS Domain of Connections to Others	
Communication Skills	Teamwork
Problem-Solving	Responsibility

ESSENTIAL CONNECTION SKILL: CONNECTIONS TO OTHERS

Collaboration skills are important for success in the real world. Many professions require teams of individuals to work together to solve complex problems and to creatively identify potential solutions or alternatives to the way things have been traditionally done. Some of the many fields that include a need for these skills are business, research, engineering, medicine, education, science, and politics. Research shows that employers value those individuals who can work effectively with others. With the increasing prevalence of artificial intelligence in the workplace, employers are placing an even greater importance on soft skills such as the ability to form human connections and effectively communicate (Cardon, 2024). Human interactions, collaboration, and the ability to develop trusting relationships that bring out individuals' talents and creativity will continue to be the foundation for successful businesses and organizations.

As our world continues to become increasingly connected, the students of today, more than ever, need to have the skills necessary to collaboratively solve problems with individuals who are different from themselves. Being able to work together as a part of a team, with teammates from different cultures, backgrounds, and perspectives, is vital. A study highlighted by *Forbes* (Lyons, 2021) showed that decisions made and executed by diverse teams delivered 60 percent better results than decisions by more homogeneous teams. Individuals who are adept at problem-solving and who can include others in the process are valued employees. Those who take responsibility for their portion of a project—who are reliable and organized—are recognized as desirable to work with and the type of employee to be sought out and hired. In teaching these skills and providing opportunities to apply them, we are preparing our students to be successful in their future workplace.

There are even more benefits to including these skills within our instruction. This chapter centers on structures and strategies that will provide students with meaningful opportunities to form connections with others while working together to tackle and solve problems or work toward a shared goal. Transforming certain instructional activities from independent work to team-based learning brings about multiple benefits. It immerses students in an environment where they develop a shared understanding of a problem and then collectively explore potential solutions by combining their distinct perspectives, knowledge, and strengths. Furthermore, students have the opportunity to build connections with each other while they learn.

Some educators continue to dedicate significant time and effort to managing and limiting the amount of student talking that takes place during their lessons instead of utilizing this natural inclination to enhance their instruction. Research indicates that students exhibit more interest and motivation when they collaborate to accomplish a meaningful objective together (Sun et al., 2022). Additionally, incorporating friendly competition among groups often amplifies the energy and motivation for the learning task. According to Vygotsky (1978), "By giving our students practice in talking with others, we give them frames for thinking on their own" (p. 19). By engaging with academic content in a more profound manner, students not only have increased opportunities to develop language and ECS but they also acquire valuable skills that will contribute to their success beyond the classroom. This is truly a win-win situation!

Even though there will always be value to students accomplishing tasks independently, there are many missed opportunities in classrooms to enhance learning and student engagement through collaborative experiences. These opportunities provide engagement in the content while helping students develop interpersonal skills such as active listening, openness, empathy, nonverbal communication, and conflict resolution. Students benefit from connecting with each other to accomplish specific tasks. They will have to navigate their collective approach to the project, use the appropriate language to convey their ideas, and listen to the contributions of others. There are many opportunities to easily adapt more conventional projects by using the strategies in this chapter.

THE IMPORTANCE OF BUILDING CONNECTIONS WITH OTHERS

As we have shared, through our visits to numerous classrooms we have witnessed the shift to students spending much of their school day working on computers; in small, teacher-directed groups; or independently applying skills. When you break from this and provide your students with opportunities to connect and learn together, you are shifting instruction from passive to active learning, which has been shown to have a positive impact on both student achievement and student skill development (Yannier et al., 2021). Students themselves, as reported both in our own interviews and in outside research, share that they enjoy learning the most when they interact with their peers. Connectedness with others makes learning more engaging and also deepens their learning and understanding of the content being explored. The students build knowledge through their interactions with others in the group, which then translates to improved individual learning outcomes.

Beyond academics, those students with more peer and adult connections at school have better school attendance (Eklund et al., 2020). Across the United States, chronic absenteeism, defined as missing 10 percent or more of a school year, surged from 15 percent in 2018 to 28 percent in 2022. These numbers are staggering, and the impact on these missing students will be ongoing. For those students that are in attendance, the work of Immordino-Yang (2016) highlights that the cognitive processes associated with learning are inextricably linked in the brain to emotional ones, indicating that connections are a necessary precondition both for learning and for the students' overall well-being.

The interruption to in-person learning during the pandemic had both an impact on our students' academic achievement and also a lasting effect on students' social skills. Even before the pivot to remote learning in the spring of 2020, there had been debate around the hours children of all ages were spending immersed in screen time. There was a call by many to reduce time on devices and to encourage kids to get outside and to spend time with others in real life (IRL). Students themselves acknowledge that the majority of their social interactions outside of school take place over the phone or within gaming platforms and that they struggle to connect with others IRL (Abi-Jaoude et al., 2020). Not surprisingly, with diminished social skills, schools have seen a significant spike in student misbehavior (Perera & Dilliberti, 2023). We have the opportunity to strengthen our students' abilities to form and sustain in-person connections with others, which helps to minimize disruptive behaviors.

BUILDING CONNECTIONS TO OTHERS IN CONTENT INSTRUCTION

The strategies included in this chapter will help you build meaningful opportunities for your students to practice and increase their ability to connect with others. Within this ECS domain there are four key areas: communication skills, teamwork, problem-solving, and responsibility. The strategies that follow can be used across grade levels and content areas to give your students opportunities to learn while forming connections with others. Examples are shared to help you start to envision how these tools or strategies may be used with your own students. Please also keep in mind that Chapter 6, "Connecting to All Learners," will give you additional strategies and adaptations for your students with varying needs.

PLANNING FOR CONNECTIONS TO OTHERS

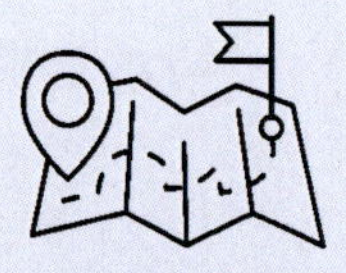 **Where Are You?** **Where Are You Headed?**	**What:** Your first step in planning is determining which of the four key areas and its components you will be focused on within your instruction. All of the strategies will provide your students with team-based learning experiences that integrate connections to others. As the teacher you will determine the area(s) the students in front of you need to develop the most.
 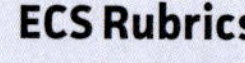 **ECS Rubrics**	**Rubrics:** Use the rubrics that follow for each of the four key areas within the essential connection skill of connections to others—communications skills, teamwork, problem-solving, and responsibility—to plan the specific focus area as you implement the strategy.
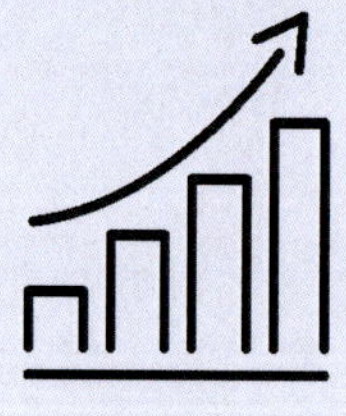 **Skill Target**	**Baseline data and goal setting:** Use the rubric and observations to determine the starting level of your students within the specific competency area that you have chosen. Plan for how you will move each group of students forward. For those that demonstrate exemplary skills, how will you move them to the next level? **Post-assessment data:** Through additional observations, what growth is noted in your students? Which areas will need continued focus and more opportunities for development?
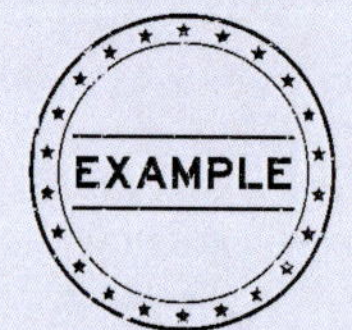	**Classroom example:** Based on observations of my class, it is clear that an area of need is improved listening skills. My students often miss key information that is shared from adults or peers. **Key area: communication skills: *listening*** • Baseline data: Using the rubric, students are identified as Level 4, Exemplary; Level 3, Proficient; Level 2, Developing; or Level 1, Emerging as their starting point.

Image Sources: Istock.com/Turac Novruzova; Istock.com/Miray Celebi Kaba; Istock.com/bgblue;Istock.com/bankrx

	• Skill targets: Within each band, plans are made for moving students into the next developmental band: ○ Students starting in Levels 1 and 2 will have small-group or individual conferences to support their listening skills development. ○ Those in Level 3 will be supported to increase active listening and demonstrating respect for the ideas of others, including self-reflection. ○ Those students in Level 4 will continue to build active listening by summarizing information and making explicit connections to prior knowledge. • Post-assessment data: Which students have demonstrated growth? Which will require additional opportunities for development? What will new goals be?

KEY AREA 1: COMMUNICATION SKILLS

Our students come to us with a wide range of communication skills. As a teacher you have a crucial opportunity to help all of your students to become effective communicators. By helping to develop their active listening skills, enabling them to successfully convey their messages orally or in writing, and encouraging them to initiate and sustain conversations, you will provide them with a lifelong advantage. According to Stott (2018), teachers should explicitly describe and model what good communication looks like across different contexts. This includes consideration of body language and the speaker's use of language; the ability to build on, challenge, question, or summarize the ideas of others; and building depth of listening and the ability to effectively respond to others.

Empowering your students with effective communication skills and multiple opportunities to practice and apply these skills has numerous benefits. Not only will this increase your students' interaction with content and provide depth of learning but it will also support students' behavior. When students are able to communicate effectively, they are less likely to engage in disruptive behaviors. They can express themselves and seek help constructively. This clarity in communication and ability to engage in conversations with others also reduces misunderstandings that can lead to escalated conflicts. Building this competency contributes to a more productive and positive classroom environment, which supports the development of prosocial behaviors.

Preparing your students for the ECS lesson by establishing a specific focus, building a shared understanding of the component, modeling both what to do and what not to do, and then having students set an individual focus will help them to get the most that they can from the lesson. According to Zwiers (2020), "Language development was never meant to be separated from content learning, nor vice versa" (p. 1). Integrating the intentional development of language skills within content learning through a collaborative focus will maximize your students' growth across the board and will improve their learning outcomes. Explicitly highlighting these skills and having each student set their own intentional goal within the lesson (and providing an opportunity to reflect after the lesson) will help set the stage for your students to learn and grow their language skills.

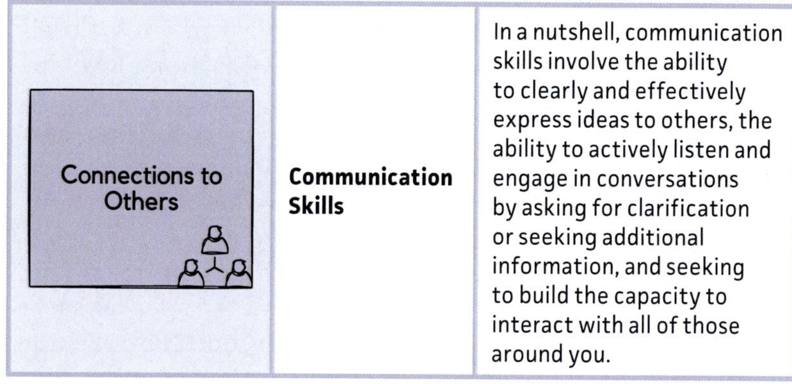

Connections to Others	**Communication Skills**	In a nutshell, communication skills involve the ability to clearly and effectively express ideas to others, the ability to actively listen and engage in conversations by asking for clarification or seeking additional information, and seeking to build the capacity to interact with all of those around you.

Sample Formative Assessment Tool for Communication Skills

	LEVEL 4 EXEMPLARY	LEVEL 3 PROFICIENT	LEVEL 2 DEVELOPING	LEVEL 1 EMERGING
Verbal Communication	Speaks clearly and confidently Uses appropriate volume and tone Use of eye contact	Speaks with some clarity and confidence Appropriate volume Some eye contact	Speech may be unclear or hesitant Peers or teachers ask for clarification Limited eye contact	Hesitant to speak with others Low volume Minimal or no eye contact

	LEVEL 4 EXEMPLARY	LEVEL 3 PROFICIENT	LEVEL 2 DEVELOPING	LEVEL 1 EMERGING
Listening	Listens actively and attentively Remains focused and shows respect for others' ideas	Demonstrates active listening skills Will occasionally lose focus	Demonstrates limited active listening skills May become distracted	Seemingly not engaged in listening Appears distracted
Conveying Information	Uses a variety of vocabulary Communicates ideas effectively using relevant details and examples	Uses basic vocabulary Shares ideas with some relevant details and examples	Uses simple vocabulary Often struggles to share ideas effectively, lacking details or examples	Limited use of words Off-topic
Questioning	Asks clarifying questions Seeks additional information when needed	Occasionally asks clarifying questions Seeks additional information at times	Rarely asks clarifying questions Does not typically seek additional information	Limited asking of questions Does not seek additional information
Participating	Engages in turn-taking Actively participates in discussions Sustains discussion Provides thoughtful feedback	Occasionally needs reminders to take turns Overall stays engaged in discussions Provides some feedback to peers	Often needs reminders to take turns and stay engaged in the discussion Provides minimal feedback to peers	Requires direct prompting and encouragement to participate in discussions

Image Sources: Istock.com/da-vooda;Istock.com/Blankstock; Istock.com/Esra Sen Kula; Istock.com/phototechno;

KEY AREA 2: TEAMWORK

The *Merriam-Webster Dictionary* (Merriam-Webster, n.d.-d) defines teamwork as "work done by a group acting together so that each member does a part that contributes to the efficiency of the whole." Providing students with opportunities to collaborate in team settings is the best way to help them understand the importance of an effective team and the qualities needed to be a valuable team member. Integration of teamwork into core instruction provides students with practice and application of communication and interpersonal skills. Teamwork is an element in many facets of life. As educators we can empower our students through experiences both as team leaders and as members of a group that works together to achieve a common goal.

According to Duckworth (2021), including teamwork in learning can help learning feel more connected to the real world. In the workplace, people frequently work together to accomplish a project. Providing open-ended tasks and problems that students must collaborate on to solve mirrors what they will most likely encounter in a future workplace. Incorporating teamwork helps students to learn problem-solving skills and develop firsthand experience with group dynamics, and it provides elements of autonomy as they choose how to move forward toward their goal. This formatting engages students in the content, and they report having more fun when they can interact with their peers.

Students have shared that they often feel uncomfortable asking their teacher a question, especially when it is something they think they should already know, but working in a team provides them with the ability to ask each other. Others have reported they like accomplishing something together rather than feeling like they are trying to outperform all of their classmates. Through randomizing the teams that students work in, they will interact with individuals they may not typically seek out on their own. Increasing interactions with a wider range of peers helps them to gain insights through hearing multiple perspectives and developing an open mind to new ideas. These opportunities help to foster empathy and respect for individuals from diverse backgrounds and will often result in new friendships.

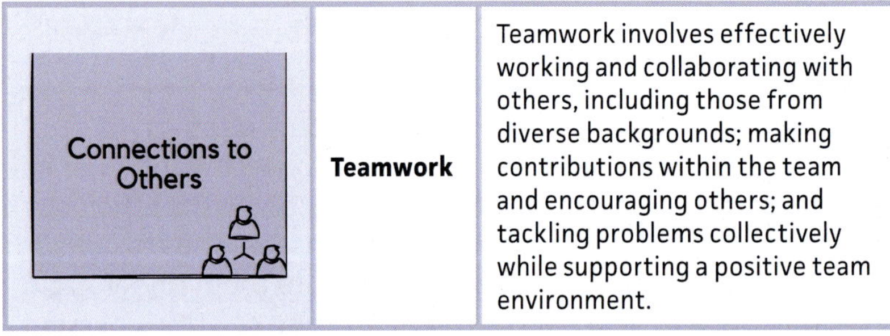

Connections to Others	**Teamwork**	Teamwork involves effectively working and collaborating with others, including those from diverse backgrounds; making contributions within the team and encouraging others; and tackling problems collectively while supporting a positive team environment.

Sample Formative Assessment Tool for Teamwork

	LEVEL 4 EXEMPLARY	LEVEL 3 PROFICIENT	LEVEL 2 DEVELOPING	LEVEL 1 EMERGING
Collaborating	Actively collaborates with others Encourages and supports the participation of others	Collaborates with others on the team Listens to teammates' ideas and respects diverse views	Participates but may need prompting of roles to take Listens to ideas of others but not always respectful of different viewpoints	Requires guidance to share responsibility within the group Struggles to listen to others
Contributing	Contributes multiple ideas Communicates effectively Demonstrates flexibility	Contributes ideas toward the team's goal Communicates clearly	Will contribute occasional ideas May not always be clear in sharing ideas	Requires prompting to share ideas Sharing of ideas is limited
Encouraging	Encourages, welcomes, and acknowledges the contributions of others Contributes to positive team atmosphere and celebrates achievements	Supportive of the contributions of others Maintains a positive team environment Acknowledges team achievements	Minimal recognition of the contributions of others Recognizes some team achievements	Support for the contributions of others may be limited or absent Lack of recognition for team achievement
Solution Seeking	Demonstrates flexibility and adaptability Resolves conflicts constructively; seeks win-win solutions	Demonstrates some flexibility Resolves conflicts with guidance; adheres to agreed-upon solutions	Has limited flexibility Requires guidance to resolve conflicts; may not move forward with solution	Lack of flexibility; can become stuck Requires significant guidance to resolve conflicts with peers

Image Sources: Istock.com/phototechno;Istock.com/Giorgi Gogitidze; Istock.com/Yuriy Altukhov

KEY AREA 3: PROBLEM-SOLVING

Integrating problem-solving within our classroom instruction supports our students' development into critical thinkers. Problem-solving is a skill that becomes better with practice and application. As students become more comfortable with addressing a problem head on, generating innovative solutions, analyzing potential outcomes, and thinking critically throughout the process, they are more likely to use this approach independently. The goal is for our students to routinely use their curiosity to analyze the world around them, ultimately arriving at their own conclusions about what they observe and experience.

Across grade levels there are tremendous gains in both academic performance and emotional intelligence when problem-solving is thoughtfully integrated into learning (Marshall, 2022). Not only is this a skill that actively engages students in their learning, it is also one of the top skills highly sought by future employers. When individuals become adept at problem-solving, they become effective collaborators, they develop their creativity, and they are more likely to display perseverance when facing challenges. We have both observed countless students who shut down at the first sign of feeling "stuck" or who seek out immediate help from someone else before trying an approach on their own. Those students with problem-solving skills tend to step back and take another look at the problem at hand and explore potential steps to try next.

Providing students with a basic framework for problem-solving that they can apply both in their learning and in resolving social conflicts is powerful. Teaching and modeling for our students how to stop and think to identify a problem, brainstorm innovative solutions, evaluate potential outcomes, review and adjust as they apply their ideas, and then stay with it and persevere through the process is invaluable. Walking students through the steps of problem-solving and then giving them repeated opportunities to apply the process will help them grow as critical, independent thinkers who are more likely to address learning challenges and social conflicts on their own. This prepares our students to successfully navigate the problems they will face both in the classroom and beyond.

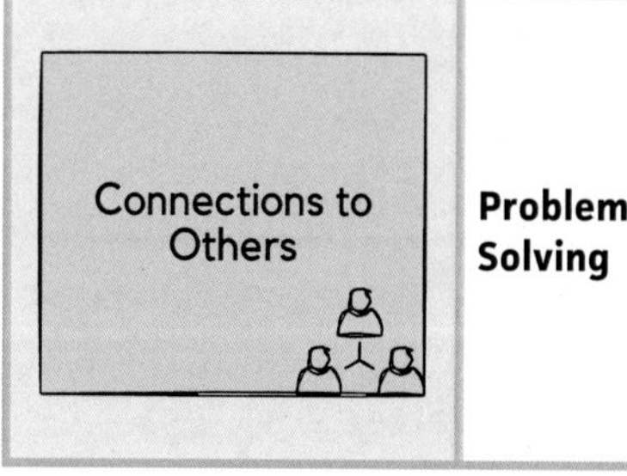	**Problem-Solving**	Problem-solving is the ability to clearly identify a problem, generate innovative solutions, and evaluate potential outcomes. Problem-solvers have the capability to review and make adjustments as well as persevere in the face of challenges. Problem-solving gives consideration to the perspectives of others.

Sample Formative Assessment Tool for Problem-Solving

	LEVEL 4 EXEMPLARY	LEVEL 3 PROFICIENT	LEVEL 2 DEVELOPING	LEVEL 1 EMERGING
Identifying the Problem	Analyzes problems effectively Identifies key issues Considers multiple perspectives	Identifies problems accurately Considers relevant factors Considers perspectives	Identifies problems with some guidance May overlook important factors or perspectives	Struggles to identify the problem Requires significant guidance to recognize issues
Innovating	Generates multiple creative and innovative solutions Ideas suggested are both logical and feasible	Generates creative solutions Ideas suggested are logical	Generates basic solutions May not be overly creative Ideas may be less practical	Presents limited ideas Limited creativity Suggestions are not practical
Evaluating	Applies critical thinking skills to evaluate potential outcomes Carefully and thoughtfully considers each potential solution	Analyzes potential outcomes Considers the advantages and disadvantages of potential solutions	Will attempt to analyze potential outcomes with some guidance	Struggles to analyze potential outcomes Has difficulty identifying outcomes without significant guidance
Reviewing and Making Adjustments	Independently implements and evaluates solutions; makes adjustments as needed Reflects on the outcomes and suggests future improvements	Implements and evaluates solutions with guidance; makes some adjustments if needed Reflects on the problem-solving process and suggests improvements	Requires support to implement and evaluate solutions; limited ability to make adjustments Shows some awareness of the problem-solving process; requires guidance for reflection	Requires support to implement and evaluate solutions; limited ability to make adjustments Shows minimal awareness of the problem-solving process
Persevering	Demonstrates persistence and resilience in finding solutions Remains committed and focused	Demonstrates some persistence in finding solutions Remains focused; may become discouraged	Demonstrates little persistence with challenges May become distracted; may show frustration	Gives up easily when encountering challenges May lose focus and have a tendency to give up

Image Sources: Istock.com/Turac Novruzova; Istock.com/-VICTOR-; Istock.com/-VICTOR-; Istock.com/PeterSnow

KEY AREA 4: RESPONSIBILITY

Teaching our students the meaning of responsibility provides them with a foundation for academic and life success. Taking ownership of their actions, prioritizing tasks, and following through on responsibilities will help them across all areas of life. Integrating responsibility within core instruction empowers students to become more independent and will help them to gain confidence in their own abilities. Considering how your words, choices, and actions will impact others is supportive of healthy relationships and successful work partnerships. This cornerstone skill is far too important to be left to chance and should be explicitly addressed within our classrooms.

In a recent *New York Times* article (Davis, 2023), students themselves pointed out the importance of teachers helping their students learn the value of responsibility and accountability. As one student put it, "Self-accountability, discipline, and order is vital to furthering your education and or just life in general." Creating an environment where students are accountable for their work helps them to take increased ownership of their learning and instills habits for success. Giving students opportunities to reflect on their progress or on the impact their actions have on others provides them with opportunities for growth. Teachers can provide and model the use of organizational tools, checklists, and reflection sheets to help students grow in this area.

To successfully form connections with others, our students need to be aware of how their choices in words and actions impact those around them. In working as a part of a team, students need to take responsibility for their portion of the work as others will be counting on them. In addition, students who are collaborating with others know that their ideas and work will be shared right away with their peers, which provides a different level of accountability than working on a task independently in a workbook or on a digital platform where their effort will only be known by their teacher. We have seen this structure motivate students to give their best effort because they know that others will be hearing and considering their contributions. When students grow in responsibility, they take pride in their work and they experience satisfaction with their accomplishments.

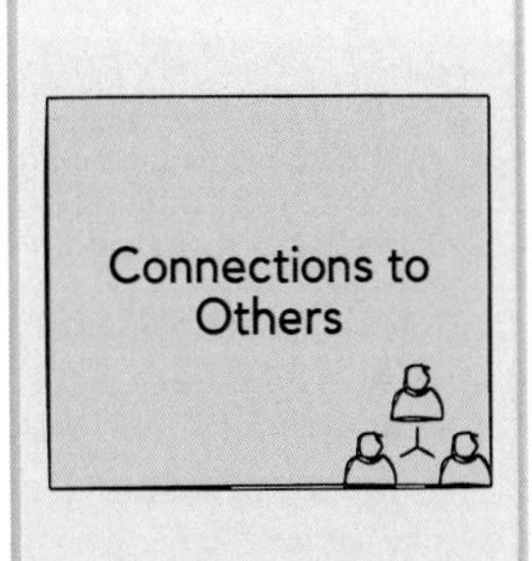	**Responsibility**	Responsibility entails having ownership and accountability for actions; being viewed by others as someone they can count on; having high levels of self-motivation; being organized and using time efficiently; and having the ability to manage reactions to others and across a variety of circumstances.

Sample Formative Assessment Tool for Responsibility

	LEVEL 4 EXEMPLARY	LEVEL 3 PROFICIENT	LEVEL 2 DEVELOPING	LEVEL 1 EMERGING
Accountability	Takes ownership of actions, choices, and commitments Accepts and acknowledges consequences, both positive and negative	Mostly takes ownership of actions, choices, and commitments Accepts consequences, both positive and negative, most of the time	Demonstrates occasional ownership of actions, choices, and commitments May struggle to accept consequences, both positive and negative	Rarely takes ownership of actions, choices, and commitments Struggles to accept consequences, both positive and negative
Reliability	Consistently fulfills responsibilities without needing reminders Takes ownership of tasks and always follows through	Usually fulfills responsibilities without frequent reminders Takes ownership of tasks and has reasonable follow-through	Requires occasional reminders to fulfill responsibilities Takes ownership of some tasks; may need assistance with follow-through	Requires frequent reminders to fulfill responsibilities Struggles to take ownership of tasks
Taking Initiative	Demonstrates a proactive attitude toward tasks and responsibilities Takes independent action with high levels of self-motivation	Often takes initiative toward tasks and responsibilities Requires occasional reminders to take independent action; satisfactory level of self-motivation	Occasionally takes initiative toward tasks and responsibilities Needs assistance or direction to take independent action; developing level of self-motivation	Rarely takes initiative toward tasks and responsibilities Requires significant assistance to take independent action; minimal level of self-motivation

(Continued)

(Continued)

	LEVEL 4 EXEMPLARY	LEVEL 3 PROFICIENT	LEVEL 2 DEVELOPING	LEVEL 1 EMERGING
Utilizing Organizational Skills	Consistently demonstrates excellent organizational skills Manages time effectively and prioritizes tasks efficiently	Usually demonstrates good organizational skills Manages time effectively and prioritizes tasks appropriately	Demonstrates some organizational skills but improvement is needed May have difficulty managing time effectively and can struggle to prioritize tasks	Displays limited organizational skills and significant improvement is needed Finds it challenging to manage time and struggles to prioritize tasks
Using Self-Control	Demonstrates consistent control in managing emotions and impulses Makes thoughtful, well-considered choices	Usually maintains control in managing emotions and impulses Generally makes thoughtful, well-considered choices	Demonstrates some control in managing emotions and impulses Makes an effort to consider choices and decisions; may act impulsively	Displays limited self-control in managing emotions and impulses Rarely makes thoughtful choices and decisions; often acts impulsively

Image Sources: Istock.com/Maksym Drozd; Istock.com/Artco; Istock.com/-VICTOR-; Istock.com/da-vooda; Istock .com/appleuzr

STRATEGIES FOR DEVELOPING THE ESSENTIAL CONNECTING SKILL OF CONNECTION TO OTHERS

The strategies within this section utilize small-group structures. There are many advantages to providing opportunities for students to work together. First, within these smaller structures, all students become actively engaged within the content, which serves as a sharp contrast to passively working on one's own. Students are exploring, considering, and discussing the information together. This enables them to learn from each other and to know the content at a deeper level as they participate in these conversations. Second, the students are able to grow in their social skills. They become directly involved in navigating group dynamics, communicating their ideas, and learning from the perspectives of others. These structures deeply engage students in their learning while simultaneously promoting their social growth, all while increasing the enjoyment of their time in school!

The table on the next page presents considerations to follow when placing your students into teams and setting them up to work together successfully.

Considerations for Effective Student Teams

<table>
<tr>
<td>Step 1:
Create Student Teams
</td>
<td colspan="2">Create student teams: The first step will be placing your students into teams. The ideal size for a team to work together is three to five students. With smaller groups such as this, each student will be actively engaged in the team's work. When the team is larger, even with assigned roles, it can be easier for some students to remain under the radar with less engagement.

Randomized groupings: Placing students into random teams can offer several advantages:<ul><li>It ensures that students will work with a more diverse group of peers, potentially interacting with those they typically would not seek out on their own. This may also help to reduce preconceived stereotypes and support the formation of new friendships. At a minimum, students gain better insights into each other, and these interactions help to develop an overall supportive community and increase inclusion within your classroom.</li><li>When students continue to work with varying peers, it continues to push them in developing effective communication skills. What worked in sharing your ideas last time may not work this time. Students learn to tailor their approach to working with new peers. This is also more reflective of work they will do throughout their learning and one day in the workplace. These groups provide practice in working with a range of personalities and people from diverse backgrounds.</li><li>This approach balances skills and strengths across groups and provides the students with the opportunity to make their own contributions within the team. This variety of perspectives promotes effective problem-solving and expanding one's thinking.</li></ul></td>
</tr>
<tr>
<td rowspan="3">Step 2:
Team Roles and Responsibilities
</td>
<td colspan="2">Roles and responsibilities: For teams to function effectively, it is important to assign specific roles or allow the teams to determine their own roles within the group. You may want to have a card for each role with bullet point reminders of the responsibility for that role; these cards can also be used by teams to randomly draw roles.

It is important for everyone to be able to experience the different roles within the team as they work in new groups. This rotation of responsibilities supports a collaborative and inclusive environment. Below are some roles to consider.</td>
</tr>
<tr>
<td></td>
<td>Leader/Facilitator: This person helps to ensure that the team stays on track and focused on the task at hand. This individual is also tasked with ensuring that each team member's voice is heard and considered. They are also responsible for guiding the team through resolving conflicts.</td>
</tr>
<tr>
<td></td>
<td>Recorder/Note Taker: This individual takes notes for the team. They can capture ideas, summarize key points, and record the team's progress. This individual helps with organization and documentation.</td>
</tr>
</table>

(Continued)

(Continued)

<table>
<tr><td rowspan="3"></td><td></td><td>Timekeeper: This individual is aware of the time allotted for the work. They can issue gentle reminders about the time remaining and the remaining tasks. This person can offer suggestions on how to use time effectively.</td></tr>
<tr><td></td><td>Presenter/Spokesperson: This person is responsible for sharing the team's work or providing a status update. This person can help to organize any visual aids or artifacts that the team will use to share their ideas or conclusions.</td></tr>
<tr><td></td><td>Researcher: The researcher will help to guide members of the team in seeking out the information, facts, or resources they will need to accomplish their work. They may help to divide the work and ask team members to share their findings. They can identify the areas where more information is needed.</td></tr>
<tr><td>Step 3:
Team Expectations
</td><td colspan="2">Team expectations: Once the team members have their individual roles, it is important to set the overall expectation for the team. This will serve as the foundation for the team to work together successfully to complete the objective. Here are some possible expectation options for you to consider:
• Respect: Treat each member on your team with respect. Listen to everyone's ideas, value their contributions, and use polite words. Be kind to all team members.
• Participation: An effective team takes everyone working together and sharing in the work. The team is stronger when everyone contributes.
• Cooperation: Work together and be a team player. Offer to help others, consider their ideas, and be willing to compromise.
• Organization: Organize your work so that you can share back with other team members. This helps the team to complete the task effectively in the time provided.
• Flexibility: As the team works together, you may decide to take your work in a new direction. Remain open to new possibilities and the perspectives and viewpoints of others on the team.
• Resolution: Remain calm and respectful as conflicts come up in the group. Step back and consider how to best move forward. Look for common ground, try to compromise, and seek the teacher's help if needed.
• Support: Actively support and encourage your fellow team members. If you see someone who is stuck, jump in to help. Provide positive feedback and acknowledge the contributions of others.
• Reflection: As a team, take the time to reflect. This does not have to wait until the project is over; check in to see what is going well and consider opportunities for improvement. Celebrate the team's achievements!</td></tr>
</table>

Step 4: **Effective Team Models** 	**Effective team models:** Even with set roles/responsibilities and reviewing the expectations for your teams, providing models for your students will help them to better visualize the ways in which an effective team works together. There are several ways to accomplish this: • Create videos of an effective team working together. You can create a short video modeling different components of an effective team with teacher colleagues. • Role-play specific elements of a team working together. You can provide students with a specific scenario and coach them through with think-alouds. • Stop and celebrate! As you see teams successfully navigating elements of group work together, have the class pause and celebrate and take the opportunity to share an exemplar. • Video student teams. As your students become more adept at working effectively together in teams, capture some video to use in future years with students. Capturing these examples of students can help future students better visualize what effective teamwork looks like.

Image Sources: Istock.com/appleuzr; Istock.com/Bulgakova Kristina; Istock.com/Designer; Istock.com/muhammad sukron makmun; Istock.com/appleuzr; Istock.com/da-vooda

EDU Showdown! Fueled by Friendly Competition

STRATEGY **EDU Showdown!** 	**What:** Students are grouped together to enhance learning through friendly competition. Each student addresses the task independently and then the students work together to consider each option and determine which response they want to move forward in the EDU (**E**ngage, **D**emonstrate, **U**nderstand) Showdown! Students further their understanding of the task at hand by discussing each individual option and collectively evaluating which response they should use in the competition. This provides both immediate accountability for each individual's work and active engagement with the content. **Bonus:** Having students work together in small groups fosters the development of social skills and dynamic interaction with the content. This structure allows students to learn from their peers and to practice their communication skills. This structure creates an inclusive environment where each individual's voice is heard and everyone belongs to a team. The students themselves report that learning is much more fun when they have the chance to work together. They also share that the friendly competition is motivating!
Step 1: **Build an Understanding of Friendly Competition** 	Your students will need an understanding of friendly competition before they can participate successfully in an EDU Showdown. Students should understand that it is a contest that takes place in a friendly and supportive atmosphere. This includes demonstrating respect, fairness, and collaboration with your team. The main focus should be on growing through teamwork, having fun, and striving to do your best together rather than just focusing on winning. Another expectation is for all teams to demonstrate good sporting behavior. This includes treating teammates and competitors with kindness and consideration regardless of the final outcome. It includes celebrating the work of the team and graciously accepting either victory or defeat.

(Continued)

(Continued)

<table>
<tr>
<td></td>
<td colspan="2">To demonstrate this you might use clips from a TV show such as Throwdown! With Bobby Flay. For those of you unfamiliar with this show, chef Bobby Flay challenges someone to prepare the food they are best known for in their area. He then goes to their town to challenge them to a friendly competition. A person known for making the best blueberry muffins, for example, might find themselves going up against the famed chef. This is an opportunity to discuss that while they will be using some of the same ingredients, each competitor will be putting their own twist on the muffin version they create. The judges then vote to determine which muffin they think is the best without knowing who created each one. The competition ends with the competitors shaking each other's hands and complimenting each other on their creations.

You might find different instances of friendly competition from your local area, school, or even a book that the class has recently discussed together.</td>
</tr>
<tr>
<td>Step 2:
Determine the Task or Problem
</td>
<td colspan="2">This should be something that the students can first attempt individually. This strategy typically centers around a single task or question that will allow students to have the opportunity to first work alone and then meet with their team and evaluate options. After consideration, each team extends together their choice for the showdown. This is all done within the same class period.

Variations: Once your students become familiar with the overall structure of EDU Showdowns and participate in them, you can consider the following:
• Tasks that will go beyond one class period
• Increasing the complexity of the tasks, such as providing specific academic vocabulary that must be included in their responses
• Adding in an additional "team combo" step where the teams are able to combine aspects from their individual responses to create a collaborative answer that they will move forward in the showdown
• Have the students suggest the topics or questions for upcoming EDU Showdowns</td>
</tr>
<tr>
<td rowspan="3"></td>
<td colspan="2">Content-Related Topic Examples</td>
</tr>
<tr>
<td>Science
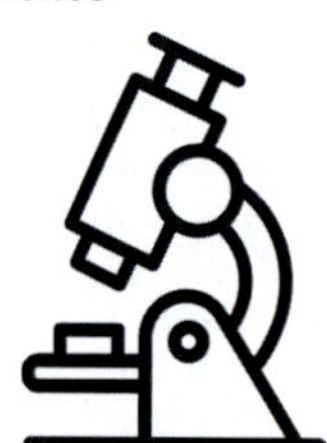</td>
<td>• Create a hypothesis to be answered by an experiment. Have students share the rationale for their thinking.
• Ask students to explain a scientific phenomenon. Which summary is the clearest and easiest to follow?
• Have students create an analogy to help others understand a science topic recently explored.</td>
</tr>
<tr>
<td>Social Science
</td>
<td>• Ask students to compare and contrast two separate historical events that you have discussed.
• Have students answer a question through the lens and voice of a historical figure.
• Provide a short answer to a prompt related to a recent class topic.</td>
</tr>
</table>

	Math	• Ask students to solve a problem and share the strategy they used. • Share a word problem and ask students what the problem is asking for and how they would solve it. • Ask students to create sample problems based on your current unit of instruction.
	English Language Arts 	• Have students write high-quality sentences or paragraphs using specific words or topics provided. • Ask for a fact and an opinion on the same subject. • Ask students to write a sentence in varying tones or from different perspectives.
	Specials   	**PE:** • Ask students to provide a step-by-step breakdown of a game or sport recently played in class. • Have students explain what it means to demonstrate fair play in sports. • Describe examples of healthy lifestyle choices. **Music:** • Ask students to write down their reaction to a piece of music. • Have students describe various musical genres. • Ask students what is needed to become a good musician or singer. **Art:** • Have students summarize a recent art history lesson. • Ask students to write a review of a famous piece of artwork. • Have students try to capture what message or feeling the artist is trying to evoke through their work. **STEM:** • Ask students to share an innovative solution to a current environmental challenge. • Have students take an existing invention and share potential improvements. • Ask students to summarize a recent lesson in a way they can teach others.

(Continued)

(Continued)

Step 3: **Students Work Independently** 	After sharing the task or question and ensuring that all students have a solid understanding of what is being asked of them, provide students with independent work time. You may consider using a timer while remaining flexible based on how the students are working. Check in to support students as needed and provide options for those who finish earlier than others, such as reading a book or creating a second response to the question.
Step 4: **Team Time!** 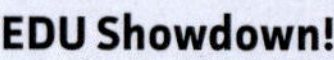	Once students have finished their individual responses, have them come together to share their work with their team members. Provide the teams with time to go through each individual response and determine which one to move forward in the EDU Showdown. **Variation:** You may ask the team to determine what they like best about each response and work together to create one new collective response by combining elements from each answer.
Step 5: **EDU Showdown!** 	After each team has decided on their chosen response for the EDU Showdown, collect all of the responses. • If possible, you will want to have a "judge" come into the classroom to review the responses and select the winner. This can be a teacher on plan time, a school or district administrator, a custodian, someone from the main office, a recess or lunch supervisor, or the school's librarian. • If no judge is available, you can lead your class through discussing what they like about each response and guide them to consensus on the winner. • You may have the judging take place in another class where those students will vote on their favorite response and share why they made their selection.

Image Sources: Istock.com/appleuzr; Istock.com/anttohoho; Istock.com/bsd studio; Istock.com/da-vooda; Istock .com/dejanj01; QIstock.com/Ideas; Istock.com/Jane_Kelly

EDU SHOWDOWN EXAMPLES

CLASSROOM EXAMPLE: ENGLISH LANGUAGE ARTS

A content goal within an English language arts classroom was to help students improve their writing skills with a back-to-basics focus on constructing solid sentences. In a more traditional approach, the students would have been provided with direct instruction on constructing a high-quality sentence and then been given pages to complete in a workbook or asked to create several sample sentences to be turned in to the teacher. If we put ourselves into the shoes of those students being asked to practice forming sentences independently without an engaging focus for the task, we can quickly see how they might be tempted to get the assignment over with without giving their best effort. Now let's keep the same content objective and see what happened when a teacher integrated the EDU Showdown strategy!

After explaining the concept of friendly competition to the students, the teacher pulled out a special file folder labeled "EDU Showdown" that contained the day's challenge. The teacher provided the students with words that they needed to use in creating their sentences. The energy and engagement in the classroom could be felt as the students worked on their own sentences in their respective teams. It was easy to see the students' excitement as they shared their sentences and evaluated them together to decide which one to put forward in the EDU Showdown. The students were excited to write and to share with their teammates, which was far different from practicing on their own. The students worked together, communicated their thoughts with each other as they made their decision on what to move forward, and they all gave their best effort knowing their peers would be reading their sentences.

Once the students became familiar with the structure of the EDU Showdown, the teacher was able to use it for increasingly complex content tasks, such as writing a fact or an opinion or a paragraph. The students would enter the classroom and ask excitedly, "Teacher, do we get to do an EDU Showdown today?" In essence, they were asking, "Teacher, can we please practice our writing skills today?" Through the use of this structure, the teacher was able to help the students accomplish the content goal of improving writing while the students were highly engaged. The evaluation of the sentences in a collaborative group helped the students to internalize the qualities of a strong sentence, which was a skill they then continued to apply in their own independent writing. Mission accomplished without boring worksheets or student eye-rolling. This level of engagement with the content helps students to learn and acquire skills in a way that stays with them, and it has the added benefit of providing students with opportunities to connect to others.

CLASSROOM EXAMPLE: MATH

In math instruction students are asked to solve multistep word problems posed with whole numbers and having whole number answers using the four operations of addition, subtraction, multiplication, and division. While it is important to see where students are individually in working toward mastery of these word problems, they can learn and grow in their math abilities while having opportunities to work together. Creating a classroom environment where students feel safe to make mistakes and to learn from them sets the foundation for working through problems collaboratively.

In order to shift from having students solve multistep word problems individually to completing them in an EDU Showdown, the teacher needs to be intentional in setting up the teams and the purpose of their work together. The focus in each group should be to listen to each other's ideas and then collectively decide how to solve the problem. The team should also be able to clearly explain their thinking and rationale for their approach to tackling the problem and then to clearly explain the steps that they took. The focus is not on plugging numbers into one way of solving equations to arrive at an answer but to showcase the team's thinking and then highlight the multiple ways teams may approach solving the same problem.

In the EDU Showdown approach to solving multistep word problems, the teacher finds or constructs high-interest word problems by presenting scenarios that are connected to real-world problems of interest to the students. Some examples include saving up to buy a video game, a class bake sale project, a library reading challenge, or a sports challenge related to a favorite team or a competition in a PE class. The teacher shares the goal of the challenge, including how the teams will earn points for clearly explaining their thinking and the steps they took to solve the problem. The teacher also shares any time limits to complete their work. The teacher may also ask the students to assign roles, such as choosing students who will take notes and capture their work and students who will be ready to share out the team's work.

The teacher observes the teams as they work through the problem, taking notes on their approaches to predetermine the order in which the teams should share their work. Once the time is up, the teacher asks the teams to share their problem-solving approaches as well as their solution to the problem. The teacher then guides the review and reflection of the approaches the teams took, highlighting similarities and differences while connecting the work to the lesson's objectives. The EDU Showdown has several benefits here, including exposing students to multiple approaches to solving the same problem and helping those students who have strong math ability to reflect on and explain their thinking and to model problem-solving steps for those still working on independently solving the problems.

This structure also provides all students with the opportunity to interact with each other and utilize the language needed to collaborate and share their thinking while navigating decisions together. The competition element also adds a layer of motivation and increased engagement that would be missing if students solved the same problems independently for the teacher to review and eventually provide feedback on. The EDU Showdown structure provides a valuable opportunity for students to experience collaborating with others, compromising when needed, and learning through peers while addressing the content standard.

TEAM Discovery: Collaborative Inquiry

STRATEGY **TEAM Discovery** 	The newly termed TEAM (**T**ogether, **E**ngaging **A**cademic **M**inds) Discovery approach has students working together to learn more about a topic through asking questions, gathering information, analyzing, and then actioning their findings. **What:** This strategy integrates a collaborative structure to transform a more traditional individual learn-and-report project. In a typical approach, students are provided with a topic and the format they need to use to report back their findings. When the students have finished, it is common for each student to have an opportunity to present their report—an approach that has each student sitting through twenty-plus presentations. **Build an understanding:** Support students' understanding of engagement to include being both involved and interested in what they are learning. This includes a focus on discovery and building on their own curiosity. It can be compared to the feelings they might experience when they are engaged in a favorite hobby, such as a sport, dancing, playing a video game, or reading a book in a series they enjoy. Discuss how these higher levels of engagement help them stay focused and invested in their learning. The term *academic* in the name's approach refers to the continuous process of expanding one's knowledge and mind. It includes engaging in activities like reading, writing, listening, and speaking as we explore different subjects and master new skills while becoming better learners. Those engaging with an academic mind remain open to new ideas and give consideration to the experiences and perspectives of others.
Step 1: **Identify an Inquiry Topic** 	Based on the content area that you are teaching, identify the topic area that your students will be exploring. • Review the standards and learning objectives for your grade level and content area. • Give consideration to the interests of your students and the real-world relevance of the potential topics. • Brainstorm topics to explore that will both meet the learning objectives and be of interest to your students. • Collaborate with your students to finalize the topics and consider topics that your students may generate on their own.

(Continued)

(Continued)

<table>
<tr><td rowspan="3">Step 2:
Generate Options

Providing students with the choice of how they want to present their findings increases their ownership of the work.

Keeping the audience in mind and having an authentic purpose for their project is far more motivating than completing it only for a grade.</td><td colspan="2">Collaborate with your students to explore the potential options for how they will share the information after their collaborative inquiry. What audience beyond the classroom would find the information of interest? Collaborate on lists of options for teams to choose from in their TEAM Discovery project.</td></tr>
<tr><td>Potential Formats
</td><td>• Presentation: created using a digital slide deck such as Google Slides or PowerPoint.
• Posters: either one overall visual or separate smaller posters for sharing different aspects of the work.
• Videos: use of video editing software or tools such as Screencastify to capture and share information.
• Graphic novel: a digital or print version of a graphic novel to present the team's work.
• Website: use a free tool such as Google Sites to create a website to present and share information.
• Brochure: a print or digital brochure to present the team's work.</td></tr>
<tr><td>Potential Audiences
</td><td>• Students: can include older or younger buddy classes or high school students.
• Leaders: depending on the topics, the audience could be school, district, or community leaders who may be asked to take action based on what is shared.
• Field experts or community members: students can present their information to community members with a connection to the content or virtually to experts in the field for feedback and additional insights.
• Showcase: the information could be shared through a showcase format, with parents, families, and community members being invited to attend.
• Local media outlets: such as the local newspaper or city bulletin; some local communities host closed-circuit TV shows where the students' information can be shared.</td></tr>
</table>

<table>
<tr><td>Step 3:
Select Teams and Share Expectations
</td><td>Select your students for each TEAM Discovery group. Review the expectations for the following:<ul><li>Working as a team: Over time, these reminders for working as an effective team should be led by the students themselves, with you as the guide when needed.</li><li>Working on their project: Review the expectations for the project with the teams. This should include the following:<ul><li>Review the selected topic(s) together.</li><li>Collaborate on the questions the students want to answer about the topic through their discovery.</li><li>Discuss to determine the target audience for their work. What is the purpose of what they will share? Is it to inform, to inspire, or to persuade, or is it a call to action? Will their project result in potential action steps to make change?</li><li>Determine the initial format they will use to share their information and ideas about the topic, knowing that this may shift as they continue to do the work.</li><li>Set clear deadlines and checkpoints for the project based on your students' age and grade level. With younger students, you will want to provide clear expectations for each class session where they work on their project, highlighting specific tasks. For older grades, you may consider a review of deadlines and check-ins, giving them more room to manage the flow of the project.</li></ul></li></ul></td></tr>
<tr><td>Step 4:
Provide Timely Feedback
</td><td>Check in with the teams to get a status report on their projects. Once you have the overall flow of their work set, the team-generated questions they are working to answer and their goals for formatting their work provide an opportunity for timely feedback. The feedback can include the following:<ul><li>Provide guidance on the team's approach to the work or resources they may not have considered yet.</li><li>Review the work completed so far, asking questions and sharing positive feedback and suggestions for consideration as they continue their work.</li><li>Provide an overall team check-in. How do they feel their team is doing together? What is something that is going well? Have they encountered any challenges? Are all team members being provided with an opportunity to contribute to their project?</li></ul></td></tr>
<tr><td>Step 5:
Feedback on Final Project
</td><td>Build in time for the teams to receive feedback on their final project and allow time for them to make any last changes based on the feedback they receive. Providing students with the opportunity to act on feedback rather than assigning a grade once a project is turned in is a powerful way to help them in their growth. The feedback may come from the following:<ul><li>You as the teacher, a paraprofessional, or regular volunteers within your classroom</li><li>Their peers or other teams, who provide balanced feedback to include what stands out to them as positives about the project as well as any questions they still have or suggestions for improvement</li></ul></td></tr>
</table>

(Continued)

(Continued)

Step 6: **Share With the Intended Audience** 	Once each team has finalized their project, they are ready to share it with their audience! Support the students during this publishing or presentation phase, providing any guidance as needed.
Step 7: **Reflection** 	This step helps students to become self-aware and supports ongoing improvement. Two levels of reflection are: • **Team reflection:** This should include a celebration of both the work that they completed together and the outcome. What did the team do best together? How did the members overcome any conflicts or challenges? How would they rate themselves as an effective team? What is something they might do differently next time? What goal would they set as a team if they were to work together again? • **Individual reflection:** What contributions did the individual members make to their team? How did they support the work of others on the team? Which qualities of being a strong team member did they display? What goal will they set for themselves the next time they work in a team?

Image Sources: Istock.com/SirVectorr; Istock.com/-VICTOR-; Istock.com/da-vooda; Istock.com/fonikum; Istock .com/Yuriy Altukhov; Istock.com/Illustrator de la Monde; Istock.com/ilyaliren; Istock.com/appleuzr

TEAM DISCOVERY EXAMPLE

CLASSROOM EXAMPLE: RESEARCH PROJECT

A teacher shared that in the past she used to have each of her students select an animal from a list of possibilities to research. Most years, several students would choose the same animal to learn more about. She would guide her students through each part of their research, and they would all create a poster to present and share with the class. When everyone had completed the project, each of her twenty-plus students would take their turn at the front of the class. The other students would sit on the rug while three to five classmates shared their presentations each day. She said it was a nonstop battle to try to have the students sit up, pay attention, and keep their hands and feet to themselves. The teacher shared that she herself was challenged to look interested by about the third or fourth report on rabbits.

Although initially unsure if her students would be capable of the TEAM Discovery approach, she finally decided that it was worth giving it a try. The biggest shift was to take the time to set the foundation for her students to work effectively in teams. She shared that she had her students start with smaller tasks initially, gradually working toward the overall collaborative approach to the yearly animal report. It was also helpful that she had saved a few examples of the animal reports from previous years to help guide the students as to the types of questions they might like to ask about the animal they chose to explore.

The teams of three to four students each chose a different animal to investigate. The teacher admitted that it was a challenge for her to set the teams up to work together and then step to the side as a guide rather than leading them step-by-step through the process as she had done in the past. She provided each team with a project checklist to help guide them in their work and to keep them focused on the project. The teacher checked in with the teams and offered guidance or support whenever needed. In general, she was astonished by the students' ability to work together in teams and by how much they were able to accomplish with minimal intervention from her.

The teacher saw many benefits to shifting the annual project to the TEAM Discovery approach. One of the key differences was the amount of communication taking place and the meaningful interactions occurring between her students. In the previous model, the majority of the time she was talking at the students while they worked independently. She would pull small groups of students to check in on or she would hold individual conferences. With the team approach, the students were there to support each other, and they were often able to answer each other's questions. She also shared that their excitement about working together as a team was clear to see throughout the project.

The student teams often came up with unique questions that were different from the ones she had her students answer each year about their animal. The teams also enjoyed looking for ways they could help their animals. Some teams wanted to collect items such as food or blankets for the local animal shelters; others created bookmarks and small posters with reminders to not litter in forests or oceans to help protect animals. Teams created slides, posters, or clay representations of their animals with information miniposters next to them. When the teams shared their projects, all students were engaged and they wanted to learn about all of the different animals and see how the teams chose to present their information. While it was a huge shift on the part of the teacher, the payoff was there, and she is looking for more team opportunities for her students.

Muralscapes: Collaborative Content Insights

<table>
<tr><td>STRATEGY
Muralscapes
</td><td colspan="2">What: Students are engaged with core content through working together to explore a topic and then collaboratively represent it in a mural format. These projects foster equity of voice and ask for each student to share their perspective.
Build an understanding: Provide your students with varying examples of murals to help them build an understanding of what a mural is and how it can be used to share a story or information. One way to explore the potential of murals is by conducting a web search on Judy Baca, an incredibly talented artist who has produced over four hundred murals. Many of these projects included bringing together thousands of participants across several decades.</td></tr>
<tr><td rowspan="7">Step 1:
Select the Learning Objective
</td><td colspan="2">The teacher identifies a learning objective for the grade level and content being taught. The topic, essential question, or concept should be one that will provide enough material for students to review and collaboratively consider.</td></tr>
<tr><td colspan="2">Sample Topics Across Content Areas</td></tr>
<tr><td>Science
</td><td>• Scientific method
• Contributions of scientists
• Exploration of scientific topics including current challenges</td></tr>
<tr><td>Social Science
</td><td>• Themes or topics related to history, geography, culture, or sociology
• Making connections between past and present
• Sharing historic or current events through multiple perspectives</td></tr>
<tr><td>Math
</td><td>• Represent mathematical concepts or practices
• Tools or steps for problem-solving
• Highlight math-related careers</td></tr>
<tr><td>English Language Arts
</td><td>• Represent literary elements
• Showcase authors or characteristics of genres
• Highlight reading or writing strategies</td></tr>
<tr><td>Specials
</td><td>PE:
• Topics related to health and safety
• Highlight fair play within sports
• Showcase athletes or related careers</td></tr>
</table>

<table>
<tr><td></td><td>

</td><td>Music:<ul><li>Explore musical genres and history</li><li>Highlight various instruments</li><li>Show emotion and feelings related to music</li></ul>Art:<ul><li>Represent historical periods in art</li><li>Highlight various mediums and tools to create art</li><li>Showcase artists</li></ul>STEM:<ul><li>Display tools and technology used within STEM</li><li>Showcase engineering and design</li><li>Highlight innovation through STEM</li></ul></td></tr>
<tr><td>Step 2:
Outline Project Details
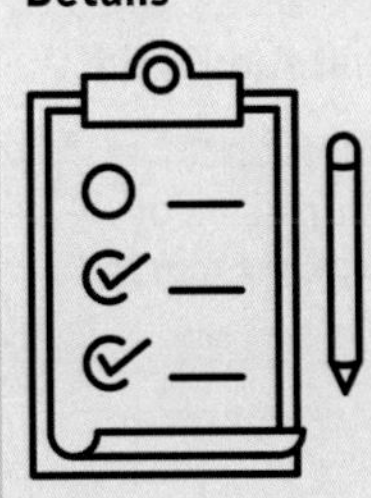</td><td colspan="2">Once the topic or learning objective has been shared and discussed with your students, move on to the details of the project:<ul><li>Muralscapes rubric: The student teams will need to know the expectations for their work. This can be provided or co-created with your students.</li><li>Materials: Clarify the materials and formats available to the teams as they create their mural. Will this be on physical paper with paint or images placed onto the paper? Is there an option to create the mural digitally?</li><li>Duration: What is the timeline for the creation of the mural? Which classes will be used for the project?</li><li>Display: How will the murals be shared? Will physical murals be displayed in the school or community? Will digital murals be shared through a newsletter or websites?</li></ul></td></tr>
<tr><td>Step 3:
Teamwork
</td><td colspan="2">After the details for the muralscapes have been shared, place your students into their teams. Review the class expectations for working effectively in teams. This should emphasize the importance of actively including all team members and their unique perspectives within the project.
Either provide or co-create a team checklist specific to this project that will do the following:<ul><li>Provide a space for identifying the role(s) of each team member</li><li>Highlight the steps and decisions the team will need to make to successfully create their muralscape, including the opportunities for individual work and for every student to contribute to the final product</li></ul></td></tr>
<tr><td>Step 4:
Checkpoints
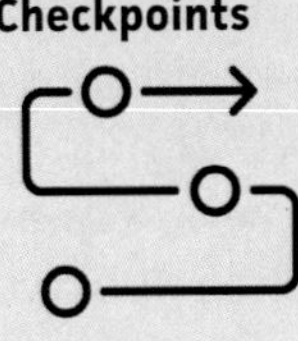</td><td colspan="2">Continue to check in with your student teams to see how they are progressing, providing timely feedback or helping to problem-solve as needed.
Encourage the teams to pause and check in with each other as they work. This is an opportunity for them to provide positive feedback to each other, ask for help, or share new ideas.</td></tr>
</table>

(Continued)

(Continued)

Step 5: **Feedback** 	Provide an opportunity for the team members to receive feedback on their muralscape, with time to make adjustments as they choose, before they finalize their work. The feedback can come from teachers, peers, other teams, or other classes.
Step 6: **Make It Public** 	Once the muralscapes are completed, it is time to share them with others! In order to help ensure that the muralscape represents the views of the team, the members should include a brief description sharing their process, their interpretation of the topic, and how they chose to represent the topic within their muralscape. They may highlight or point out specific features or give the viewer things to look for. Then you may do the following with the muralscapes: • Display them within the school where they can be viewed by others. • Hold a showcase where families and community members have the opportunity to view and learn through the muralscapes.
Step 7: **Evaluate and Reflect** 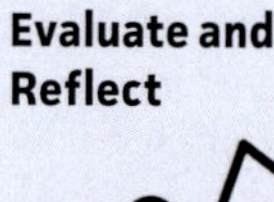 	Once the finish line is reached on the project, it is time to evaluate and reflect! • **Team reflection:** The team should reflect together using the rubric. What are their celebrations as a team? Were they able to address all of the success criteria as outlined in the rubric? What do they like the most about their muralscape? • **Audience feedback:** Provide an opportunity for the audience to highlight what stands out for them the most about each muralscape. • **Teacher feedback:** Highlight celebrations for each group based on their team's collaboration and their final product. Share constructive feedback and future considerations through the rubric.

Image Sources: Ilstock.com/Ali Kerem; Istock.com/Miray Celebi Kaba; Istock.com/Stockyarder; Istock.com/Chanathip Pedruang; Istock.com/StudioU; Istock.com/iconsimo

MURALSCAPES: COLLABORATIVE CONTENT INSIGHTS AND EXAMPLES

CLASSROOM EXAMPLE: ENGLISH LANGUAGE ARTS

One of the speaking and literacy standards includes the use of visual displays to enhance the development of main ideas or themes. Instead of taking the conventional approach of having each of the students read a book and create their own display to capture the key takeaways from the text, a teacher decided to have groups of students work together to create a muralscape for a shared text that they had read in their book group. In previous years the students would work on their own and the teacher would display their projects around the room. The class would then rotate through a gallery walk to see what their peers had accomplished. Shifting from the traditional approach of students working on this individually to a collaborative group project had many advantages that elevated the typical outcome of the same project.

The students in each group first engaged in meaningful conversations around the main idea and themes within the book they had read as they started to plan their muralscape. Some of the groups had highly energetic conversations until they were able to come to a consensus on the main idea that they wanted to represent. Then the groups moved on to discuss the themes. Once they had a map of what they wanted to share, more conversations and negotiations were needed to determine how the ideas should be represented. Most groups decided to work in pairs on specific parts of their project and then put them all together to create their final project. The teacher checked in with the groups as they worked, providing timely feedback and asking guiding questions.

The students were engaged in meaningful uses of language throughout the project. This element would have been missing if the students had been left to complete it individually. The students also developed a deeper understanding of the main idea and themes themselves through their active engagement in conversations as they navigated the project as a team. Many of the students shared that they started with one idea about the book but that idea changed or strengthened based on the conversations with their team members. If the students had been left to complete this project individually, they would have missed out on that level of thinking. The students connected with their classmates as they completed the work to accomplish their shared common goal with a tangible outcome. The teacher noted that the students became much more invested in the project when it was transformed from an individual project to a shared muralscape.

CLASSROOM EXAMPLE: SOCIAL SCIENCE

A class was working on a geography standard in social studies that required them to compare and contrast the cultural and environmental characteristics of various regions and places. The teacher decided to use a muralscape approach to having the students work toward this standard. Each group chose the regions they wanted to represent within their project. The students had to figure out how to depict a comparison between the two regions in their mural that would be clearly understood. They also collaborated on a paper that explained the comparison in depth and served as a reflective tool for the group to capture and reflect on their decision-making process.

One group chose to share a comparison of Mexico and the United States. They represented each country through an intentional selection of colors, using warmer colors for the landscape of Mexico and cooler colors for the landscape of the United States. The group included traditional crops, landscape features, and animals commonly found in each country. Their paper went on to share a more in-depth analysis of how the natural resources available in a region impact the regional economy and position within global trading. Planning the visual image captured within their muralscape provided the students with the foundation for their paper. The conversations and decisions they negotiated to create the muralscape provided rich language that was centered within their content. Each student brought their unique backgrounds and experiences to the project, allowing them to make and share connections with the content. This collaboration helped create a more authentic outcome.

Another group chose to represent children from various countries exchanging traditional greetings while dressed in traditional clothing. This group used their muralscape to showcase their own native languages of English, Spanish, and Urdu. Their paper provided more in-depth information about the environmental influences on traditional clothing and varying customs related to greetings. The students learned more about the cultures and traditions of their classmates as well as successfully accomplishing tasks related to a specific social science standard. Each student could have completed their own project, but this format provided an opportunity to practice social interactions and collaborative decision-making, and it increased the use of language throughout the project.

This teacher added another layer at the completion of the project. The individual students were asked to complete a reflection on what they learned about collaboration through their participation in the muralscape project. They were asked what they liked most about working in a group as well as any aspects that frustrated them. The teacher asked them to describe the characteristics of someone they would want to work with on a team. Finally, the teacher asked each student to identify their own strengths and to set an individual goal for the next time they participated in a group project. This reflection gave the teacher valuable insights and provided a reflection opportunity to help students identify their personal strengths. It also helped to raise awareness regarding individual responsibilities within a highly effective team.

CHAPTER SUMMARY

Connecting to others is one of the most essential skills in all of life. Experiences in school can significantly enhance the growth of this skill, which consists of four key areas: communication skills, teamwork, problem-solving, and responsibility. These four areas can and must be interwoven with academic learning tasks in order to maximize students' overall development for the future.

Reflection Questions

1. What are you already doing in classrooms to foster the essential skill of connecting to others?
2. Reflect on the impact of teamwork and collaboration on student engagement. How can these strategies and practices be used to improve both academic outcomes and social-emotional development?
3. Which of the four key areas (communication skills, teamwork, problem-solving, and responsibility) need to be developed in your setting?
4. How will you evaluate the effectiveness of these essential connection skills when students work with others?
5. Consider the EDU Showdown strategy introduced in the chapter. How can friendly competition among teams enhance student motivation and deepen their understanding of content? Identify an upcoming lesson where you will try an EDU Showdown with your students.

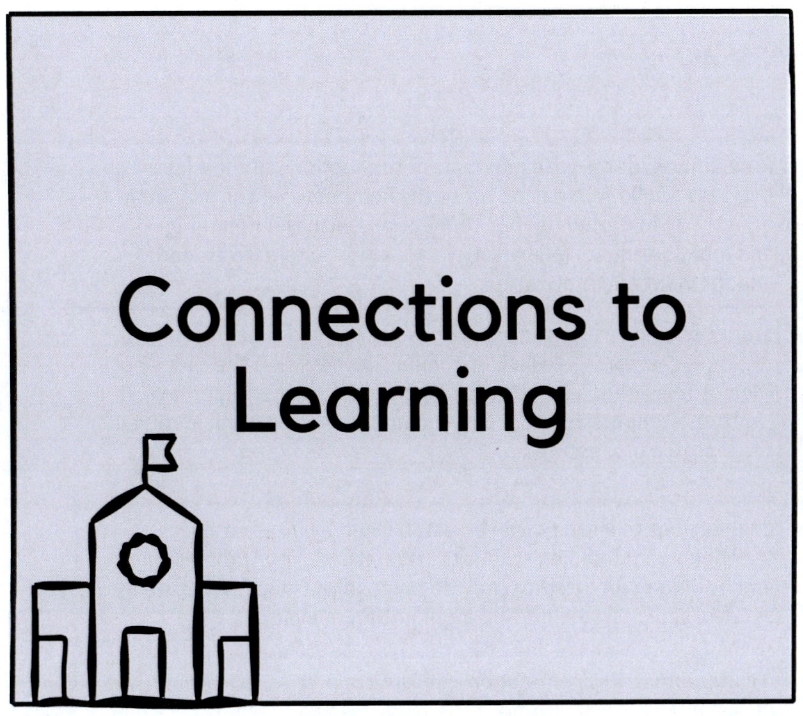

CHAPTER 4

> ***"Tell me and I forget. Teach me and I remember. Involve me and I learn."***
>
> **—Xun Kuang, Confucian Philosopher**

Your Snapshot Guide

Connections to Learning

WHAT?	Providing students with meaningful connections to their learning provides a solid foundation for both their personal and academic growth. By fostering deeper connections with their learning and highlighting its relevance, we are able to increase student engagement and motivation.
WHY?	Students who struggle in school have expressed that the main reason is the perceived lack of connection between their life and their studies. When we shift to a connected learning approach, it captures students' interest and encourages active participation in the learning process.
HOW?	Connections to learning can be established by integrating strategies that build on students' natural curiosity through inquiry, embedding practices that provide personalization, making use of asset-based goal setting, and highlighting relevance.
BONUS	A classroom with a connection-centered approach to learning offers many benefits for both the students and teachers. Emphasizing connections to learning creates a positive, inclusive learning environment that promotes lifelong learning, which is critical to success in an ever-changing world.

Four Key Areas Within the ECS Domain of Connections to Learning	
Curiosity and Inquiry	Personalization
Relevant Learning	Goal Setting

ESSENTIAL CONNECTION SKILL: CONNECTIONS TO LEARNING

One of the greatest opportunities we have as educators is to empower our students to become lifelong learners. By teaching our students how to ask questions, seek out and evaluate information, and make informed decisions or determine action steps, we are setting them up for success in the future. When individuals view themselves as lifelong learners, they become less afraid of change, more open to acquiring new skills, and better prepared to step outside their current comfort zone. Engaging in lifelong learning enables individuals to address stressful situations for themselves or others, to avoid feeling stuck, and to embrace new possibilities. It also prepares them for adapting to the constantly changing world and workplace.

Students themselves are sharing that one of their top struggles in school is not seeing the relevance between their studies and the real world (Ascione, 2022). Students do not see how what they are learning in school will ever be used in their lives outside of the classroom. While some students are motivated by grades or a report card, others cite frustration and do not want to put effort into work that "really doesn't matter." As educators we can help our students find the value in the content and skills that they are learning in the classroom. Helping our students to build meaningful connections to what they are learning is critical!

The essential skill of building connections between students and what they are learning helps to close the relevance gap. Through a focus on helping students see the potential application for what they are learning, we shift from a grade-based motivation to a more authentic purpose for students to invest their time, energy, and effort into their learning. Intentionally bridging the gap between classroom instruction and students' real-world lives, experiences, and goals helps to create an inclusive learning environment where all are encouraged to find meaning in the content, with a focus on the learner rather than on a reported grade. Future readiness brings connection to potential careers associated with the content being taught, providing students with possible pathways they may have never known about or envisioned for themselves.

The focus on real-world application of knowledge and skills equips students with the agility to transfer what they are learning and apply it beyond the classroom. This includes consideration of the ways the content, information, or critical thinking skills may benefit them in the future. Students should be able to reflect on their ability to connect and navigate relationships within the classroom and on how these prosocial skills will extend beyond school. As educators we are also able to use these connections to learning to personalize instruction. Meaningful connections to learning are made when we provide opportunities for students to view what they are learning in a way that is authentic to them by allowing them to explore topics and content through a lens that resonates with their identity, interests, and future aspirations.

THE IMPORTANCE OF BUILDING CONNECTIONS TO LEARNING

I (Anne) recently spoke with a student and asked her what she might like to do when she gets older. She looked at me, shrugged her shoulders, and said, "I'm not sure. What will I really be able to do?" This statement was heartbreaking on so many levels! Here was an extremely bright student with an outgoing personality who did not yet envision what a future beyond school might look like. Many of today's students have the same uncertainty or apathy when asked that same question. At the end of the day, even with a stellar report card, what connections was this student making with what he was learning? Academic proficiency or improvement on standardized achievement measures is not enough! As educators we must help every student make meaningful connections to what they are learning, including establishing potential goals for their lives beyond school and their time with us.

There are multiple benefits when teachers utilize strategies and teaching frames that create connections between their students and what they are learning. Providing students with authentic ways to connect with what they are learning and to see the value it holds specifically for them pays a number of dividends. This focus helps to build on our students' natural curiosity as they develop inquiry skills, it helps us to personalize learning, it can be used to help students set meaningful goals, and it highlights the relevance of what students are learning. When students are supported in this essential connection skill, they are more likely to see connections between subjects, concepts, and related experiences, which helps to build a more in-depth and comprehensive understanding of what they are learning. As students see the relevance and applicability of what they are doing in school, it increases their motivation and enhances long-term retention of the material.

Providing opportunities for students to explore questions and topics related to your content increases intrinsic motivation for learning, develops their ability for inquiry, and fuels an interest in lifelong learning. Encouraging a high level of connection helps to build students' natural curiosity. This increases both engagement and ownership of their learning. This shift enhances the students' overall learning experience and elevates the purpose for their learning to be authentic and meaningful far beyond any grade or report card provided.

BUILDING STUDENTS' CONNECTIONS TO LEARNING WITHIN CONTENT INSTRUCTION

It is the teacher who plays a critical role in helping students to see that what they are learning has relevance. Helping our students to make these connections is not often outlined in teachers' manuals, which are designed to cover content and increase test scores. And, while one key aspect of teaching is to help improve student learning outcomes as measured by assessment measures, providing the best education for our students goes beyond those numbers. As we have stated, we need to balance educating both the mind *and* the heart. While the human/heart side of education is harder to measure, we must elevate its importance.

Education holds the possibility to address deeply entrenched inequalities that have been standard practice for years and that have roots in long outdated practices and structural inequities. During the Industrial Revolution, schools were used to prepare students to become factory workers or managers based on their social status. While we live in a very different, complex, ever-changing world and society, we need to ensure that our students are not limited by deeply rooted, outdated practices. As educators we hold the power to ensure that each of our students finds meaning in what we are teaching them and that they see a world of possibility for their future based on their own passions, talents, and choices. We can empower our students to not only see but navigate beyond any systemic limitations they may encounter. We should help each and every one of our students to have multiple visions for their future based on their strengths and interests!

Providing ECS within our classrooms prepares all students to have the range of skills and competencies needed to confront barriers. This includes developing critical thinking and problem-solving skills to analyze challenges and identify innovative solutions. Students also need self-advocacy skills to speak up for themselves and to set goals even when faced with obstacles. Developing emotional intelligence, including resilience and self-regulation, prepares students to learn from setbacks and to continue toward their goals. Cultural competency helps students to both understand and challenge social systems and sources of power within our society. Cultivating curiosity and a lifelong love of learning prepares our students for the futures they envision for themselves.

Many schools have gifted programs in which some students have project-based learning opportunities or career exposure that others do not receive. As an educator, you have the ability to place every learner at the center of the learning experience. Through intentionally building connections for your students with what they are learning, including potential career pathways and personal growth goals, you are planting the seeds of possibility that may never have been even remotely contemplated by your students. How can you imagine yourself in a role or career when you are not even aware that it exists? Our students have limitless possibilities, and we have the chance to help them understand their own potential.

Teachers can create a learning environment that values curiosity and inquiry, personalization, and goal setting and that highlights the relevance of what students are learning. The extent to which teachers can develop meaningful connections between what the students are working on in school and the students' own lives, interests, backgrounds, and aspirations is hard to measure. However, promoting these connections through strategies and practices within instruction enhances any curricular program by boosting student engagement and ownership while also being inclusive of all learners. Furthermore, when we intentionally build in connections to learning, students can achieve improved academic outcomes. This also supports their personal growth and fosters opportunities for them to explore potential career pathways that align with their strengths and interests.

The strategies and instructional frames within this chapter will support you in helping your students to develop connections to their learning. These strategies can be used across multiple grade levels and content areas. The strategies include aspects of the four key domain areas within this essential connection skill: curiosity and inquiry, personalization, goal setting, and relevant learning. All of us should be able to ask any of our students what they might like to do when they get older and have them excitedly share some potential options with us. While they may change their minds multiple times along the way, even through adulthood, we want to do our part in helping them to see multiple pathways now to a bright, fulfilling future!

KEY AREA 1: CURIOSITY AND INQUIRY

How would you define curiosity? The *Merriam-Webster Dictionary* (Merriam-Webster, n.d.-a) defines curiosity as a "desire to know." Loewenstein (1994) proposed curiosity as a deprivation that arises based on a perceived gap in knowledge or understanding. This concept was furthered by Litman and Jimerson (2004) to identify two types of curiosity: one based on interest and the other on deprivation or a gap. Most researchers today also include active behaviors that are associated with curiosity. And now, pause and think for a moment. When was the last time you were curious about something? What was it and how did you go about seeking information?

Chances are the topic of interest you just thought of was something that you identified on your own and not for a class. Now, what is something you really have no interest in? For some of us that might be tax law; for others it could be sports-related statistics or the latest information on fashion trends. Even if you were provided multiple sources of information on a topic that does not naturally appeal to you, chances are you would take a pass on learning more or would merely skim some of the key points. As educators, we must put ourselves in our students' shoes: Do they have an interest in the information you are about to provide them, or will they be inclined to take a pass? What steps can you take to actively engage them and to build their curiosity?

Many of us feel the need to "cover" the standards and to teach at a rapid pace so our students do not fall behind. This overarching sense of not having enough time encourages us to teach directly from the manual without taking steps to connect the learning with the students in front of us. In reality, if our students' curiosity is not there and they are not invested in what we are trying to teach, our impact will be limited. Creating a classroom learning environment that prioritizes engagement through curiosity and inquiry and that continues to connect students with our content will allow them to learn at a deeper level and to gain the skills and mindsets of active learners.

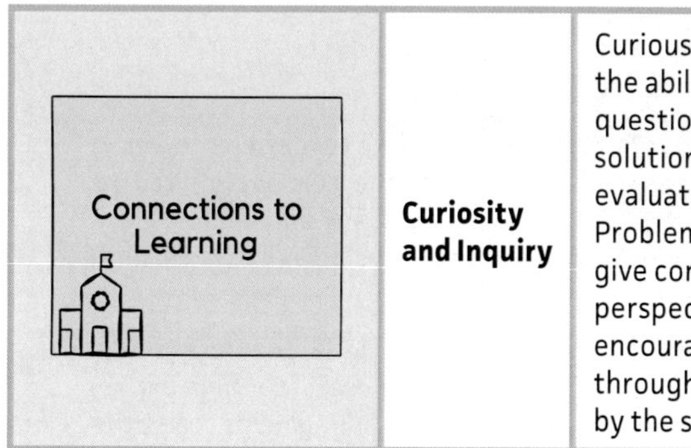	**Curiosity and Inquiry**	Curioussity and inquiry involve the ability to clearly identify questions, generate innovative solutions to problems, and evaluate potential outcomes. Problem-solving and exploring give consideration to the perspectives of others and encourage deeper learning through exploration directed by the students.

STRATEGIES FOR BUILDING CURIOSITY AND INQUIRY

Exploration Zone

STRATEGY **Exploration Zone** 	**What:** This strategy enables teachers to enhance learning provided through curricular materials by leveraging their students' natural curiosity. After an introduction to the topic or material, students share their questions and the subtopics they would like to explore further. This strategy helps students to become actively involved in their learning by providing choice and increasing student ownership. Including this strategy within your instruction increases students' investment in the topic as they augment their knowledge of the content through an exploration of self-identified subtopics. **Bonus:** Many teachers struggle to find meaningful "center work" for their students to complete as they work with small groups. Along with fun yet often surface-level activities, students may work on devices with predetermined lessons. Incorporating the Exploration Zone provides another opportunity for students to engage in meaningful learning while you work with small groups. Students can work independently or in small groups to research their identified questions and to format the resulting information in a way that others can access it.
Step 1: **Introduce the Topic, Skill, or Learning Standard** 	**Give them just enough:** Provide your students with just enough information to engage them with your content. Well-intended teachers will often provide the students with the learning target right away, sometimes driven by an explicit "I can" or "Students will be able to" statement. There are benefits to co-generating and sharing the learning target later within the lesson or unit. Shifting this practice to introducing the content without the explicit learning target at the start of the lesson gives students the opportunity to explore the content and have them help to identify the target. This practice can lead to a more student-centered approach that increases engagement and helps to develop students' critical thinking skills.
Step 2: **Spark Curiosity** 	**Wait, what?** This is where you start to pique your students' interest and investment in the topic. You can share a thought-provoking picture, video clip, story, song, news story, analogy, or initial questions that will start to get them thinking!
Step 3: **Generate Questions, Statements, or Connections** 	**What questions do you have? What would you like to learn more about? Share the connection:** After you have provided the introduction to the content, provide your students with time to form any initial questions they may have or determine any subtopics they would like to learn more about. Students can also consider why they think the material they will be learning might be important and how it might be useful to them in their lives. This reflection and time for independent thinking helps to set the stage for learning.

Step 4: **Post to the Exploration Zone** 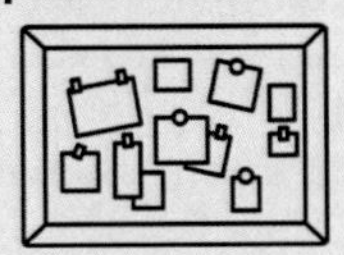	**Share your thinking in the Exploration Zone:** The next step is for your students to be able to review their notes and to share them with the class. The Exploration Zone could be a physical bulletin board within your classroom, or it could be a digital version through a platform such as Padlet, Google Slides, or FigJam. Students should include their names or initials so that those interested in the same topics can choose to explore them together. It will also help you to connect with any students who haven't contributed to the board and encourage them to add in their ideas. You can divide the space into three sections: questions, topics to explore further, and possible connections to real life.
Step 5: **Organize Your Zone** 	**Review the information and form related groups:** Depending on your grade level, you may choose to do this step together with your students or, after modeling, you may assign this to students on a rotating basis. Within each area of the Exploration Zone, look for questions or statements that are similar and group them together. You may even choose to note the names of the students who fall into the same question or statement grouping so they can explore the topic together.
Step 6: **Exploration and Research** 	**I would like to know more about:** In addition to your lessons on the content or topic, provide your students with opportunities to further explore their self-identified interest areas. This exploration can take place as a center rotation or it can be assigned to a specific day during your small-group rotations. Many teachers have shared that their students became so invested in their topic that they spent time at home researching their questions. You can help to build this connection by having a template for students to capture and share their Exploration Zone area of interest with families/guardians.
Step 7: **Share Their Findings** 	**Check this out:** Students should have multiple ways that they can share their information and their takeaways on the topics with the class. This may be a physical written paper that can be checked out by other students from the Exploration Zone classroom library, or it may be a digital version attached to the original question set on the digital Exploration Zone platform. It might also be an opportunity during class for individuals or teams to share what they discovered. As the information is shared, the students may want to generate additional questions on what they discovered to share with their classmates. You may create interactive opportunities for this, such as having them write down or share their own predictions before the information is shared or having them complete a quick survey afterward about what they would still like to know or any connections that they made.
Step 8: **Reflection and Insights** 	**What is the takeaway?** As the topic is closing out, revisit the Exploration Zone to reflect together on the learning. Was anything surprising or unexpected? What are the key takeaways to remember from this unit? Based on the information gained, are there new topics or questions that students might like to explore?

Image Sources: Istock.com/lokomotif; Istock.com/appleuzr; Istock.com/Marvid; Istock.com/bsd studio

Questioning Bootcamp: Building Capacity to Explore and Learn Through Questions

<table>
<tr><td>STRATEGY
Questioning Bootcamp
</td><td>What: The ability to generate and ask questions is an important skill set for all of our students. Individuals who are able to effectively generate or ask questions are more likely to become lifelong learners who are able to successfully navigate learning as well as the complexity of the world around them. Questioning is a highly important skill that is often assumed within our education system rather than being explicitly taught and discussed.

Through an intentional focus on building our students' ability to ask questions, we are fostering their sense of curiosity and building their critical thinking skills. Generating and asking questions also builds their communication skills and their confidence in interacting with others. The ability to ask effective questions on their own also actively engages students in their learning.</td></tr>
<tr><td>Step 1:
Build an Understanding
</td><td>Why is questioning important? It is important for students to understand why it is important for them to build their questioning skills. Questioning skills are useful in the following settings:

• In school: Being able to ask questions helps with learning. When you are stuck, you can pause to think about what questions may help you to move on. Having questions about your learning answered helps you to gain a better understanding of and make connections to what you are learning. These connections help you to remember new information.

• In conversations: When you are able to think of questions, including follow-up questions to something someone has shared, you are better prepared to interact with others. When you can confidently ask questions, you can learn from others and better understand their perspective.

• In life: When you are able to generate solid questions, you can find your way through new places and situations. Share a few examples of how asking questions is helpful in new situations, such as when getting your driver's license and needing to know about the test protocol and necessary documents. Another example could be getting your first job offer and asking questions so you have the information you need before you decide to accept the position.</td></tr>
<tr><td>Step 2:
Explore Question Types
</td><td>What should I ask? Explicitly teach your students the many types of questions they can ask. This should include providing examples, modeling, and discussion around when they may use a particular type of questioning.

You may keep a chart, physical or digital, where you can add the types of questions as you introduce them. In your instruction highlight the types of questions being asked to continually reinforce students' understanding of them. You can also ask students to generate specific question types within your lessons.</td></tr>
<tr><td colspan="2" align="center">Types of Questions</td></tr>
<tr><td>Factual Questions
</td><td>Type: Factual questions seek concrete information and specific details.

Examples: What is the capital of France? When did dinosaurs live?</td></tr>
</table>

Clarifying Questions	**Type:** Clarifying questions seek to clear up confusion or gain a better understanding. **Examples:** What does *photosynthesis* mean? What did you mean by ____________? I'm still not clear about ____________, so can you please tell me more about that?
Open-Ended Questions	**Type:** Open-ended questions cannot be answered by a simple "yes" or "no." They encourage deeper thinking and engagement. **Examples:** Why do you think plants need sunlight to survive? How do we use patterns to predict the next numbers in a sequence? What are the elements of a good story?
Opinion Questions	**Type:** Opinion questions ask for an individual's opinions or beliefs. **Examples:** What is your favorite book and why? Do you think teachers should give homework every day?
Probing Questions	**Type:** Probing questions push for more information, details, or depth on a topic. **Examples:** Can you explain why you took those steps to solve that word problem? Can you tell me more about the hibernation of some animals during winter?
Prediction Questions	**Type:** Prediction questions ask about what might happen in the future, including the potential outcome to a situation. **Examples:** What do you think will happen in the next chapter of the book? What do you think would happen if we stopped recycling?
Comparing Questions	**Type:** Comparing questions compare and contrast two or more elements. **Examples:** How is an alligator different from a crocodile? How does the concept of place value differ when working with decimals versus whole numbers? How does the lifestyle of those in rural areas compare to those in urban areas?
"What If" Questions	**Type:** "What if" questions pose a hypothetical situation or scenario to encourage critical and/or creative thinking. **Examples:** How would life be different if people could fly? If all of the numbers in the world disappeared, what would be different? If you could travel in time, which person from history would you like to meet and why?
"What Next" Questions	**Type:** "What next" questions build on previous information or questions to establish a sequential order. **Examples:** What comes next after the caterpillar forms a chrysalis? What is your next step in solving this equation? Can you share the steps you should follow for planning a persuasive essay?
Reflection Questions	**Type:** Reflection questions encourage thinking about an individual's experiences, feelings, and key takeaways. **Examples:** What was the most interesting thing that you learned today? Do you think you will follow the same steps in solving a problem like this next time? What did you learn about yourself as a learner from this assignment?

(Continued)

(Continued)

Step 3: **Teach and Model** 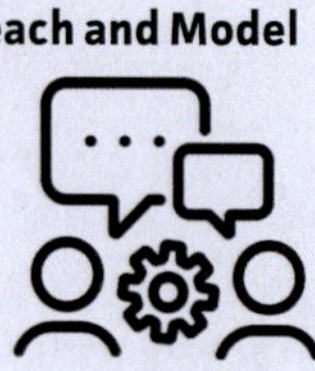	**Which type of question would fit here?** As you introduce your students to the types of questions, model their effective use. This includes the use of follow-up questions. Help your students see how they can connect with both content and others through their use of questions. List the question types on a physical chart or digital resource that your students can refer back to. You and your students can continue to add examples during your instruction, which will help solidify their understanding of the intent and purpose of the questions in each category. As questions are posed in your class, pause and ask the students to identify the type. You can also pause your instruction and ask students to write down one or more of a specific type of question to give them additional practice and to help build their questioning agility.
Step 4: **Role-Play and Journal** 	**And pause . . . what question would you ask here and why?** The use of role-play scenarios can help build your students' capacity to ask effective questions in a variety of situations. This can include both academic content discussions and social situations. Providing your students with multiple examples of scenarios and opportunities to practice their questioning skills will have many benefits. Students that can ask the right questions have more agency over their learning, can advocate for the information they need to move forward, and can use questions to be agents of inclusivity by engaging all in conversations. You can start by creating the role-play scenarios and then provide your students with opportunities to create their own or to generate them with you. Making use of an actual remote control to "pause" the scene and ask which question should come next helps students connect to the pause in a concrete way. You can also provide opportunities for your students to reflect and journal about their growth as questioners. Do they find conversations with others becoming easier? How do questions help with their learning? Give them a space to record powerful questions from texts or interactions with others. Does all of this have anyone else thinking of the Dave Matthews Band's song "What Would You Say?" If you don't know the song, this might be a good place to give it a quick search. Gina—you know who you are—we recommend you give this band another try! A good follow-up question might be "Which bands do you prefer and why?"

Image Sources: Istock.com/appleuzr; Istock.com/Jane_Kelly

KEY AREA 2: PERSONALIZATION

How can we add elements and strategies into our instruction that will help every learner connect to the content? Rather than teaching the material directly as it is organized within the teacher's edition textbook, what can be done to help the students in your class at this point in time make connections to what you are learning? When our students feel connected to what they are learning, they are more likely to be engaged in the lessons and become more motivated to learn. These connections and increased engagement provide increased ownership, deeper learning, and better retention of the material. When we intentionally seek ways to personalize our instruction, we are including our students' languages, backgrounds, cultures, interests, and unique perspectives. This builds and models the creation of an inclusive environment where all individuals feel welcomed and valued.

Personalized learning can be defined as the customization of learning opportunities in response to individual student needs, strengths, interests, and passions, which also takes into account student diversity and equity (Gunawardena et al., 2024). As we have shared throughout this book, there is currently a predominant use of adaptive technology as a means of "personalizing" instruction to meet students' needs by providing web-based lessons that fill in students' skill gaps based on adaptive assessments. While there is value to the balanced use of these technology tools, truly connecting our students to our content and within our instruction involves providing ways for them to reflect, identify, and share their own unique connections based on their life experiences and who they are as individuals.

How do we provide our students with the best possible learning outcomes? According to continued research, there is not a strong correlation between student performance and school resources (Handel & Hanushek, 2022). So if the impact of learning is not significantly impacted by spending, what else can we control? A research study by the RAND Corporation showed that students who experienced personalized learning made gains of approximately three percentage points in reading and math over those in traditional settings; over time, those students who started below national norms were able to meet or surpass them when engaged through personalized learning (Pane et al., 2017). Regardless of your classroom, school, or district budget, you can make a difference for your students by adding in elements that provide them with stronger connections to what they are learning.

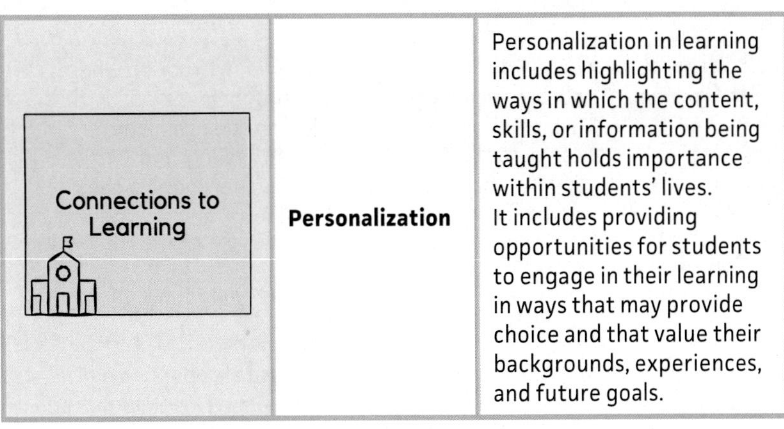

Connections to Learning	**Personalization**	Personalization in learning includes highlighting the ways in which the content, skills, or information being taught holds importance within students' lives. It includes providing opportunities for students to engage in their learning in ways that may provide choice and that value their backgrounds, experiences, and future goals.

STRATEGIES FOR PERSONALIZATION

Discover Your *Why*: Identifying Purpose, Goals, and Aspirations

<table>
<tr><td>STRATEGY
Discover Your Why</td><td colspan="2">What: Helping students to reflect and identify their why cultivates a sense of purpose and deeper motivation for their learning. It helps them to build personal connections with the content they are learning in school.
This inclusive strategy emphasizes the uniqueness of each student. Each individual's why is connected to their own strengths, interests, background, experiences, perspectives, and aspirations for their future.
Bonus: This strategy enables you as the teacher to know your students at a deeper level and for the students to learn more about each other.</td></tr>
<tr><td>Step 1:
Build an Understanding</td><td colspan="2">Sharing the concept of a student's why is the first step. Explain that it is the reason that motivates and inspires a student to learn and to give their best effort. This why may change over time.
You can share examples of your own why and how that motivated you to choose teaching for your career. In what way does your why continue to guide you? This may include hobbies or activities you have outside of school. This helps your students gain a better understanding of the concept while getting to know you better as an individual.
Examples of the why: You can also share the motivation that inspired some well-known people through sources such as addicted2success.com or from the books and stories you share as a class.</td></tr>
<tr><td rowspan="6">Step 2:
Interests, Passions, and Values</td><td colspan="2">Discover interests, passions, and values: Students of all ages can engage in these reflection activities. Based on your students' grade level, you can use any combination of the tools below to help them discover their why.</td></tr>
<tr><td>Journal Prompts</td><td>Ask questions that help students identify their interests. These can be answered in written or digital format. You can ask new questions throughout the year to help students continue to build or adapt their why.</td></tr>
<tr><td>Exit Tickets</td><td>You can incorporate exit tickets that encourage your students to reflect on their strengths, interests, and goals. The questions can draw on the content taught in class as a basis for exploring connections in these areas or for prompting students to consider potential career interests.</td></tr>
<tr><td>Collaborative Reflection</td><td>Build intentional pauses into your instruction where students can reflect and discuss their answers with a partner or small group. Sharing their thinking can help students solidify that thinking, and follow-up questions by peers further support their understanding of themselves.</td></tr>
<tr><td>One-on-One Conferences</td><td>You may choose to have brief, informal conversations with your students that will help them think about and identify their why.</td></tr>
<tr><td>The Why Catcher</td><td>A basic organizer, either on physical paper or a digital version, can help students organize their thoughts and remind them of their current why.</td></tr>
</table>

Step 3: **Vision Board** 	**Let's see it:** Once students have identified what makes up their *why* as well as any related aspirations for their future, provide options for them to create a visual reminder. This may be a miniposter that they create by printing, drawing, or cutting out images, or you may provide a digital option that they can store online or print to have anytime access. These visuals help to remind students of those factors that motivate them and encourage them to invest in their learning. These images can be revisited and adjusted over time with future reflections and as the students make new discoveries about themselves and the world around them. You may also provide opportunities for the students to share their visions for the future with peers or their families. This deeper-level sharing provides students with greater insights into their classmates and gives parents or guardians a glimpse into their current hopes and dreams.
Step 4: **Build Connections** 	**Will this be possible?** Once students have identified their *why* as well as some future goals, you can better help them to make connections within the learning content. As you introduce new learning objectives, intentionally build in time for your students to identify how what they will be learning might be connected to their *why* or to their future goals. For those who struggle to see the connections or bridges to the content, encourage collaboration with peers or provide direct guidance or the use of prompts to help them.
	Sample connection prompts: • How will learning about __________ help you achieve your goals? • How can __________ help you make a positive difference in the world? • How can __________ help you become who you want to be in the future? • What interests you the most in learning about __________?
Step 5: **Conferences** 	**Can you tell me more?** One-on-one conferences allow you to connect with each of your students to learn more about their *why* and their goals. It also provides you with an opportunity to share any potential commonalities you have with their goals, passions, or interests. During the conferences you can ask students to share more about the connections they were able to identify between their *why* and the learning content.
Step 6: **Reflections** 	**Has your thinking changed?** Providing your students with ongoing opportunities to revisit their *why* and to consider shifts as their motivations and interests continue to evolve is one way to empower them and to maintain connection within their learning.

(Continued)

(Continued)

	Sample reflection prompts: • Have your interests or passions changed from the start of the school year? • Think of a time/topic when you were most engaged and interested in learning. Is this something you might like to pursue further or add to your *why*? • Think about a skill or strength you would like to develop. What actions can you take to make this happen? • Imagine yourself ten years from now. What do you think will be important to you?
Step 7: **Celebrations** 	**Personal growth:** Build in celebrations to recognize students' progress, achievements, and growth as they connect their learning to their *why* to help them see the impact of their efforts. You can recognize and reward students as they demonstrate commitment to and enthusiasm in pursuing their interests and connecting their learning with their purpose. This can be in the form of a shout-out or certificate to help them step back and celebrate their progress and ownership of learning.

Image Sources: Istock.com/shopplaywood; Istock.com/appleuzr

In Your Own Words

STRATEGY **In Your Own Words** 	**What:** This strategy is used to enable your students to connect the academic content to their own lives, communities, or futures. This enhances overall student engagement, making it more meaningful. **Bonus:** This is an inclusive strategy that provides an intentional opportunity for all students to share their lived experiences, backgrounds, and perspectives related to the content they are learning.
Step 1: **Introduce the Content** 	**Share the learning objectives:** The foundation for the use of this strategy is engaging the students with information related to the standards and learning objectives that you are teaching. Students will need to have an understanding of the content as well as resources and materials they can reference as they start to build their connections to the content. Checking for understanding and clarifying misconceptions before moving on to the strategy is an important step.
Step 2: **Make Your Connections** 	**How do you relate to the content?** Use a graphic organizer and model for your students how to identify and record connections to the content. Discuss and share several possible connections to help your students get started. **Examples:** • **Kindergarten:** In learning about the life cycle of plants, a student makes the connection to helping her grandmother in Mexico water her garden.

	• **Third grade:** While learning about fractions in math, a student makes a connection with making a pizza at home and then cutting it into pieces. • **Sixth grade:** In social science class, a student makes a connection between Greek architecture and the columns found in an area museum and library.
Step 3: **Map It Out** 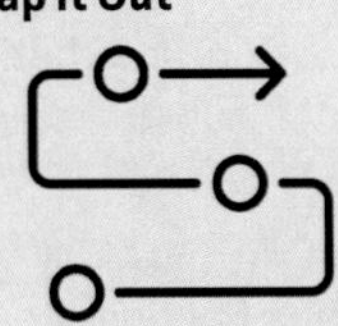	**Provide a graphic organizer:** Share the organizer tool to help your students reflect on and capture their connections to the content. **Potential connections:** • Lived experiences may be related to the content. Students can share or highlight something from their life that directly relates to what is being taught. • Community connections may include observations of area weather, local buildings or organizations, community spaces such as parks or gardens, or area businesses. • Future goals or aspirations can be related to the instructional content. Students can identify how they might use this information in the future.
Step 4: **Support the Connections**  	**Let's connect:** Help to support students as they make their connections. Review and provide timely feedback on the connections that students have made. Also provide time for the students to share their potential connection with a partner or small group for feedback or questions; they can use this feedback to help strengthen or clarify the connection that they will work from.
Step 5: **Sharing Your Connections**    	**How will you share your connection?** Provide your students with multiple options and choices for developing and sharing their connection with others.
	Write a story: Students can write in a variety of formats, such as a short story, an article, a graphic novel, or a letter.
	Breaking news report: Students can create and record a news segment highlighting the content and the local community. Students can write a script and record either themselves or puppets representing in-studio journalists and on-site reporters sharing the news.
	News reporter: Students can script out an interview related to the content. This format can help them share their own personal connections by writing the questions of the reporter and answering from their perspective, or they may create an imagined interview script with other stakeholders.
	Show me: The students may choose to highlight their connections in a diorama, poster, digital slide, or drawing. Students should be prepared to share the meaning behind their image.

(Continued)

(Continued)

Step 6: **Share Your Work** 	**Here's how we connected:** Provide a time for students to share their connections with the class or have a digital space where their recordings can be viewed. Include ways for parents and guardians to see their child/children's creations. **Example projects:** • The student that remembered helping her grandma with her garden in Mexico could draw a picture that shows planting the seeds, small sprouts growing, watering the plants, the plants flowering, and then her and her grandma picking the flowers. The student could provide details about her experience when sharing the picture. • The student who connected fractions with making and cutting pizza at home might choose a news report format highlighting fractions in daily life. • The student who recognized Greek architecture in local buildings might create a mock interview with an architect centered on the influence of ancient civilizations on modern architecture.
Step 7: **Reflect and Assess** 	**What is our takeaway?** Provide your students with an opportunity to reflect on their connection and the way they chose to share it with others. What did they learn? What went well? What would they do differently next time? What did they learn from their classmates? **Assess:** Now that you have gained insights into your students' thinking, is there anything you would adjust in presenting the content next time? Were students able to make personal connections with the content? Did this strategy impact their engagement or overall understanding? Consider saving exemplars to share with future classes so that they can see how other students their age were able to make connections.

Image Sources: Istock.com/appleuzr; Istock.com/RLT_Images

KEY AREA 3: RELEVANT LEARNING

"When will I ever use this?" and "Why do I need to know this?" are age-old questions that some of us may even remember asking back in the day when we were students. This element of relevance remains present for today's students too. Especially when learning new information or skills is challenging or frustrating, it becomes much harder to convince our students to invest their time, energy, and effort into staying with it when they do not see the relevance of what we are teaching. Former teacher and neuroscientist Willis (2011) shares that the brain is "wired" to stop expending energy when there is a low probability of success. This brings us full circle to the point we made earlier that not all students are motivated by grades or test scores. We need to acknowledge the existence of a "relevance gap" and then actively work to address it.

A perceived lack of relevance between what students are learning and their real-world lives is a hurdle we can work to reduce or eliminate. As educators we need to prioritize working with our students to build personal connections to our content. When learners see that what they are learning is relevant to their lives, they become more emotionally invested in the content, which increases their overall engagement (Blue, 2022). If our students are unable to see how what they are learning can be applied in the real world, they are less likely to put in effort to learn it. Most of you are familiar with the saying "In one ear and out the other"; this section will provide you with strategies for the ECS domain of connections to learning, which will help the information you are presenting connect with your students rather than just flowing in one ear and out the other.

Incorporating relevance into learning includes building explicit bridges to real-world application, creating opportunities for learning to extend beyond the four walls of the classroom, and including your students' interests and aspirations in your lessons. How many of you have been in a back-to-school presentation for teachers focused on tapping into your *why*? The teaching profession is simultaneously one of the most challenging and most impactful careers in our society. Addressing the daily challenges in teaching, such as meeting the diverse needs of your students, managing students' behaviors, handling pressures to increase standardized test results, and navigating parental involvement, can lead to teacher stress and burnout. Remembering your *why* can help you step back and keep the larger picture in mind while connecting you to the reasons you chose this profession. This can increase your resilience and renew your determination to face the inherent stressors.

Similarly, when we can help our students identify their *why* it helps them to find their purpose and motivation for learning. Through the intentional layering of these strategies into our instruction, we can increase students' investment in their own learning. Helping our students identify their *why* and having conversations with them about their goals and purpose also helps us to strengthen our relationships and connections to them as individuals. Students have reported the increased motivation they feel when teachers take the time to get to know them as people rather than only as learners. When students are clear on their *why* it also helps them to handle any setbacks or challenges they may encounter, similar to teachers getting through the many challenges they face by focusing on the bigger picture.

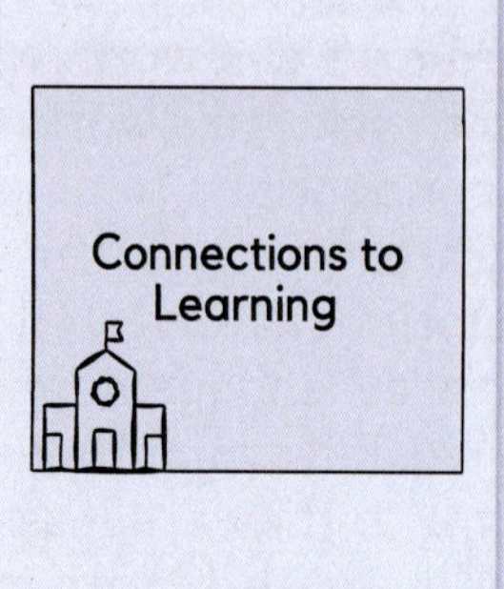	**Relevant Learning**	Relevant learning involves making academic content relevant for students by providing learning opportunities that are directly meaningful and applicable to a student's interests, life, or future goals. This learning connects content to real-world contexts, helping students to understand the importance of what they are learning.

STRATEGIES FOR RELEVANT LEARNING

From Learning to Living: How Could I Use This in the Real World?

STRATEGY **From Learning to Living** 	**What:** Introducing your students to a wide range of career possibilities connected to the instructional content can inspire them to dream big. Through this highlighting of potential career pathways connected to what they are learning, students can see the relevance of the instruction and start to envision their possibilities. **Bonus:** As educators, the more we can break down the walls between the classroom and the real world, the more we will be able to engage our students in our content. By broadening our focus beyond students' performance on high-stakes assessments to include the potential use and application of the material in their lives, we will increase student investment and ownership in their learning.
Step 1: **Review Curriculum Content** 	**Identify core focus areas within the curriculum:** As you review your upcoming unit of instruction, identify the key skill areas or the specific focus of the content. Create a list of the key areas of focus as well as any cross-curricular relevance that will help you identify the areas to narrow in on when seeking potential career connections in the next step.
Step 2: **Connect Relevant Careers** 	**Potential career pathways:** Research and compile a list of careers that are related to your identified content. You can use a range of resources to generate your list, such as career websites, educational platforms, and professional organizations. You may also choose to have your students involved in this step, asking them to include anyone they might know with a job or career that is related, to make connections with characters from books, or to suggest people they have learned about in science, social science, or other fields.

Step 3: **Career Cards** 	**What are the highlights?** Create a template styled like a baseball card that is either printed or digital to keep track of and organize highlights of careers related to the content you are teaching. You may create the career cards or enlist your students to help with the creation. You can print and share or save in a digital database that all students can access. **Possible card features:** • Job description • What people enjoy the most about the career • Some of the career challenges • Required education or degree • School subjects to focus on for this career pathway
Step 4: **Careers in the Spotlight** 	Consider highlighting a different career each week related to the content you are teaching. You can build it into a weekly routine, such as having "Motivation Mondays" or "Future Me Fridays." Along with the career cards, you can use video clips, snips of recorded interviews, articles, or virtual tours to help your students develop an understanding of the career. Ask your students to share their thoughts, ask questions, and share what they find interesting about the career in the spotlight.
Step 5: **Connect to Learning** 	Highlight the ways the spotlighted career is directly related to the content that you are learning. Explain how the skills and knowledge within your current lessons are directly connected to the career. **Examples:** • Connect math knowledge to a career in culinary arts, engineering, or installing HVAC systems. • PE class content can connect to a career as a personal trainer or physical therapist. • Writing can extend to becoming a reporter, becoming a manager who shares information in reports, or becoming a home inspector who shares written findings.
Step 6: **Career Exploration** 	**I might like to become ______________:** Provide opportunities for your students to learn more about the careers that interest them. Or help them to identify potential pathways that build on their strengths, their areas of interest in school, or their *why*. **Possible resources:** • Invite an individual with that career to visit class in person or virtually (see next strategy). • Help students find books or articles related to that field. • Guide students in writing letters to professional organizations for that career so they can ask questions and request recommendations for learning more about that career.

(Continued)

(Continued)

Step 7: **Career Journals** 	**This might be the career for me:** Provide your students with a way to track their potential career interests. This can be in the form of a notebook or a digital journal. This provides students with a way to remember the related careers and to track their potential interests over time. You can help students develop a coding system, such as rating careers with one to five stars, to reflect their level of interest in that career path. The system can also include a space to take notes to capture their thinking at that time.
Step 8: **Career Shares** 	Provide opportunities for students to share their career interests with others. This can include sharing with the class, sharing with a partner or in small groups, or writing a letter to share with their families. As students share their interests, you can consider related fields that they may not yet be aware of and share these additional possibilities with them. You can track the careers you have shared in a database that you can also use in future years as a starting point with new students.

Image Sources: Istock.com/JDawnInk; Istock.com/Anton Porkin; Istock.com/RLT_Images; Istock.com/Turac Novruzova; Istock.com/JDawnInk

Learning Beyond the Classroom: Let's Ask the Experts

STRATEGY **Learning Beyond the Classroom** 	**What:** Learning beyond the classroom means connecting students with professionals, community members, organizations, and guest speakers to enhance their learning experience and help them see the relevance of what they are learning in school. **Bonus:** Extending learning beyond the classroom walls by inviting in experts and community members enriches the student experience by highlighting real-world application of learning. These interactions can help cultivate curiosity and inspire students by sharing career path opportunities they may not have known existed.
Step 1: **Identify Learning Objectives** 	Once you have determined the learning goals and standards of your unit of study, you can brainstorm how a guest speaker may be able to enhance understanding of the content or highlight a career or community connection. You may choose to co-plan with your students by sharing a preview of the learning ahead and having them join in on planning for potential connections outside of the school walls. **Examples:** • An upcoming unit on ecosystems could involve a biologist discussing their work in conservation. • A focus on writing descriptions and the use of adjectives could include a realtor discussing word selection in property listings.

Step 2:

Research and Select Beyond-the-Classroom Connector

Locate the expert: Once you have identified some potential options for including experts or guests in your instruction, start to reach out and explore potential connections.

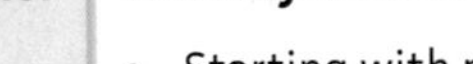

This may include:

- Starting with people that you or others in your school might know
- Reaching out to local businesses or area universities
- Searching for potential guests or experts that may be willing to meet with you and your class virtually

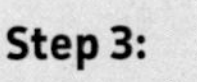

Step 3:

Coordinate Scheduling

Strategic scheduling: Once you have identified the individual that will be adding to your content, you will need to work around their availability and your instructional timing to make the most of their time with you.

Considerations:

- You may have them speak to the class toward the start of the learning to generate interest in the topic.
- Toward the middle of the learning, students will have some information and will have a basic foundation to form questions to ask the guest.
- A speaker at the conclusion of the unit of study can help students have a working knowledge of the potential application of what was learned in the real world.
- Be sure to prepare the speaker with information about the learning your students have done up to this point. Possibly share some sample text excerpts or student writing to give them a feel for where the students are in their understanding. You may want to encourage the use of visuals or realia if possible. Be clear on the structure and time allotment for their visit.

Step 4:

Prepare Your Students

Always be prepared: In order to provide the conditions necessary to make the most of your interaction, it will be important to prepare your students for the visit:

- Inform your students about the guest speaker, sharing information on their background and reviewing the purpose of their time with you.
- Provide an opportunity for the students to prepare questions in advance.
- Have the students remind each other about, and clarify, expectations for behavior when the guest is with the class.

Step 5:

Build Into Instruction

Intentional planning: In order to make the most of the outside connection, build related activities into your instruction leading up to and then after the visit.

Example: Before a visit with a city planner, have the students create their own city maps. After the visit, compare and contrast how real-world planning compares with their own mapping process.

(Continued)

(Continued)

Step 6: **Facilitate the Interaction** 	Make sure that everything is set up for either the virtual or in-person visit, ensuring that both sides have all of the necessary information, including virtual links or information for school sign-in. **During the session:** Be prepared with a brief introduction along with the purpose of the visit. You should also be ready to redirect the guest as needed. For example, they may be sharing information in advanced terminology that your students have difficulty understanding, or they may start to lose the students' attention if speaking too long on one component. You can help the guests be successful by cueing them to move on or asking questions to help your students understand better.
Step 7: **Create Opportunities for Interaction** 	**Avoid a one-way lecture:** Create opportunities for students to ask questions and engage with the speaker. The speaker may also use interactive elements such as having students write down predictions or using tools like Kahoot. **Examples:** • Have students take turns asking questions from their groups that you have previewed. • You may have your students create a chart of the top five things they would like to know from your guest. • Have some questions prepared that will help students make the connection between the guest's time in school, what they learned, their current role. • Ask the guest to share advice or recommendations for any students who may be interested in their field. • Have students share their work or projects related to the content for feedback from the expert.
Step 8: **Reflect and Assess** 	**Takeaways and future planning:** You can lead your class through a reflective discussion about what they learned from the speaker and how it connects to their learning. You can use the students' reflections to assess the impact the speaker may have had on your students or their learning. **Next time:** What went well with your guest session? Is there anything you would communicate differently to the guest ahead of time? Did the structure of the visit work? What would you change?
Step 9: **Send Thank-You Notes** 	**Show your gratitude:** This is an opportunity to teach your students about gratitude by having them write thank-you notes to the guest speaker. These may be handwritten, digital, or one giant thank-you from the class signed by all. Ask the students to highlight something they learned or their favorite part of the guest's visit. You may also consider sharing a picture of the speaker with the class to go along with the written thank-yous.
Step 10: **Maintain the Connection** 	**Let's do this again!** If all went well, you may consider staying in touch with the guest speaker for future visits or asking for their involvement in extended learning projects. The speaker may also have colleagues in related fields that would be interested in sharing information with your students. Maintaining connections with solid speakers will help you moving forward. You may want to send an occasional class newsletter to the speaker or highlight the connections students made to what they shared.

Image Sources: Istock.com/milkghost; Istock.com/appleuzr; Istock.com/lushik; Istock.com/bankrx; stock.com/fonikum

KEY AREA 4: GOAL SETTING

Another way to help our students build connections to their learning is by engaging them in the identification of individual goals to achieve within their learning. This process creates a clear, individualized purpose as well as shifting some of the responsibility for the learning process to the students. Layering goal setting into instruction also provides a concrete, tangible way for students to track their progress, to advocate for their needs as they encounter obstacles, and to help them celebrate their accomplishments. This should be an ongoing process that is embedded into your units of instruction rather than something that only takes place at the start of the year or each trimester.

When students set attainable goals (e.g., SMART goals) and make significant progress toward them or reach them, it helps to build both their self-efficacy and self-confidence. A focus on setting, working toward, and achieving goals positively impacts overall student achievement and helps to build individualized connections to the content. According to the Midwest Comprehensive Center (2018) at American Institutes for Research, students are up to three times more likely to be motivated to engage in activities that are related to working toward the goals they have set. This highlights the importance of supporting your students in developing their own goals and determining the pathways to reach them.

Along with short-term goals related to the content you are teaching, you can start to work with your students on future forward goals. The concept behind this type of goal setting is related to each individual's current vision for their future. What do they see as their current career goal? What are their current strengths and interests, and how would they like to build those into their plans for the future? A teacher shared an example of one of her students, Roberto, giving minimal effort in her class, often shutting down at the first need for any cognitive sweat. She made time to speak with him one-on-one. He started out resistant and stated, "I guess I'm in trouble." The teacher surprised him by asking what he thought he might like to do as he got older. Roberto became very animated and spoke about an uncle that had his own small restaurant and how he wanted to one day open his own. He said he would specialize in different chicken recipes and call it the Chick Inn Palace. This was something he had clearly been thinking about.

Once the teacher was aware of Roberto's potential vision for his future, she asked him for even more details. Then she helped him connect his dream to how what he was learning in school would be able to help him make his restaurant possible. They discussed several examples of how both math and reading skills would be needed to help him achieve his goal and to run his business successfully. After his teacher helped him to make connections between his learning and his future forward goals, Roberto became much more engaged in his schoolwork, asking for help when he needed it rather than shutting down. The teacher continued to meet with him to discuss both his learning and his future—she also requested an invitation to the opening day of his restaurant!

This focus on what our students envision for their future is a key lever for helping them connect to their learning. There is no one way to define success; it looks different for each individual. As educators we need to adopt a much broader definition of success that stretches far beyond the numbers on a standardized assessment measure. While these data have relevance and are important in overarching accountability, we need to take the steps to connect with each of our students to show that we believe in them and that we know they are capable of anything they set their minds to! This is one of the greatest gifts we can give our students: an unwavering belief in the strengths, talents, and passions of every one and a prioritization of their future forward goals in our instruction. We can give our students hope, help them to see a world of possibilities, and support them in building the connections between their learning and their current vision for themselves. We can make these slight changes and adjustments in our practice that can make all of the difference for our students and their futures!

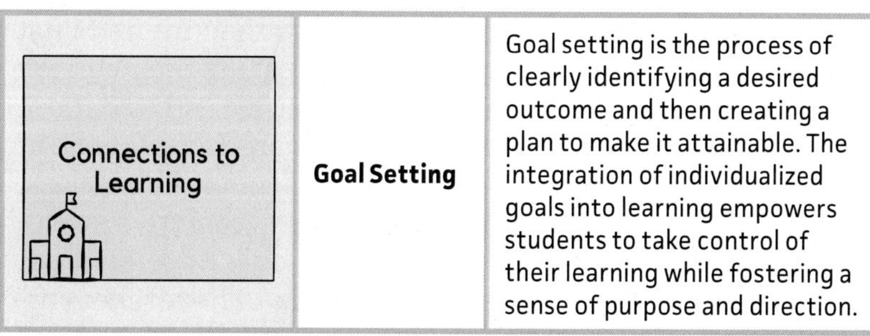

Connections to Learning	**Goal Setting**	Goal setting is the process of clearly identifying a desired outcome and then creating a plan to make it attainable. The integration of individualized goals into learning empowers students to take control of their learning while fostering a sense of purpose and direction.

STRATEGIES FOR GOAL SETTING

Success Steps: Incorporating Short-Term Goals Within Your Instruction

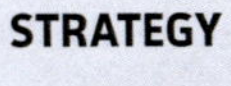 **STRATEGY** **Success Steps** 	**What:** Incorporate short-term goals set by your students within your instruction to increase ownership and further connections with their learning. This also increases their focus as they engage in the unit of instruction. **Bonus:** Enhancing your instruction through short-term goal setting helps to build students' confidence by providing them with a sense of accomplishment. Goal integration also encourages students to think about the ways they learn best and fosters an overall growth mindset.
Step 1: **Build an Understanding** 	**What are short-term goals?** Help your students to develop an understanding of short-term goals. You can share that setting a goal is like having a plan to reach a target. Goals help us to stay focused on what we want to achieve. **Share examples:** • For someone to earn a black belt in a martial art, they learn specific skills and they achieve different colored belts that show their progress and growth as they work toward becoming a black belt. • A student who wants to read more books may set a short-term goal of reading one book each week. As you reach a goal, you may consider focusing on a new goal or increasing your original goal. In this case, the student may want to start reading two books each week.
Step 2: **Share the Purpose** 	**Why add in goals?** Once students have an understanding of goal setting, you will want to help them understand why they will be setting goals to work toward in their learning. **Points to share:** • Setting goals helps us to focus on what we want to achieve. • Goal setting can help make learning exciting as it helps you to see the progress that you are making. • When we reach our goals or show growth, it helps us to feel proud of our effort and accomplishments.
Step 3: **Brainstorm Goals** 	**Brainstorm potential goals:** Have a class discussion to collectively brainstorm possible goals related to the current content. Encourage students to think about what they would like to learn or improve in. Model the thought process that you use when identifying short-term goals that you would like to achieve within your own life. You can share a range of content-related goals to help students start to narrow in on their area of focus.

(Continued)

(Continued)

<table>
<tr><td>Step 4:
Create Short-Term Goal
</td><td>Establish a short-term goal: Provide a template for students to develop their short-term goal. The areas to build out include the following:<ul><li>Goal: What do you want to learn or improve?</li><li>Why: Why is this goal important to you? Why did you select this area?</li><li>How: How will you work to reach your goal? How will you measure your success?</li></ul>Examples:<ul><li>Goal: Learn all multiplication tables up to ten.</li><li>Why: Because it will help me to solve math problems faster and with fewer mistakes.</li><li>How: I will practice my facts daily with flashcards and Reflex on the computer. I will take weekly quizzes to track my progress.</li></ul></td></tr>
<tr><td>Step 5:
Monitor Goal Progress
</td><td>Am I making progress? Provide your students with ongoing opportunities to reflect on their progress toward their goals:<ul><li>What is going well?</li><li>What are my challenges?</li><li>What adjustments can I make, or should I stay the course?</li><li>When you reach your goal, celebrate and adjust the goal or set a new one.</li></ul></td></tr>
<tr><td>Step 6:
Goal Reflection
</td><td>Reflect on the goal process: Help your students to pause and reflect on the goal process. Encourage them to think about what worked and what they might do differently when setting the next goal. Ask:<ul><li>Did you achieve your goal?</li><li>What helped you to be successful?</li><li>If you didn’t reach your goal, what might you do differently next time?</li><li>What progress was made?</li><li>Did you discover anything about yourself as a learner?</li></ul></td></tr>
<tr><td>Step 7:
Celebrations and Next Steps
</td><td>Celebrate! One advantage to setting and working toward short-term goals is that it can provide our students with concrete, tangible celebration points as they continue to learn.

Taking the time to celebrate growth and progress helps to motivate students and helps them to see themselves as capable learners. Give recognition to their hard work and effort as they work on their goal.

Provide students with a means of tracking their goals so they can see their growth throughout the year. This progression of short-term goals can also be used to help them identify their next area of focus.</td></tr>
</table>

Image Sources: Istock.com/Ideas and Istock.com/appleuzr

Future Forward Goals: Career Kickstarters

STRATEGY **Future Forward Goals** 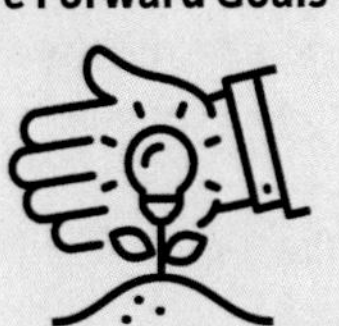	**What:** This strategy helps students to understand the relevance of education by building connections with their future careers and the pathways needed to get there. This strategy helps to develop important life skills from an early age, including goal setting, resume building, and job interview skills. Discuss the process involved from identifying a career to being hired for that role. What are the steps in between? **Bonus:** Including these opportunities within core instruction from an early age helps to empower our students with the skills and knowledge they will need to successfully navigate the world ahead of them. Through integration within traditional classes, we help to build students' confidence and help to make the process less daunting. This also helps students to envision their futures and encourages them to make the most of their education.
Step 1: **Career Possibilities** 	**Review of career possibilities:** Based on how much you have integrated the connection of potential careers into your students' learning, either review or introduce the concept of careers. **Explore:** Explore potential careers together using resources such as careeronestop.org or mynextmove.org.
Step 2: **Introduction to Resumes** 	**Capturing your background and experience:** Explain what a resume is and why it is so important when searching for a job. Provide students with some sample resumes to help them gain a better understanding of the information on a resume and some of the basic formatting options. **Experiences and resume builders:** Help students understand that often potential employers will look for individuals that were active at their school by belonging to teams or clubs, or they may look for those who volunteer and give back to their community. **Student resume:** You can provide your students with the experience of creating a resume by giving them a template that has sections for name, skills, interests, languages spoken, and any relevant experience, such as school projects or responsibilities at home.
Step 3: **Job Applications** 	Provide students with some sample job applications in either print or online format. Discuss what the individuals in the hiring role are looking for when they review a resume. **Classroom jobs:** Have your students fill out an application designed for various roles within your classroom. These roles may include technology specialist, director of classroom operations, or learning environment curator. As you rotate these jobs throughout the year, students can reapply or try for a new role. Ensure that everyone has one or more jobs throughout the year.

(Continued)

(Continued)

Step 4: **Preparation for Job Interview** 	Share the process for successfully preparing for a job interview. **Provide models:** Find or create short videos showing an interview. What do the students think went well? If they were to coach the candidate, what feedback would they provide to help them improve in their next interview? Some of the areas to highlight may include the following: • Explain how your education, experience, and skill set make you the ideal candidate to fill the position. • Learn more about the company, its goals, and specifics about the role. • Come prepared with questions to ask the interviewer at the end of the interview. These questions should reflect what you learned about them and display your genuine interest in the role. • Practice through interview role-plays. Have students practice interviews with each other and provide resources for family members to help students practice at home if they choose.
Step 5: **Job Interviews** 	**The job interview experience:** Discuss the elements of a successful job interview, such as making eye contact, offering a solid handshake, and addressing the question asked and not going off topic. Run your students through interviews; these can be for either the classroom job they have applied for or a mock interview based on a potential career goal. Start with a handshake and introductions, ask questions, and provide them with an opportunity to ask their questions. End with the final handshake and concluding remarks.
Step 6: **Reflection and Feedback** 	Have the students reflect on how they think their interview went: • What went well? • What would they do differently if they could do it over? • How were they feeling during the interview? Do they have strategies they can use to feel less nervous? Provide your students with your feedback once they have shared their reflection. Share their strengths (their "glows") during the interview as well as any areas to continue to work on (their "grows").
Step 7: **Future Forward Goal Setting** 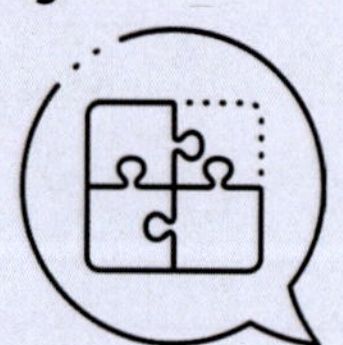	Provide students with a space to reflect on their job-centric experiences, including tips for their future selves that they would like to remember. Students can set goals such as seeking volunteer opportunities or joining a certain number of clubs or activities to ensure that they are having well-rounded, diverse experiences. You can help them identify options based on their *why*, passions, or interests.

Image Sources: Istock.com/appleuzr; Istock.com/StudioU; Istock.com/fonikum; Istock.com/matsabe

CHAPTER SUMMARY

Connecting to learning is a powerful skill that teachers and students need to develop every year. The more engaged and connected students feel to the learning, the more lasting the learning becomes. Teachers play a large role in the growth of this skill, which consists of four key areas: curiosity and inquiry, personalization, relevant learning, and goal setting. These four areas can and must be interwoven with academic learning tasks to help students engage in deep and enduring learning.

Reflection Questions

1. What are you already doing in classrooms to foster the essential skill of connecting to learning?
2. How can curiosity and inquiry enhance students' motivation and lead to lifelong learning? Provide examples of how you can incorporate these elements into your lessons.
3. How can you connect what students are learning in the classroom to real-world applications? Why is this essential for maintaining student interest and investment in their education?
4. Reflect on the importance of goal setting as discussed in this chapter. How can helping students set short-term and long-term goals increase their ownership of learning and provide motivation to succeed?
5. Which of the strategies suggested in this chapter do you plan to use in your setting?

Connections to Community

CHAPTER 5

"A true community is not just about being geographically close to someone or part of the same social web network. It's about feeling connected and responsible for what happens. Humanity is our ultimate community, and everyone plays a crucial role."

—Yehuda Berg

Your Snapshot Guide

Connections to Community

WHAT?	As educators, we have numerous ways that we can grow connections between our students and the community that are directly related to learning standards. In addition to increasing students' academic skills, providing these opportunities helps to build their self-esteem and self-confidence, and it enhances their life satisfaction.
WHY?	These enriched educational experiences contribute to greater engagement in learning and a deeper understanding of the world around them. These learning experiences also lay the foundation for our students to become responsible, informed, and active citizens.
HOW?	Building connections between our students and their community extends learning experiences beyond our classroom walls. Through authentic learning projects, service-learning opportunities, and school–community partnerships, we deepen content learning and help students' holistic growth.
BONUS	A classroom environment that includes community connections is highly engaging and motivating for your students. All of these strategies can be implemented at a wide range of levels within your instruction (e.g., exploring, integrating) and can be layered within any curriculum across content areas.

Four Key Areas Within the ECS Domain of Connections to Community	
Belonging	Advocacy
Social Responsibility	Global Community

ESSENTIAL CONNECTION SKILL: CONNECTIONS TO COMMUNITY

Enhancing instruction in grades K–6 through the inclusion of community connections has a profound impact on both academic learning and personal development. Including authentic learning projects, providing service-learning opportunities, and building school–community partnerships helps to make learning more relevant and meaningful. These hands-on, experiential approaches lead students to deeper comprehension and increased retention of what they have been learning. In addition to academic gains, community-integrated learning provides multitiered opportunities for personal development in areas such as empathy, self-confidence, leadership, critical thinking, and collaboration skills.

The four key areas within this ECS domain center around belonging, advocacy, social responsibility, and the global community. Through integration of instruction that includes bridges with the community, our students learn more about what it means to be a member of a group, how to speak up and take action for themselves and others, how to consider ethics in decision-making, and how to seek ways to grow their knowledge and awareness of the global community and their place within it. These experiences have a lasting impact on students as well as energizing and motivating their learning and school experience in the here and now.

When students have more agency and play an active role in decision-making during instruction, they understand more about themselves as learners. In a recent study by KnowledgeWorks (Kuhlmann, 2024), when student-centered practices that included authentic options to apply and demonstrate learning were included in instruction, there was a significant increase in student outcomes as measured on nationally normed assessments. Teachers also observed that more choices for students brought increased growth through productive struggle as students themselves navigated decisions and outcomes related to their learning. This state of engagement is where students experience growth.

Another approach to learning that builds connections with the community is service learning. The National Youth Leadership Council (n.d.) defines this as teaching and learning in which students use academic and civic knowledge to address genuine community needs. These opportunities involve application of what the students have been learning combined with empowering them to make a real difference. Students themselves report feeling motivated by the opportunity to help others, and several said they would continue to find ways to help and support others within their community. Embedding service learning into instruction "connects students to each other and to the world around them while providing the skills necessary to succeed in school and beyond" (Meuers, 2023).

The National Math + Science Initiative (2023) also recognizes the potential of community partnerships for students. The initiative highlights that these partnerships can take any number of forms, including working with businesses, nonprofits, universities or colleges, government agencies, or community members. All of these options have a common purpose of working together to improve students' educational outcomes by partnering with diverse community resources for a more supportive, inclusive, and engaging learning experience. Studies show that including community engagement often results in higher student achievement and provides real-world learning experiences that are not available through traditional instruction.

THE IMPORTANCE OF BUILDING CONNECTIONS TO COMMUNITY

When the essential connection skill of connections to community is woven into classroom instruction, there are several benefits. Multiple research studies show that students are motivated by hands-on activities that have a real-world connection (Farber & Bishop, 2018; Gupta, 2019). Integrating connections with the community enhances both the academic (mind) and personal (heart) development of our students. These opportunities help to transform classrooms from spaces that are solely focused on grades or test scores to being more practical and engaging, with real-world relevance that helps students develop essential life skills and a sense of civic responsibility.

Students themselves have reported that they appreciated the opportunity to interact with their classmates while they worked together as a team on a community project (Paonessa, 2023). It helped them to make lasting friendships. The students also shared that even though the project wasn't for a grade, they put more time and effort into it knowing that what they were doing would be seen by others. Not only did working together on these projects increase the connections with their community but it also strengthened the connections within the classroom, including the relationship between the teacher and the students. The students acknowledged that it took some additional effort on the part of the teacher to make such projects possible, which they appreciated, and engaging in the work helped them all get to know each other better. The students felt respected and valued for their contributions and for being viewed as capable of "real work" by their teacher.

BUILDING CONNECTIONS TO COMMUNITY INTO CONTENT INSTRUCTION

Integrating opportunities to build connections with the community is a powerful way to enhance your instruction and have a lasting impact on your students. These connections can be built in a variety of ways across all content areas. As a teacher you may experiment with a strategy in a particular class or subject area, or you may consider forming new partnerships within your community. Any connection that you are able to weave into your instruction will add to your students' experience. You can begin planning independently or with a grade-level professional learning community team, and over time, you can empower your students to take on more responsibility for planning and directing these community connections.

Getting started will require planning and effort, but the reward for your students will be far-reaching. You will provide your students with real-world application of their studies, which will bridge the gap between learning concepts in the classroom and relevant application. While the process of planning and actioning community connections may seem daunting at first, the joy and excitement that it will bring to your classroom is contagious. The reciprocal relationship between the students and the community is powerful. Students gain a sense of purpose and relevance for their education while the community benefits from the fresh perspectives and energy of the students.

The ECS domain of connections to community supports both academic development and personal growth for your students. Through building and modeling these connections, you are providing unique experiences that will directly prepare your students to seek out, form, and maintain involvement and relationships within their community. According to the Mayo Clinic (Thoreson, 2023), by volunteering and becoming involved within their community, individuals reduce overall stress and some risk of physical and mental health problems. Providing these community-connected experiences for our students as a part of their learning is setting them up for continued involvement as they go through life.

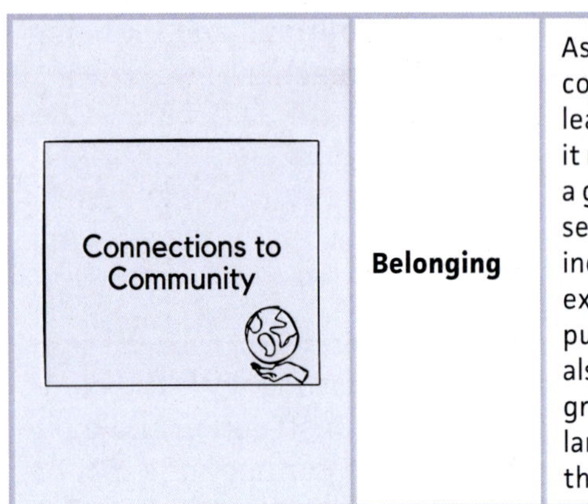 Connections to Community	**Belonging**	As students engage in community-integrated learning, they explore what it means to be a member of a group or community. Their sense of classroom community increases through shared experience and sense of purpose. These opportunities also help students develop a greater understanding of the larger communities to which they belong.

KEY AREA 1: BELONGING

The key area of belonging within connections to community is an essential human need. The *Cambridge Dictionary* (Cambridge University Press, n.d-b.) defines belonging as "a feeling of being happy or comfortable as a part of a particular group and having a good relationship with the other members of the group because they welcome you and accept you." With the increasing diversity within our classrooms, it is more important than ever to cultivate belonging within our educational ecosystems (Strom et al., 2024). Having this need to belong met impacts the students' overall well-being and their availability for learning. As educators we have the opportunity to cultivate a classroom or school community where everyone feels a sense of belonging while also helping our students develop the skills necessary to navigate and strengthen their connections with others.

Which spaces or communities make you feel the most comfortable and valued? Where or when do you experience belonging? While this may look different for each of us, we can probably all think about past or current connections that led us to feel a sense of belonging. On the flip side, we can probably all think of at least one experience where we felt excluded or as if we didn't fully belong. Sitting briefly with the feelings that those questions evoke is a simple reminder of the importance of continually ensuring that each and every one of our students feels like they fit in and belong. When you integrate belonging into content instruction you are helping to prepare your students to be empathetic, engaged members of society.

When students have this sense of belonging, of feeling safe and supported, it can increase their academic success and motivation to try their best and keep them engaged in their learning. This sense of community not only helps students feel comfortable but also fosters a sense of looking out for one another.

Consistently reflect on belonging as a fundamental aspect of your students' experience and take action when necessary if you notice any student who is disengaged. Include discussions about what belonging entails and everyone's role in creating a welcoming and inclusive environment for all. By including an understanding of the power and significance of belonging, you can help enhance your students' awareness of their actions and how they affect others, which can help to build their emotional intelligence.

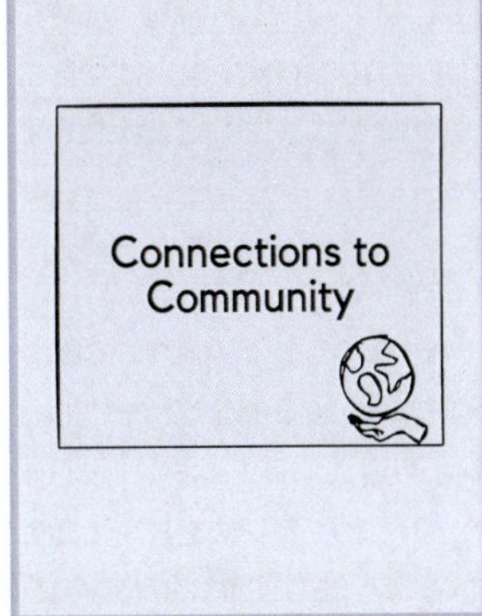	**Advocacy**	This involves students learning to voice their needs and to support others. Community-connected learning allows students to participate in activities that help them develop the skills to speak out and take action for important causes. These experiences empower students to become confident individuals who promote fairness and equity while actively engaging within their communities.

KEY AREA 2: ADVOCACY

The *Cambridge Dictionary* (Cambridge University Press, n.d.-a) defines advocacy as "public support for an idea, plan, or way of doing something." As an educator you can support your students in becoming advocates for themselves and others. This involves a number of skills and competencies, including empowering them to effectively share their thoughts, opinions, and needs. Students also need to be active listeners as they engage with others to help resolve issues or address a need. Students must have strong critical thinking and problem-solving skills in order to be able to suggest action steps or possible solutions.

One of the first steps to helping your students engage in advocacy is to help them build an understanding of what that means, which includes providing them with examples and role models. Drawing from current events, books, classroom content, or school-related scenarios, you can highlight and discuss when someone is advocating for themselves and others. You can guide your students in reflecting on what the problem or injustice was, what actions the advocate took to address the issue, the outcomes, and how the person might have felt through each stage. You can provide examples of students who advocated for their own learning needs, such as requesting manipulatives, graphic organizers, or a change in seating. Teaching self-advocacy—the ability to stand up for yourself—is an important life skill.

There are several books and videos that show children standing up for others. Picture books with this theme can be used with students of all ages to provide examples and generate meaningful discussions. Students can then create their own examples that can be used as the basis for role-plays. Through integrating these examples into your classroom and discussing them together, you are helping to normalize for your students speaking up and taking action. You can provide examples from times when you were an advocate for yourself or others. Sharing your own experiences, talking through your thought process at the time, revealing the outcomes, and relating how you felt can further motivate your students to be advocates.

Building connections within the community by identifying a need or those that would benefit from help or support can provide your students with a real-world experience with advocacy. Students can work on addressing any local environmental issues, become involved in a food drive, or advocate for the needs of younger students at your school, such as having their own books to keep at home. By including advocacy within your instruction, through both building the concept with your students and providing opportunities for them to act as advocates, you are helping students to develop important life skills, promoting their personal development, and setting the stage for them to become involved and active members within their communities.

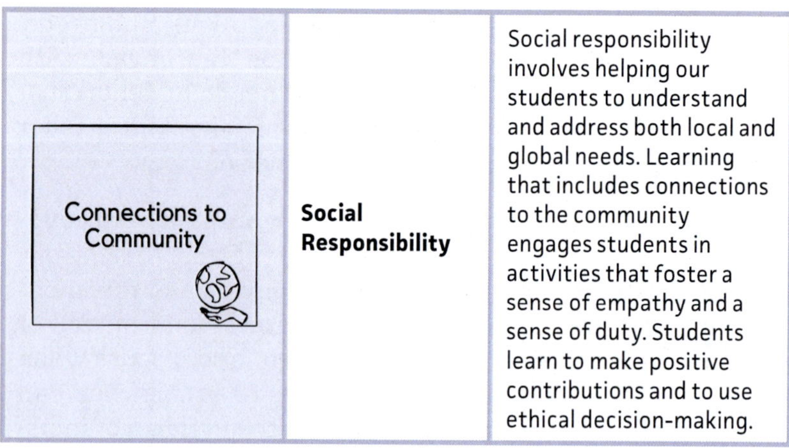

Connections to Community	**Social Responsibility**	Social responsibility involves helping our students to understand and address both local and global needs. Learning that includes connections to the community engages students in activities that foster a sense of empathy and a sense of duty. Students learn to make positive contributions and to use ethical decision-making.

KEY AREA 3: SOCIAL RESPONSIBILITY

While advocacy is focused on specific situations or injustices, social responsibility has a broader scope and includes proactive efforts and ethical decision-making that benefit society at large. The efforts within social responsibility tend to focus on longer-term, systemic changes that will have a lasting impact over time. Teaching social responsibility from an early age helps students to consider the consequences of their actions and to include ethical considerations in their decision-making. This includes giving consideration to aspects such as empathy, respect, fairness, and the consequences of actions.

You can help to build social responsibility with your students by using phrases they will easily understand, such as "taking care of our planet" and "being kind and considerate of others." You can share ways that you make socially responsible choices like recycling, supporting small businesses, engaging in acts of kindness, or supporting charitable organizations. Helping your students to understand ethical decision-making can include using principles that they can easily relate to, such as what is fair or unfair, or what is right or wrong, and making choices that align with what is important to you, such as respect and kindness. This includes thinking through how your decisions will impact others and the world around you.

As an educator you can integrate examples and discussions of ethical decision-making within your content instruction. Including examples that your students can easily identify with is a good step in helping them to consider social responsibility as it relates to decision-making. You can provide them with examples or scenarios related to putting systems and procedures in place to make the classroom environmentally friendly, such as recycling and minimizing waste, showing compassion toward others and valuing diverse perspectives, or always including the voices of everyone working in a group. Social responsibility at school includes treating the school and school resources with care and respect and using them responsibly. This can also include being a good citizen by contributing to the classroom or school community in positive ways.

Many examples of social responsibility can be found in local communities. One example is picking up litter along streets or in parks to keep spaces clean and safe. People donating unused toys, books, or clothing to area organizations is another demonstration of social responsibility. Organizations plant trees or flowers to enhance local green spaces and create areas for wildlife. There may be individuals or groups that write letters or attend meetings seeking localized change to better the environment or to meet the needs of individuals within the community. All of these socially responsible actions add up to make a difference that will have a lasting positive impact.

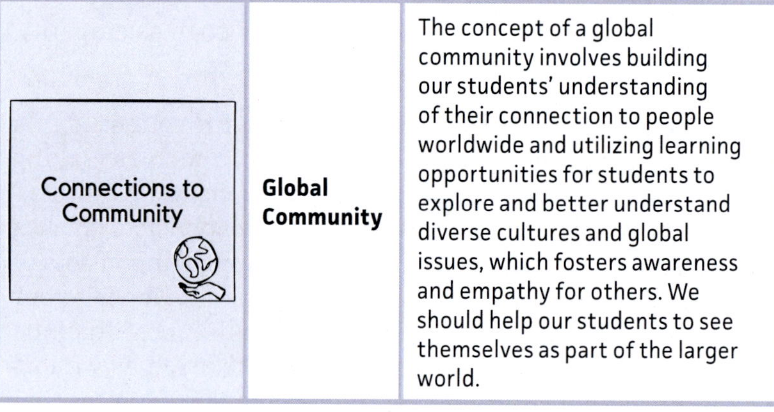

Connections to Community	**Global Community**	The concept of a global community involves building our students' understanding of their connection to people worldwide and utilizing learning opportunities for students to explore and better understand diverse cultures and global issues, which fosters awareness and empathy for others. We should help our students to see themselves as part of the larger world.

KEY AREA 4: GLOBAL COMMUNITY

More than ever there is a need for our students to understand that they are a part of the globalized world. Our planet is interconnected, and we need individuals who see themselves as global citizens with a desire to address the issues that transcend any borders. The *Collins Dictionary* (Collins, 2011) defines global community as "the people or nations of the world, considered as being closely connected by modern telecommunications and as being economically, socially, and politically interdependent." As educators we have the opportunity to help our students grow in awareness of and appreciation for varying cultural perspectives as well as have an open mind as global issues are considered (Courtney, 2024). Highlighting the global community in your instruction will help your students develop empathy and a sense of shared responsibility to address global issues.

One way to get started is by highlighting and honoring the varying heritages and backgrounds of students within your classroom or school community. Not only does this value the assets and perspectives that diversity adds to your community but also it helps make the concept of a global community relatable for all students. As students learn about the cultures of their classmates it helps them to become more aware of traditions and varying experiences that are a part of your classroom and the world at large. Recognizing and valuing diverse perspectives and celebrating diverse backgrounds helps to build a stronger community. You may consider adding elements such as a global show-and-tell where students can bring in items or pictures related to their culture. You can create an "Our Heritages" bulletin board that highlights the diversity within your classroom. These are all tangible ways to bring aspects of the wider world into your classroom.

In order to help students understand the depth of diversity and varied life experiences across the globe, you can invite guest speakers or family members to share with your students. This is an opportunity for them to learn directly from others who may have different experiences from their own. They can learn some words or phrases in a new language and hear directly about traditions and values that are important in that cultural community. Including a wide array of books and stories that reflect the cultures and backgrounds of your students as well as other cultures is another way to help your students understand the concept of global community. Celebrating and exploring the contributions of various cultures creates a foundation for developing respect, empathy, inclusivity, and curiosity about the world and the many different people within it.

There are many free resources to support teachers with bringing global citizenship into their classrooms. One example is the California Global Education Project (CGEP). This group provides a number of resources including the global competence framework, which adopted the four domains developed by the Council of Chief State School Officers and the Asia Society Policy Institute Center to foster global awareness and curiosity about the way the world works. These domains are (1) investigate the world beyond the immediate environment, (2) recognize perspectives, both your own and those of others, (3) communicate ideas effectively with diverse audiences, and (4) take action to improve conditions. The CGEP website (calglobaled.org) includes a number of resources, including posters to encourage global thinking with titles such as "Keep an Open Mind" and "Consider Multiple Perspectives and Opinions."

STRATEGIES FOR INTEGRATING CONNECTIONS TO COMMUNITY INTO INSTRUCTION

Connections to Community	
	Authentic Learning Projects
	Service-Learning Opportunities
	School-Community Partnerships

	**Authentic Learning Projects**	These projects engage students in meaningful, hands-on, real-world learning experiences that allow them to apply what they are learning. These experiences are tailored to students' interests and are connected to the world around them.

EDUPitch: Design to Meet a Real-World Need

STRATEGY **EDUPitch** 	**What:** This strategy enables students to work alone or with others as they identify real needs within the world and then design a product that will address the need. Think of it as a mini-*Shark Tank* experience for your students! This strategy requires students to use several skills, such as critical thinking to identify a need; problem-solving to design a solution; the application of literacy skills as they research the issue and then create their design; and communication skills as they share their pitch with a panel of judges. If students work with others, they are also applying their collaboration skills and utilizing communication skills as they share ideas and navigate a large number of decisions. **Bonus:** Students find the EDUPitch highly motivating and engaging. This is a unique opportunity for students to think outside of the box and use their creativity to think through and design new products.
Step 1: **Introduce the Concept of the EDUPitch** 	**Dive into the shark tank:** Some of your students may be familiar with the concept if they have watched the TV show *Shark Tank*. On the show's website, you can find clips that will help you build the concept with your students. There are also many examples of companies that started on *Shark Tank* that have a social responsibility component, such as Bombas, which donates a pair of socks to the homeless for each pair that is purchased. It is important to introduce the concept of an *entrepreneur*, or someone who starts a new business after identifying a need that is currently not being met or makes an improvement to something already in the marketplace.

Step 2: **Share Student Examples** 	**How can I do that?** While there are some clips from *Shark Tank* involving children as entrepreneurs, the majority of participants are adults. It is helpful to have at least one example of a project that students within the same age range as yours have already completed. Moving forward, it is advised to have some projects from previous years saved. You can search online for examples, create a sample that a student that age might generate, or work with children of a similar age (your own, neighbors, or other relatives) to create an initial example. Having some exemplars will help make the EDUPitch more approachable for your students.
Step 3: **Introduce the Project as It Relates to Your Content** 	**Introducing the EDUPitch!** You will want to share an overview of the project with your students, including any elements or parameters specific to your content area. You may choose to leave the projects open-ended and include a content connection within their pitch. You can introduce the EDUPitch graphic organizer and share with students the timeline, the class time they will have to work on the project, and when they will be making their pitch. Students may choose to design a product based on a need observed in their own community.

Content-Related EDUPitch Projects

Science 	You may choose to include specific science-related topics that the students have worked on in class. **Examples:** Creating new tools to support making observations in nature or eco-friendly science kits for use in homes.
Social Science 	Students may be asked to think of a product related to concepts or topics taught in social science. **Examples:** Tools to help students better understand the timeline of history or a product that helps families discover other cultures.
Math 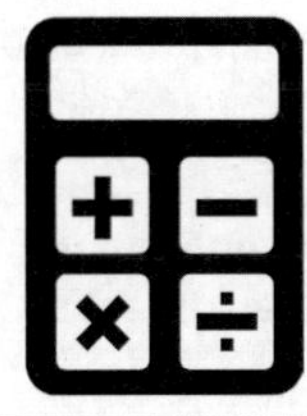	You may ask students to include aspects such as current market share of similar products, cost of a product, and the profit margin based on anticipated costs. You can also ask for math-focused products. **Examples:** Board games that can be played at home to build math concepts or visuals to help students learn about geometry in everyday life.
ELA 	Students will be highly engaged in all aspects of literacy within their EDUPitch projects. You may also request literacy-related products. **Examples:** Products that will improve the library experience or kits to help anyone be able to write their own fiction story.

(Continued)

(Continued)

	Specials	**PE:** You may ask students to create a product related to fitness or sports. **Examples:** Have students create products related to engaging kids in physical activities outside of school or have them create a new sport.
		Music: You may ask for projects directly related to experiencing or creating music. **Examples:** Have students design a product that will enable listeners to capture their feelings about specific music or have them create new instruments.
		Art: You can have students focus on concepts or topics taught in your class. **Examples:** Kits that guide individuals to create art from found objects or a subscription box that will help families create art projects with global connections.
		STEM: Projects may be based on your class content. **Examples:** Creating kits or a board game that families can play to introduce coding or a STEM challenge game using found objects in the home.
Step 4: **Review the Graphic Organizer and Timelines**	**EDUPitch Terms**	**Preview and explain:** Review the terms within the organizer based on your students' age and grade level.
	Brainstorm	**Create a list of potential ideas:** From your list select a product with a potential name and brief description.
	Problem and Solution	**State the problem:** Describe the problem that you identified and share how your product addresses the issue.
	Target Market	**Identify your target market:** Who will your target market be? Why does this market need your product?
	Unique Selling Points	**What are the unique selling points?** What makes your product different from existing products? Is your product new? What features does it have that will interest potential investors and buyers?
	Design and Prototype	**Sketch your prototype:** Students may use digital graphics or paper and pencil to sketch their product, or they may create a version of their prototype using recycled products. Students should label any key features.
	Marketing Strategy	**What is the marketing strategy?** How will you advertise your product? Create a slogan or tagline for your product.
	Pricing and Sales	**Pricing and sales considerations:** Determine a price based on your estimated costs. Create a plan for your sales—will you be in stores or online?
	Develop the Pitch	**Pitch the product:** Prepare your opening hook to gain the judges' interest. How will you explain your product and why there is a need for it in the marketplace? Capture all key points. Prepare a strong closing to ask for investors.
		Follow the provided timeline, which is typically a maximum of five minutes.

Step 5: **Conference With Your Entrepreneurs** 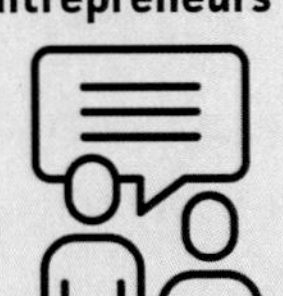	**Check-ins:** Hold conferences with your entrepreneurs to check in on their progress, provide timely feedback, and supply resources as needed. **Review deadlines:** Help to ensure that students are on track and ready for the final EDUPitch with the judges. You may choose to have students present to each other or to classes at other grade levels as they prepare for their final pitch.
Step 6: **Set Up the EDUPitch Event** 	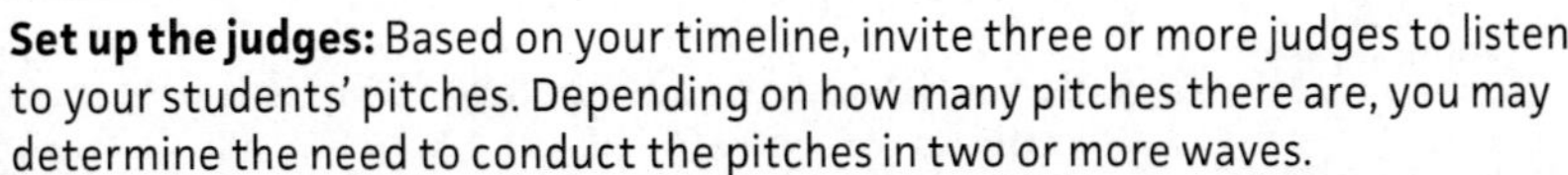 **Set up the judges:** Based on your timeline, invite three or more judges to listen to your students' pitches. Depending on how many pitches there are, you may determine the need to conduct the pitches in two or more waves. If conducting pitches over more than one day, you may look for different judges for each event. These can be school or district administrators, city officials, or representatives from area businesses.
Step 7: **Experience or Prizes?** 	**Will the experience be the reward?** Some EDUPitches are conducted with the idea that the experience and satisfaction that comes from participating in the project is the end goal. Other EDUPitch events have certificates that are awarded based on the voting by the judges or audience. These awards can include the following: • Most Creative • Best Pitch Hook • Best Protype • Award-Winning Slogan • Most Likely to Be in Demand Some EDUPitch events take place annually and solicit prize money from business sponsors or local organizations and provide oversized checks to the winners of each category.
Step 8: **EDUPitch Reflection** 	**What are the takeaways?** Provide your students with the opportunity to reflect on their EDUPitch experience: • What went well? What are they proud of? • What was the hardest part? • What would they do differently next time? • Has this experience motivated them to consider entrepreneurship or related fields such as design or marketing? As the teacher, pause for a reflection process so that you can remember any changes you would like to implement the next time you engage students in the process. Consider soliciting feedback from your students as they may be able to provide insights you have not considered on how to make improvements.

Image Source: Istock.com/Pavel Sevryukov

Community Passport: Taking Learning Into the Community!

<table>
<tr><td>STRATEGY
Community Passport
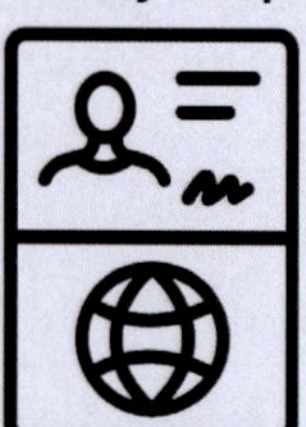</td><td>What: This strategy provides students with authentic hands-on learning experiences that are integrated in their community. The Community Passport extends learning beyond the classroom through real-world experiences.

Students have the chance to explore spaces and aspects of their community that they may not typically encounter. It will be important to offer a range of activities so that all students have ways to participate even if an adult is unavailable to take them to visit listed location options.

Bonus: Students have agency within this project to select which activities they would like to participate in or to suggest activities to be added to the passports. Completing activities listed in the passports helps students to deepen their connection to their community.</td></tr>
<tr><td>Step 1:
Identify Learning Objectives
</td><td>Integrate content objectives: How will the Community Passports project directly relate to your curriculum? Once identified, you can integrate your grade-level content standards into the tasks provided to your students from the passport activities.

Examples:
• Students can engage in math-related tasks at the community garden.
• They can look for a date and historical facts related to a local statue.
• Several tasks can incorporate writing, such as capturing an interview or listing what was observed at a specific location.</td></tr>
<tr><td>Step 2:
Create the Community Passport
</td><td>Begin by introducing the concept of a passport to your students. Explain it is a way to track where you have traveled and to indicate your nationality. You can explain the idea behind the Community Passport project and tell them the passports will identify them as members of your classroom community.

You can collaborate with your students on the formatting of the passport. You can determine a design for the cover together and provide space for each person to draw or insert a picture of themselves on the inside cover.

Having a physical passport can make it easier for students to bring it to different locations and will more closely mirror a real international passport.</td></tr>
<tr><td>Step 3:
Involve Parents and Community Members
</td><td>It takes a village! The Community Passport project is a great way to get parents, guardians, and community members involved in student learning.

Create a letter sharing the details of the project and asking for ideas from families or a willingness to participate from area businesses and local government. Highlight that students will be in locations with adult supervision.

You can follow up with a phone call or a quick visit to explain further and address any questions they may have. By involving more voices, you might come up with ideas that you had not considered.</td></tr>
</table>

Step 4: **Identify Community Locations and Tasks** 	**The places we'll go!** Once you have all of the ideas gathered for places to include in the Community Passport, start mapping out the potential tasks and their connection to your learning objectives. You may start to plan for any clues that will be left at specific locations if that is agreeable to the business or location.
Step 5: **Include Student Choice** 	**Do you have any ideas?** Provide an opportunity for students to share their own ideas for community engagement. You can also leave some blank pages in the passport labeled as "Student's Choice" so that each student has the option of adding in their own activities once the project gets started. Leaving some pages open encourages students' creativity and ownership of the project.
Step 6: **Develop Clues and Riddles or Location Objectives** 	**Now that I'm here:** Now that you have the locations identified and the involvement of parents or community members secured, it is time to map out what the students will do at each location. For some locations you may create clues or riddles for the students to solve based on where they are. **Examples:** • At the library, have the students go to the children's check-out desk and show their Community Passport. The librarian will give them an envelope with clues that lead them to different spaces in the library. • A riddle at the local park may lead the students to a plaque featuring the date the park was opened. You can have students write down the date and complete math tasks based on the numbers in the date. Another option is to have students complete tasks at various locations. **Examples:** • **Interview:** You may ask the students to conduct a brief interview with a business owner or an individual who works for the city. • **Public art:** Have the students find local artwork, such as a mural or statue, and then research the artist. They can take a picture, write a description, or draw their version of the art. • **Nature walk:** In any green space, the students can describe or draw some of the plants or animals they encounter. It will be important to have at least three activities that students can complete from their homes. Not all students may have an adult available to take them to other passport locations. **Examples:** • Have watercolors, markers, or colored pencils that students can check out in order to depict the houses or buildings on their street, thus creating a snapshot within the community. • Students can write a poem or a description of the sounds they hear just outside their windows. • Students can create an ad campaign for their community, capturing the elements and features that make it unique.

(Continued)

(Continued)

<table>
<tr><td>Step 7:
Set Clear Expectations and Guidelines
</td><td>Once the passports are ready, the next step is to provide a timeline and clear expectations for your students:
• Will they have one or two months to complete the passport, or will this be an activity that lasts throughout the school year, with students bringing in projects as they are completed?
• What is the expectation about the number of tasks to be completed? Will each student be asked to complete a minimum of three with any additional being optional?
• Make safety a top priority when exploring the community. Make sure students only visit locations with an adult present or, if this isn't possible, consider exploring the activities that can be done from home. Communicate with families about the project, review expectations, and emphasize the importance of safety.
• Explain how to approach community members during the tasks, including role-playing with the students introducing themselves and saying "Please" and "Thank you."
• Review options for recording their experiences.
• Discuss the purpose of the project—explain that this is a way for students to get to know their community better as well as meet some of the people who live and work there. Remind them it is not a competition but a way for each student to have new experiences while interacting with different elements within the community.</td></tr>
<tr><td>Step 8:
Incentives
</td><td>Get that stamp! If possible, bring in your passport or ask a well-traveled colleague if they would be willing to bring theirs to show the students how people receive stamps in their passports as they visit different countries. You can also find digital images of stamped passports to show students.
Provide any willing community partners with a stamp that they can use to mark the student's passport when the student visits their location.
For other activities, including the community-related ones completed at home, students can bring in their project to receive a passport stamp from you.</td></tr>
<tr><td>Step 9:
Reflection and Passport Presentations
</td><td>What did you learn? Leave a space in the passport for reflection or ask students to complete a separate reflection form. This should provide an opportunity for them to share their thoughts about the experiences they had while completing the Community Passport activities.
Provide opportunities for your students to share what they learned and how they engaged with their community.
Reflect on the project overall so that you can decide what went well and what you would like to do differently next time. Consider gathering feedback from the students, the families, and the community members who were involved.</td></tr>
</table>

Image Sources: Istock.com/Mariia Lov; Istock.com/LueratSatichob; Istock.com/krugli; Istock.com/spiralmedia

	**Service-Learning Opportunities**	This involves combining community service with classroom learning, integrating learning objectives, and fostering reflection. These opportunities enhance problem-solving, communication, collaboration, and leadership skills.

EmpowerED: Teaching Through a Cause

STRATEGY **EmpowerED** 	**What:** This strategy entails engaging students in learning through the integration of service-learning opportunities. Through collaboratively working with your students, you are able to provide them with meaningful ways to have a positive impact within their community. These projects involve both the minds and hearts of our students! Service-learning opportunities include a wide range of options that can connect with any content-area learning objectives. Students have the opportunity for real-world application of what they have been learning that extends far beyond the school's walls. **Bonus:** Students themselves report putting much more effort into projects that will be seen by others and have a real impact in the community. This is not surprising—few would be more motivated by completing a page in a workbook! These projects are highly engaging, build bridges within the community, and create bonds between the participants. They provide an authentic purpose for the students' work and will often have a lasting impact on them.
Step 1: **Know the Benefits** 	**Why would you do that?** It will be important to both know and be able to speak to the multiple benefits of integrating service learning into your instruction. When asked by any stakeholder, or when sharing your plans, you should be able to highlight the many reasons why you are providing this experience for your students. Some of the many benefits include the following: • Promotes critical thinking and problem-solving skills • Fosters connections between the classroom and real-world experiences within the community • Enhances student engagement and motivation for learning • Cultivates a sense of agency and empowerment • Provides meaningful reasons for collaboration and communication • Promotes ongoing responsibility for the welfare of the community • Students involved in these projects have high attendance rates and enhanced overall well-being

(Continued)

(Continued)

	There are many resources available to help teachers get started with service-learning projects and to provide some examples. These include the following: • youth.gov: "Service Learning" • illinoiscivics.org: "Service Learning Toolkit" • dropoutprevention.org: "Service Learning" • education.nationalgeographic.org: "Service Learning Toolkit"
Step 2: **Identify Learning Objectives** 	**Application of learning objectives:** The first step in planning a project is identifying the specific grade-level content standards that can be met through the service-learning project. The learning targets will serve as the foundation for the project itself. Having these objectives in mind from the start and sharing them with your students will help guide you as you determine how to address the problem or need within the community that you have identified.
Step 3: **Engage Students in Identifying Needs** 	**How can we help?** Collaborate with your students to identify needs within your community. You can discuss local issues and brainstorm potential projects. During this step you will focus on your students' areas of interest and their passions as well as on the potential ways to have an impact within the community. Once you have a few feasible ideas identified, talk through them with your class and collectively determine which project you would like to move forward for actioning.
Step 4: **Connect Your Content Objectives** 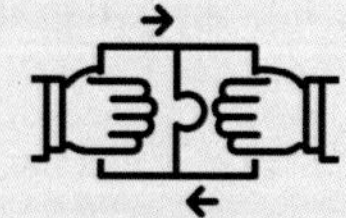	**How will we apply our learning?** Now that you have the problem or need you will address through the service-learning project, it is important to revisit the learning objectives with your students. The learning objectives, as well as the goals of the service-learning project, will be the foundation for your project design. All students should be able to speak to these components in order to effectively participate in the co-planning of the project.
Step 5: **Co-Plan the Project With Your Students** 	**Now what?** Once you have the need identified, have reviewed the learning targets, and have some initial thoughts as to how you can help, it is time to plan out the steps of the service-learning project. Collectively map out the action steps you will take and assign any roles. Once you have an overall project plan in place, you will want to identify initial timelines and steps needed to work with any community partners or organizations to put the project into place. Also be aware of any permissions that you may need to secure before moving forward with the project as planned. There are many ways to have an impact that can be done from school as well as other opportunitie where the students actually go out into the community.

Step 6: **Collaborate With Community Partners** 	**We have an idea:** Once you have a draft of the service-learning project outlined, you will need to reach out to any community organizations, local businesses, or individuals that can support the project. You will want to solicit feedback on your plans and collectively make adjustments as needed based on the information you receive. Examples of organizations you may be working with are area senior living centers, food banks, temporary housing facilities, or animal shelters.
Step 7: **Journal to Capture Pre-Project Mindset** 	**Gather your thoughts:** Provide your students with an opportunity to think through how they are feeling about the project. They can record their thoughts or feelings in a notebook or digital document. At the conclusion of the project, they will be able to go back and review their initial thoughts before the project and incorporate that into their overall reflection. Some students shared how they were nervous about not knowing how to interact with the seniors or that the project for the food pantry might not raise enough money. Some were anxious about speaking to people they didn't know or about sharing an announcement on the project over the school's intercom. Others just weren't sure what to expect. Having the opportunity to go back and read their own words once the project has ended helps students to reflect on their growth or what they learned through the experience. This helps them to build confidence as they move forward and face similar situations.
Step 8: **Implement the Project** 	**Let's do this!** Once everything is in place, it is time to guide your students through the implementation of the project. As much as possible, move to a co-collaborator role. Guide them through the steps in the project. Provide support and supervision as needed but allow your students to take the lead on the project. Ask them guiding questions or help them to determine any adjustments that may need to be made to the original plan as the project gets underway. If students have been assigned specific roles or aspects of the project, clarify the expectations and responsibilities for supporting the implementation.
Step 9: **Collect Feedback and Consider Sharing the Project** 	**Project impact:** Your students most likely will have an idea of the impact of their efforts and hard work, but when possible capture any feedback that is available so that they can hear firsthand that they truly had an impact. You may receive an email or letter that can be shared with your students that captures the impact of their work. You may have some statements shared with you verbally. It means a lot for you to share the feedback with your students. You may also consider ways to highlight the impact your students have had within the community. This can be a way to feature them within your school, which may encourage other classrooms or grade levels to take on projects of their own. This could also be an announcement or story in the local newspaper, or any newsletter put out by the organization itself. You may consider having some of the students in the role of journalists documenting the project and put together a slideshow or video that captures the planning, the implementation, and the impact of the EmpowerED experience.

(Continued)

(Continued)

Step 10: **Reflect on the Experience** 	**We did that!** Have your students return to the journal entries they wrote before the project. You may provide them with some guided reflection questions, such as the following: • What, if anything, surprised you about the experience? • As you reflect on your thoughts prior to the project and review them now that you have completed the experience, what are your reflections? • How does it feel to know you made a difference? • Do you think you will seek out other ways to help in the community? Reflect collectively as a class. This may include: • Asking if the learning objectives were met • Soliciting suggestions that they have for future service-learning projects • Guidance or tips from the students that you can share with future classes as they begin the planning process

Image Sources: Istock.com/fonikum and Istock.com/appleuzr

Grade - Level Band Possibilities for Service-Learning Projects

GRADE LEVEL	SAMPLE PROJECT IDEAS TO GET YOU STARTED!	
Kindergarten	**Caring for the Environment**	**Plant a garden:** Plant a garden in a schoolyard with native plants that will support the ecosystem by attracting beneficial insects such as butterflies, bees, and other pollinators. This can be done with the support of the PTO or local gardening groups.
	Appreciation for Community Helpers	**Say thank you!** This project can provide the kindergarten students with a meaningful opportunity to put their developing writing skills to work. Students can create cards or posters to thank the local community helpers.
1st–2nd Grade	**Recycling Project**	**Reduce, reuse, recycle!** Students can help to organize and launch a schoolwide recycling campaign. They can create posters, make sure all classrooms have a bin for recycling paper, and encourage students who bring lunch from home to use reusable containers.

GRADE LEVEL	SAMPLE PROJECT IDEAS TO GET YOU STARTED!	
	Pet Care Awareness	**Pet care reminders:** You can partner with an area animal shelter to provide students with the opportunity to design flyers, brochures, or videos that remind people about pet care tips. These can include special care based on changing weather conditions and safety and care during firework events.
3rd–4th Grade	**Community Clean Up**	**Caring for the community:** You can partner with your students and local government agencies to organize a community clean-up effort. Students can create flyers or make video clip announcements to encourage participation.
	Connect With Seniors	**Dear friend:** You can partner with an area senior living facility to have students create cards and room decorations, especially for those residents without many visitors. If possible, the students can go and visit as a culminating project to read books together or to perform a reader's theater.
5th–6th Grade	**Develop a Local Welcome Kit**	**Welcome to the neighborhood:** Your students can collaborate with the local chamber of commerce to design a new resident welcome kit. This can contain highlights of the area, typical weather across seasons, and recommendations for activities as the new residents start to learn their way around.
	Own a Book	**Books of their own:** Children who are currently in transitional housing may have limited access to their own books. You can collaborate with area housing providers to prepare book bags with books based on a child's age that they can keep with them. You may also include bookmarks made by the students, markers, pens, pencils, and notebooks.

Image Sources: Istock.com/bounward; Istock.com/fonikum; Istock.com/Artco; Istock.com/appleuzr

Building Bridges: Embracing Learning Partnerships

STRATEGY **Building Bridges** 	**What:** Including community partnerships within your instruction enriches the overall learning experience and provides your students with opportunities to learn more about different careers or cultures. Teachers may bring experts into the classroom, extend learning beyond the classroom to locations within the community, or leverage technology to connect with experts or other classrooms worldwide. **Bonus:** These bridged learning opportunities not only are highly engaging for students but also help prepare them for a rapidly changing and increasingly interconnected world.
Step 1: **Identify the Learning Objectives** 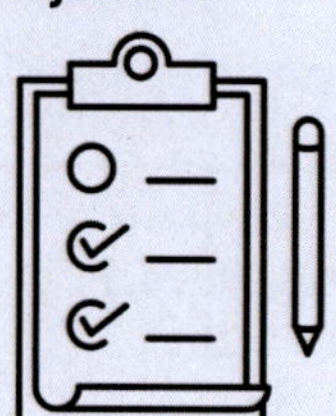	**Have a clear target:** Which standards will be addressed within the partnership being created? It will also be important to differentiate the experience to meet the needs of the diverse students in your classroom. Every Building Bridges engagement needs to have specific learning standards as the foundation for the experience.
Step 2: **Reach Out to Identify Opportunities** 	**Where are my partners?** The next step is to identify potential partners both within your local context and that you can collaborate with via virtual platforms. Once you have your learning targets identified, you can brainstorm possibilities. There are local businesses, government agencies, or organizations that may be open to a partnership. As you approach potential partners, it will be important that you share the learning objectives, potential ideas for your collaboration, and a general idea of what the scope of the partnership will be. You will also want to highlight any benefits to them for their participation, such as acknowledgment in a school or classroom newsletter. You should also consider potential partners who you can collaborate with virtually as well as the available resources for connecting with classrooms worldwide. Technology enables access to international guest speakers and learning partnerships. Global community resources include the following: • ePals Global Community (ages three to nineteen) • Flat Connections (Grades K–12) • GLOBE.gov • Flipgrid: GridPals • ditchthattextbook.com: virtual speakers and field trips

Step 3: **Develop Partnerships** 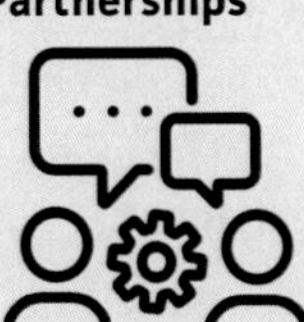	**Collaborate with potential partners:** After you have connected with your learning partners, collaborate on the learning objectives. Discuss how they can get involved in your students' learning by giving tours, providing guest speakers, or collaborating on a project with your class. The business owners, experts, or government agencies may provide ideas that you have not even considered! If you are working with teachers to connect your classrooms virtually, you can engage in collaborative planning by sharing documents to record your thoughts, the project timeline, and next steps.
Step 4: **Plan and Design Activities** 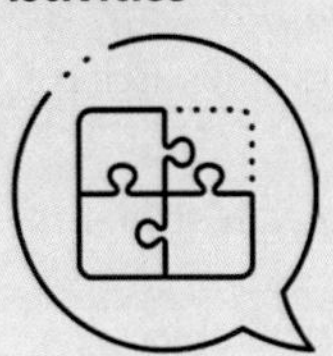	**What will this look like?** Finalize what the learning partnership will look like and specify how the learning objectives will be met through the interactions. Create a Building Bridges information hub that will organize all of the details of the project. This shared document should include specific dates and times for the activities and what the interaction will involve, and it can also be used to communicate with families about the project. Whenever possible, provide some hands-on learning activities for your students with as many real-world connections as possible. As the educator, you may need to make suggestions and work with your partners to move beyond a "sit-and-get" presentation.
Step 5: **Prepare Students** 	**Set up for success!** In order to make the most of the opportunity, you will need to set the stage for your students. Provide them with any background knowledge or terminology that will help to prepare them for the learning activity. Preview everything that will happen and explain the purpose and goals behind the activities. Review your classroom expectations for respect, safety, and active participation during the learning activity.
Step 6: **Implement Activity**  	**Let's learn already!** It is finally time for all of the collaboration and planning to pay off! Make sure that you review any checklists for the day of the learning partnership. Send any reminders to your community partners to make sure that everything is in place for the activity to run smoothly. You know that class that can be so talkative and engage in high-level conversations? Be prepared for them to be a bit more reserved or hesitant to participate. Jump in to guide their engagement and co-facilitate with the community partner to make the most of the activity.
Step 7: **Include Student Voice and Choice** 	**Not *too* planned:** Please remain flexible and go with the flow. Student questions or ideas may lead the activity in a different direction than planned. Will the learning objectives still be met? If so, then go with the flow! Offer opportunities for students to share their ideas, ask questions, or propose suggestions. Include interactive elements that will help partners gain insight into the students' understanding of the material being discussed.

(Continued)

(Continued)

Step 8: **Reflect and Assess** 	**What did you learn?** After any learning interaction, provide time for your students to reflect on what they learned and their overall reaction to the experience. Utilize the students' reflection to gain insights on both their proficiency with the academic learning targets and any personal growth or development. Be sure to gather feedback from the community partner too. This will help in your planning of future Building Bridges opportunities.
Step 9: **Share and Celebrate** 	**Way to go!** Share the details of the Building Bridges experience with your school community. Include pictures, quotes from both students and partners, and the learning outcomes. Highlight the successes and key takeaways that were noted by your students. Sharing the story may inspire other teachers to provide similar experiences for their students. Similarly, sharing information about the partnership within the community can help to encourage other potential partners to come forward for future opportunities.
Step 10: **Maintain Partnerships** 	**Let's stay in touch!** After the learning activity is over, find a way for your students to express their gratitude. This may involve drawing pictures, writing thank-you notes, or creating a poster with pictures that everyone can sign. Consider sharing occasional newsletters or updates from your school or class with your community partner to help maintain the bridge that you have created.

Grade-Level Band Possibilities for Building Bridges Projects

GRADE LEVEL	SAMPLE PROJECT IDEAS TO GET YOU STARTED!	
Kindergarten	**Healthy Foods**	**Partner with a local grocery store:** Visit a local store where students can learn more about making healthy food choices. They can partner with the store to write healthy messages on paper grocery bags or compose reminders to recycle.
	Virtual Zookeeper	**Behind-the-scenes access:** You can arrange for a virtual session with a zookeeper where students can learn more about a favorite animal and gain a glimpse into what is involved in caring for that animal. The students can create a book about what they have learned and a one-page flyer of facts that the zoo can have on display for visitors either in print or accessible through a QR code.

GRADE LEVEL	SAMPLE PROJECT IDEAS TO GET YOU STARTED!	
1st–2nd Grade	**Once Upon a Time . . .**	**Bridge with an author:** Connect with a local author or arrange for a meeting virtually. Provide your students with the opportunity to learn more about the writing process. Collaborate on an interactive learning opportunity that may include the author helping your class get started writing their own story.
	What's the Weather?	**Do I need an umbrella?** Arrange for a virtual visit with a meteorologist. Your students can learn more about what is involved in predicting the weather. Students can track the local weather and then start making predictions or forecasts of their own.
3rd–4th Grade	**City Hall**	**Is the mayor in?** You can build a bridge with your local government so students can learn more about city officials and their roles. Collaborate with city officials for an opportunity for your students to share their voices. This may involve providing feedback on a local park or ideas for an upcoming festival.
	Cultural Exchange	**Virtual pen pals:** You can leverage virtual meeting software to connect your class with students across the globe. They can teach each other some favorite games and traditions and exchange recipes.
5th–6th Grade	**Local Realtor**	**The power of word choice:** Partner with an area realtor who can share information about their profession and highlight the power of word choice. The realtor can look at house listings and explain why the words in them were chosen. The class can write some sample house descriptions with the agent and discuss which words would make the house more appealing to buyers and why. You can continue students' focus on word choice by having them select sentences from their books, exchange words in them for different words, and analyze the impact that their word choice had on the overall meaning.
	Local Museum	**Did you know?** Build a bridge with an area museum or connect with one virtually. Your learning activity can focus on a specific time in history. The curator can share more about how exhibits are developed and encourage students to ask questions about the history and stories behind the artifacts. Students can have the option to create advertising for an exhibit or to develop a true/false guessing game for museum visitors to play at specific exhibits.

Image Sources: Istock.com/LueratSatichob; Istock.com/GreenTana; Istock.com/appleuzr; Istock.com/Illustrator de la Monde

The Power of the Pen: Using Words to Build Connection

STRATEGY **The Power of the Pen** 	**What:** This strategy provides your students with an authentic reason to write. Using the Power of the Pen, students are the ones who have the opportunity to initiate a connection or to have their voices heard. Students can reach out to a variety of individuals, organizations, or businesses. The communication can take place through a number of formats, thus giving students choice. These activities support grade-level standards related to literacy and communication. **Bonus:** Students report that they enjoy the opportunity to write for a purpose. Several shared that even though the project was not necessarily for a grade, they were far more motivated because they knew it was actually going to be read by someone outside of their school. When provided the opportunity to reflect on their experiences, students acknowledged that their overall use of language and their writing skills grew through these projects. These skills led to more confidence and overall gains in their traditional schoolwork.
Step 1: **Build the Concept** 	**Share your voice!** Build your students' understanding of the concept by reviewing some of the many potential purposes an individual may have for initiating a connection through writing. These may include the following: • Expressing gratitude for help, support, a product, or a service • Providing thoughts on a product, service, or event, outlining strengths and identifying actions for improvement • Asking for information to learn more about an individual, product, or service • Asking for support with a project, for advice, or for feedback • Taking the time to congratulate someone on what they have achieved and including ways they may have inspired you It will be important to help your students understand that, with any communication that they initiate, there is a chance that they will never receive a response. While this may be disappointing, some individuals or companies receive an overwhelming amount of correspondence, making it challenging to respond to everyone that reaches out. This doesn't mean that the students' words were not received or not appreciated.
Step 2: **Safety and Policies First** 	**Prioritize safety!** When providing an opportunity for students to be in contact with individuals or entities outside of your known school community, it is of utmost importance that you protect students' safety and follow any and all school or board policies that apply to your project. • **Outline your project:** Identify the ways in which you will plan for student safety. These might include reviewing the need for safety with your students, not sharing full names, using the school address or email for all correspondence, and reviewing all content before it is sent to ensure personal information is not being shared. • **Seek administrative approval:** Share the specifics of the Power of the Pen activity that you would like your students to engage in with your administrator. Include your rationale, the learning standards being addressed, and your plan for safeguarding content and students' identities.

	• **Follow all guidelines:** In your meeting with your administrator, ask for all steps or safety measures you will need to follow in writing. These measures may include adhering to specific school board policies, such as getting written permission from parents, monitoring all replies that the students receive, and reviewing digital safety rules.
Step 3: **Identify the Audience and Purpose** 	**Who will I write and why?** Once the foundation is set, you will work with your students to identify both the audience and the purpose of the communication. **Together or individually?** Based on the meeting with your administrator, you may determine to have all students write to the same individual, organization, or business, with all communication coming directly from you without individual student identification. If permission is granted for individual students to identify their audience and purpose, you will need to follow all safety procedures and policies related to individual communication. **As a class:** You may decide as a class to reach out to a favorite author, an educational platform, or an area business. **As individuals:** You may ask your students to identify someone who inspires them or a company that they would like to reach out to in order to share their feedback.
Step 4: **Brainstorm** 	**What should this look like?** Once you have determined your audience and your purpose, you will brainstorm both the content and the format for the communication. **Content:** Clarify the purpose of your communication and outline a draft of the correspondence. This may include reviewing or introducing the parts of a letter. **Format:** Once you know both the audience and the content, you will determine the format. There are many possibilities! Some of the options include the following: • A handwritten letter that may include a drawing or painting • An email format for sharing correspondence • A Plus/Delta chart created as a class or by individuals (used to share positives about a product as well as suggestions for improvement) • Individual cards made by the students or one oversized card that all help to create • A book or graphic novel • Poetry highlighting the way they have been inspired by the audience • A sample ad campaign based on an existing or proposed product • Creating and sharing your own class or individual awards
Step 5: **Draft the Communication** 	**Create a draft:** Even when you have decided on the audience, the purpose, and the format, it can sometimes be challenging to get started. You may have an idea in your head of the final product but are stuck on how to get there. Encourage your students to just get started with a draft. Let them know that this is just a first attempt and that, once it is created, they will go back to review and make revisions before it is ready to send out.

(Continued)

(Continued)

Step 6: **Review and Revise** 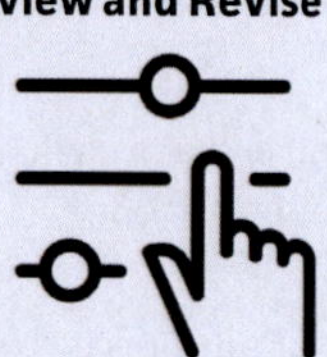	**How can I make this even better?** Guide your students through the revision process. You may do the following: • Model the revision process for them, sharing your thought process and showing how you can make changes. • You may provide or co-create a rubric or a checklist that can help guide students as they review the drafts of communication. • Hold individual conferences and guide students through the reflection and revision process. • Guide students to provide peer feedback by sharing what they like the most from another student's draft, asking questions on areas that seem unclear, or providing suggestions for consideration.
Step 7: **Finalize and Send** 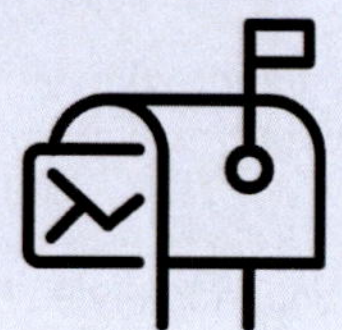	**It's ready to go!** Once the final version is ready to be sent, you may want to consider taking a picture of your students with any cards, posters, Plus/Delta charts, or artwork before they are sent. **Where does it go?** Show your students the process for locating the email addresses or physical addresses of where to send your correspondence. This will help to empower them with the tools they will need to continue to share their voices in the future. **Walk to the mailbox?** Depending on the proximity of the school to a mailbox, or the size of the correspondence being sent, you may consider a walk to a nearby mailbox where students can mail their letters. I (Anne) did this over five decades ago in kindergarten and can still remember our shared walk to the mailbox and my turn to put my letter into the box. These opportunities stay with our kids—thanks, Mrs. Melody! (A great name for a kindergarten teacher, right?)
Step 8: **Reflect and Share** 	**How did that go?** Take the time to review both as a class and individually about the main takeaways from the Power of the Pen activity: • What did the students enjoy about the project? • What, if anything, would they do differently next time? • What did they learn about themselves as a writer or a communicator? • Who might they want to reach out to next? **Share:** If a response is received, make sure to share it both with the class and with their families. If an individual letter or email is received, consider making copies for each student in the class to be able to have and share with their families. Circle back to your school administrator to show them some samples or pictures of the communication, share any responses received, and share some of the student reflections. You can share the project and any responses through a hallway bulletin board or a school newsletter.

Image Sources: Istock.com/Esra Sen Kula and Istock.com/RLT_Images

Peace One Day: Collaboration as a Global Community!

<table>
<tr><td>RESOURCE:
Peace One Day (POD)
</td><td> What: Peace One Day (POD) is a nonprofit organization founded by UK documentary filmmaker Jeremy Gilley in 1999 to inspire individuals, communities, and nations to collaborate and work toward peace through education, awareness, and action. In 2001, all member states of the United Nations (UN) unanimously adopted September 21 as the International Day of Peace. This is a self-sustaining, annual day of global unity and intercultural collaboration. In order to support this effort, POD provides several multimedia educational tools, programs, and opportunities for children and educators across the globe to become involved in these efforts. Free education resources are shared in multiple languages and provided at no cost to schools within all 193 UN member states. Bonus: POD provides educators with a number of ways to involve students in the global community. The organization shares ways to recognize and celebrate the International Day of Peace and offers suggestions for supporting students in powerful discussions on the actions they can take to bring peace to their classrooms and community. It also provides resources on antibullying, climate action, cyber peace, and antiracism. </td></tr>
<tr><td>Step 1:
Educator Account and Overview
</td><td> Get started! Visit peaceoneday.org to get started. You will be able to sign up for a free educator account. Once you have your account established, you will be able to explore the site and start to become familiar with the resources. Consider starting with a video introduction: You can view “Introduction to Peace One Day” on YouTube. This is a video introduction lasting just over five minutes that will give you the background on September 21 becoming the International Day of Peace. Film: On the POD website, you will find a feature-length documentary titled “The Day After Peace” for those who would like even more information. POD education: In this section of the website you will find a wide range of free educational resources including full lesson plans and examples from other students. You will find many lessons and activities that you can use in your classroom to involve your students in this global movement. “I commit”: This section highlights a few of the activities that are taking place around the world on September 21 to mark the day of peace. </td></tr>
<tr><td>Step 2:
Identify Activities
</td><td> Informed, inspired and engaged: The goal of POD is to raise awareness of actions we can take to help bring peace to our world and inspire other individuals to take action. Brainstorm: As you review the lessons and activities, consider which you would like to use to help your students connect with the global community. Your students can become involved in a wide range of lessons and activities to show their commitment to a more peaceful and sustainable world. </td></tr>
</table>

(Continued)

(Continued)

Step 3: **Mosquito in Your Ear** 	**Can I make a difference?** Quoting an African proverb, the Dalai Lama once said, "If you think you are too small to make a difference, you haven't spent the night with a mosquito." If students feel like they are too young to make a difference or to help support a cause in a meaningful way, this proverb serves as an excellent reminder of how even a small living creature can make a significant impact. Many of the POD activities and lessons highlight the various ways our students can make a difference in the world. The organization provides them with tools to take action and to encourage others to become involved.
Step 4: **Actioning POD Within Your Classroom or School** 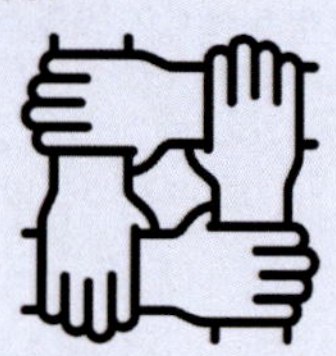	**Let's do this!** There are a number of ways that you can action POD in your classroom, grade level, content area, or school. **Collaborate with your students:** Introduce your students to the mission and goals of POD and share some of the many ways your class or school may want to become involved. Collaborate with your students on how to get started. **School leadership team:** If your school has a team of teachers or students who help to lead initiatives within your school, you and your students can introduce this team to POD and suggest ways that your whole school community can become involved.
Step 5: **Reflect and Next Steps** 	**Identifying impact:** After any POD lesson or activity, take the time to reflect with your students. These opportunities will help them to grow further through their involvement. You can use reflection questions such as the following: • What did peace mean to you before the project and what does it mean to you now? Has your understanding of peace changed? • How did participating in this project make you feel? • What role do you think kids can have in helping to create a more peaceful world? • What are the ways that you will continue to bring peace into our school, our classroom, your home, and your neighborhood? • What do you think we should do differently next time? • What projects would you like to see us do next? Do you have ideas for getting more people involved?

Image Sources: Istock.com/Fidan Babayeva and Istock.com/appleuzr

CHAPTER SUMMARY

Connecting to the community is a powerful skill that teachers should help students continue to develop every year. Community involvement is a significant force that can help students build lasting relationships and see the value of school-based learning. It can also help the community, which builds up students' sense of agency and confidence. Teachers play a large role in the growth of this skill, which consists of four key areas:

belonging, advocacy, social responsibility, and global community. These four areas can and must be interwoven with academic learning tasks to help students stay connected and see the value of working with and for the community.

Reflection Questions

1. Which of the four key areas of connecting to the community (belonging, advocacy, social responsibility, global community) need to be developed in your setting?
2. How does community-connected learning foster a sense of belonging among students, and how does this sense of belonging support their success both in and out of the classroom?
3. What role does advocacy play in building students' confidence? How can teachers support students in becoming advocates for themselves and others?
4. How can educators integrate an awareness of global community into their curriculum? Why is it important for students to understand their role in a larger world?
5. Reflect on a service-learning or community-based project that you can implement with your students. How will you structure the project to ensure it is both meaningful and connected to academic standards?

Connecting to All Learners

CHAPTER 6

> *"Everyone is unique and each experience is different."*
>
> **—Gloria Steinem**

Your Snapshot Guide

Connecting to All Learners

WHAT?	Our students come to us with a wide range of learning styles, backgrounds, and experiences. As educators, we know there is no one-size-fits-all approach to meeting the needs of the students in front of us. Knowing and valuing all of our students and their diverse needs means that we must be intentional with our planning and our approach to ensuring each student's success.
WHY?	When we seek to create learning environments that are respectful and affirming of all learners, we must give consideration to what actions we can take to be inclusive of all of our students. A commitment to engaging all learners requires reflection and intentionality.
HOW?	Taking into consideration the holistic learning needs of varying groups of students, combined with your knowledge of each individual student and the relationships you build with them, positions you for connecting your lessons to all learners.
BONUS	Establishing a classroom that operates from a strengths-based perspective of each student and the unwavering belief that every student can and will be successful creates a supportive environment and provides modeling for students of the importance of valuing and celebrating the differences of others.

ESSENTIAL CONNECTION SKILL: CONNECTING TO ALL LEARNERS

The strategies, resources, and instructional contexts provided throughout this book are all intended to help your students develop connection skills. As educators we must provide holistic instruction that values more than academic assessment outcomes, and we must also take the necessary steps to ensure that we are meeting the needs of all of the students in our classroom. We need to continue to grow in our ability to adjust and adapt our instruction in order to connect and engage all of our learners within our instruction. When we fail to recognize the strengths and needs of the students in front of us and do not make the intentional shifts they require, we leave some students behind and miss opportunities to have them fully engage and grow through accessible rigor within our lessons.

It is not uncommon to see students who do not connect with the planned instruction as delivered being targeted for repetitive instruction. Without even being aware, teachers may dilute the expectations for these students as the students spend time receiving formulaic direct instruction. On the other hand, those students who are deemed ready for extensions often have the opportunity to participate in authentic learning experiences, are provided with a choice of projects, or engage in interesting collaborative projects. But as McCarthy (2023) points out, this is like having those students who are struggling prepare to eat a white bread and lettuce sandwich while they watch the other students enjoy a savory banquet.

This book is about having all students at the savory banquet! All learners deserve to have opportunities to grow through projects, instructional strategies, and experiences that will help them to succeed not only academically but across the four ECS domains (Chapters 2–5). As an education system, when we provide these opportunities to only those students who are perceived as ready for an extension, we are imposing limits that will have a substantial impact on the majority of our students. The strategies and learning opportunities provided within the chapters of this book are intended for every one of your students as we believe they should all have the opportunity to see themselves as capable, to know and value their strengths, and to gain the critical thinking, communication, and collaboration skills they need to be successful in life.

Connecting our instruction to *all* learners requires us to recognize and embrace our students' differences and then to take intentional actions to create plans that will make the most of each individual's abilities, strengths, interests, and experiences. As teachers we are called upon to optimize the growth of all learners by accepting that every student has a different way of learning and responding to instruction (Gay, 2018; Tomlinson, 2014; Zwiers, 2024). Effective teachers know the needs of their students and then anticipate those needs within a specific lesson and plan to ensure that all students can be successful based on their distinct backgrounds, abilities, and interests.

THE IMPORTANCE OF CONNECTING TO ALL LEARNERS

Kofi Annan (1999), Nobel Prize winner and former secretary-general of the United Nations, is quoted as saying, "Education is the greatest equalizer of our time. It gives hope to the hopeless and creates chances for those without." This is only true if we meet each and every one of our students where they are and do it from a strengths-based foundation that sees diversity and unique learning lenses as assets rather than obstacles to overcome. The strategies and practices within this book will go a long way toward providing our students with equity by giving each of them a balance of both academic and personal growth. We are hoping that you will create this balance of mind and heart within your learning spaces and take any additional steps necessary to connect with all of your learners.

When we have students who are not engaged or who check out of our instruction because we are not meeting their needs, education loses its power and potential. Differentiating instruction with scaffolds, supports, and adaptability to meet the learning backgrounds, styles, and needs of our students is only the first step. Research consistently demonstrates that teachers' perceptions of marginalized students often leads to lowered expectations for these students as well as diminished confidence in the teachers' own ability to effectively instruct them (Rubie-Davies, 2010). Not only do we need to have the strategies and scaffolds in place to meet students' needs, at the core of everything we need to see them as capable and able to achieve and to be successful.

There are many well-intended educators that will make statements such as "My students aren't quite ready for that yet" or "My students just don't like to talk." As educators our perspective of our students can unintentionally build barriers and limit their potential for growth. It is our responsibility to hold high expectations for all of our learners and to hold on to the belief that they will get there. Students are incredibly perceptive and easily pick up on a teacher's frustration or dismissal of them. These subtle messages can then become a part of the students' perception of themselves and their abilities. When students encounter adults who become frustrated with them or give up before discovering alternative pathways that leverage their strengths, they may feel defeated.

Our words, actions, and body language are continually sending messages to our students. The terminology we use when referencing student groups also carries significant power and implicit messaging. For example, referring to students as *English language learners* (ELLs) has a deficit lens of "not yet English speakers." Using the more assets-based designation of *culturally and linguistically diverse* (CLD) students highlights the strength that these students have in knowing more than one language. Throughout this book we made intentional choices about the terms and language that we use based on the information that we had at the time of writing, but we acknowledge that these terms may shift and change over time. We would ask that you continue to be an advocate for all learners by using, and encouraging others to use, strengths-based language.

BUILDING A CONNECTION TO ALL LEARNERS WITHIN CONTENT INSTRUCTION

Adjusting your instruction to best meet the needs of all learners should be at the core of teaching in any classroom. By knowing your learners, leveraging their strengths and assets, and making the adjustments necessary to help them be successful in your lesson, you are working to close equity gaps. We know that a one-size-fits-all approach does not work, leaving many behind. If our only differentiation strategy is to place students into "ability groups," we may be limiting their opportunities and true potential for growth. When we make assumptions about what our students are ready for, or what they are capable of, we may be unintentionally confirming our beliefs by not giving them the chance to show us more.

The tools and strategies that follow are intended to help you differentiate your ECS-integrated lessons in ways that will provide access for all of your students. All of your learners should have experiences that allow them to deepen their connections to self, to gain the competencies needed to connect and collaborate with others, to develop connections with their learning, and to become connected within their communities. Our students grow through active participation in these ECS lessons. We need to do our best to make adaptations and adjustments that encourage all students to participate and feel safe to do so! The following strategies are intended to give you ways to involve all of your students.

CONNECTING WITH CULTURALLY AND LINGUISTICALLY DIVERSE LEARNERS

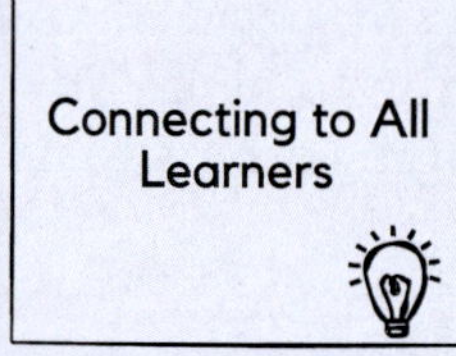	**Connecting With Culturally and Linguistically Diverse (CLD) Learners**	CLD learners come to us from a variety of cultural backgrounds and often know more than one language. These students can enrich classrooms with their unique perspectives and often require strategies that support language development.

CONNECTING STRATEGY OR SUPPORT	DESCRIPTION/EXAMPLE
Multimodal Representation	**More than words:** For those students who are adding English words into their language, presenting information in multiple ways can be helpful. Using visuals such as videos and pictures can help give background and build vocabulary association in English. **Total physical response (TPR):** This strategy includes the association of physical movements or gestures with words or phrases to help build vocabulary and explain concepts. **Show what you know:** Provide CLD learners with multiple ways to respond to and engage with the lesson. For those with initial proficiency in English, they may draw pictures or concepts to participate. Offer multiple ways for students to share their thinking.
Cultural Relevance	**Celebration of diversity:** Ensure all of the learners in your classroom can see themselves in the materials and examples that you use in your lessons. Support students in learning more about a wide range of ethnic and cultural backgrounds and contributions. **Open the door:** Invite and encourage students to share information, experiences, and traditions from their own cultural backgrounds. Create an atmosphere where all students are heard and diverse experiences and viewpoints are valued.

CONNECTING STRATEGY OR SUPPORT	DESCRIPTION/EXAMPLE
Language Scaffolds	**Building on from where you are:** Gather the information needed to have a clear understanding of the current English language development level of your CLD students. Providing students with visuals, word banks, sentence frames, or organizers may support their participation. Continue to celebrate effort, growth, and progress! **Language progression:** Look to tools such as the WIDA English Language Development Standards Framework (2020 edition). This resource is accessible online at no cost, and it can help you understand where students are in their development of English as well as how you can support them in getting to the next level.
Peer Language Partners	**We've got this:** You may consider establishing peer language partners to help support CLD students. These partnerships should take the students' personalities and potential interpersonal dynamics into consideration. It may be helpful to a CLD student to have an encouraging peer they can turn to. **Two-way partnership:** Non-CLD peers can support CLD students with English acquisition and participating in lessons, and the CLD students can share their ideas and perspectives. The CLD students can also share words and phrases from their first language with their partner.
Heritage Language	**Background and connections:** You can incorporate the use of heritage language into your lessons. Students can read passages or listen to a video in their first language, which can help provide the foundation for the lesson in English. **Building bridges:** Help students to participate in lesson activities with the use of translation tools and same-language peers, but ensure that CLD students also have opportunities to use English to continue their English language development. Use the supports necessary for CLD students to access lessons in English and to feel safe to make mistakes as they add English into their languages.
Multiple Entry Points	**Connect with every CLD learner:** CLD students have reported that some of their teachers didn't seem to realize that they were new to the country or acquiring a new language. While students often go through a "silent phase" when they are acclimating and internalizing information about a new language, it should not equate to being invisible in our classrooms. Check in with them, learn words and phrases from their heritage language, and ask how they are doing. **Which one works best for you?** Conferencing with your CLD students and offering them various participation options in the lesson will enable them to succeed in ways that they find comfortable. Students themselves may offer suggestions on which tools or supports will help them participate.

Image Sources: Istock.com/Premium Art; Istock.com/lushik; Istock.com/appleuzr; Istock.com/Lukman Hakim

CONNECTING WITH EXCEPTIONAL LEARNERS

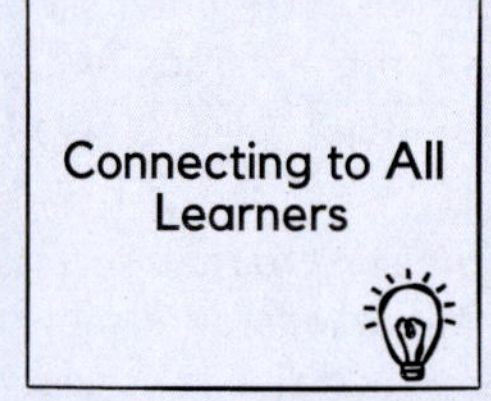	**Exceptional Learners**	Exceptional learners are students with a wide range of strengths and talents along with unique learning needs that may require specialized instruction, accommodations, or support services.

CONNECTING STRATEGY OR SUPPORT	DESCRIPTION/EXAMPLE
Collaboration	**Knowing goals and accommodations:** Any teacher working with a student who has received an individualized education program (IEP) or 504 plan should be familiar with both the student's goals and the accommodations that need to be in place in the learning environment. Take these into consideration as the foundational step for instructional planning. **Working together for student success:** Collaborating with the case managers for your exceptional learners is a key step to helping those learners be successful. Talking through the lesson and co-planning for both engagement and success will help you provide an inclusive experience.
Assistive Technology	**Setting up for success:** A wide range of available assistive technology (AT) tools can benefit students with diverse learning needs. These tools can range from low-tech graphic organizers or sensory tools to augmentative and alternative communication (AAC) devices that generate speech or closed captioning. Give consideration to any AT tools that your learners need to participate in your classroom and have those tools included in your plans and readily available during the lesson.
Strategic Groups	**Collaborative groupings:** Place students into collaborative groups by combining exceptional learners with their peers who do not have identified needs. This provides an opportunity for all students to learn from each other and to hear new perspectives. **Group roles:** Assign roles within the group based on each student's areas of strength and areas for growth. Ensure that all students have meaningful ways to participate.
Flexible Options	**Which would you like to do?** Providing exceptional learners with multiple ways to participate in a lesson or activity can help them select the option that fits them the best. Even with intentional planning, exceptional learners may prefer having a voice in how they will participate in the lesson. Having two or more options can help to provide students with ownership of learning.

CONNECTING STRATEGY OR SUPPORT	DESCRIPTION/EXAMPLE
Multiple Steps	**Break it down step by step:** Looking at the lesson or activity and breaking it down into smaller steps can help it to feel more manageable. You can provide checklists with visuals and directions to help exceptional learners navigate the lesson.
Checkpoints	**Let's check in!** Build in time to connect and check in with your exceptional students. You may want to ask the following: • **"Can you show me what you have done so far?"** This allows you to check progress and gain insight into current levels of understanding. It serves as a starting point for feedback and includes acknowledging their effort and work so far. • **"Which task has been the easiest? Which has been the most challenging?"** This is a quick way to see what the students feel are their strenghts and will help identify where they may need more support. • **"Do you remember when we discussed _______ strategy?"** This can help exceptional learners make connections with previous tools or strategies that helped them navigate earlier work.

Image Source: Istock.com/anttohoho

CONNECTING WITH INTROSPECTIVE LEARNERS

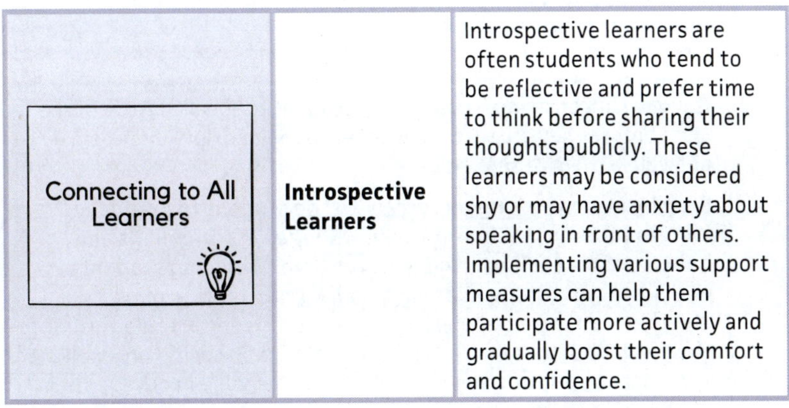

Connecting to All Learners	**Introspective Learners**	Introspective learners are often students who tend to be reflective and prefer time to think before sharing their thoughts publicly. These learners may be considered shy or may have anxiety about speaking in front of others. Implementing various support measures can help them participate more actively and gradually boost their comfort and confidence.

CONNECTING STRATEGY OR SUPPORT	DESCRIPTION/EXAMPLE
Safe Spaces	**Comfortable routines and environment:** Establish and follow consistent routines and procedures in your classroom. This predictability can help shy or anxious students feel more comfortable in your learning space. **Leave out the cold call:** Take away the stress of nonvoluntary sharing within your classroom. Provide dry erase boards so all students can have time to think and prepare their answers, and provide opportunities for sharing with a partner or in a small group.
Choice Partner	**Engagement support:** Work with your introspective learners to identify one or more classmates that they can partner with during different learning opportunities. Any choice partner should be empathetic, kind, and encouraging. The partner can be a safe entry into participation and can help their introspective peers feel more comfortable sharing ideas and more confident and open to sharing.
Journals	**Written expression:** Some learners who are hesitant to express themselves verbally, or who tend to share only a few ideas aloud, may feel more at ease sharing their thoughts through writing. **Use of journals:** Journals may be in the form of a physical notebook or kept in a digital format. With the student's permission, either the teacher or the student may share a journal entry with the class. This is a less direct but effective way to incorporate all voices in the classroom.
Participation Options	**Options for sharing:** Provide multiple ways for introspective or shy students to both participate and ask questions during a lesson. Work with students to provide them with options to ask questions, such as writing their question down to be shared by another student or read directly by the teacher. Provide options for sharing their thoughts, such as using a digital platform where they can post their thoughts or questions.
Gradual Participation	**Beyond sink or swim:** Forcing a shy student to speak in front of the class before they are ready can increase their anxiety, break trust, and cause them to shut down. **Step by step:** Working directly with the student to gradually increase their participation acknowledges their feelings and helps to grow their confidence over time. Providing students with opportunities to share in small, comfortable groups and then continue to build at a pace that is comfortable for them will help them feel less overwhelmed. Focusing on small successes and reflecting on these together will encourage their continued growth.

Image Source: Istock.com/Maksim Ankuda

CONNECTING WITH ENTHUSIASTIC LEARNERS

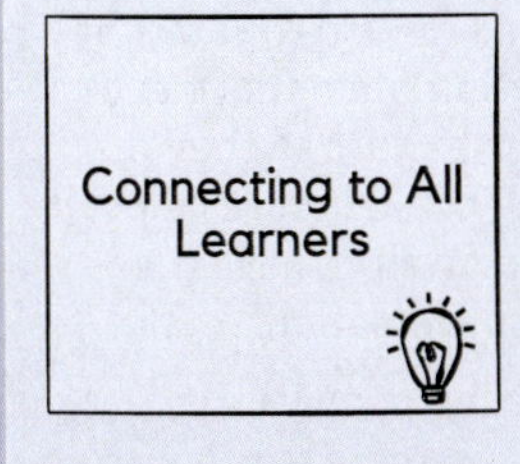	**Enthusiastic Learners**	Enthusiastic learners bring a high level of energy into the classroom and are always eager to participate. However, at times they may not realize that their enthusiasm can limit opportunities for others to contribute and so they might miss out on hearing the insights of their peers.

CONNECTING STRATEGY OR SUPPORT	DESCRIPTION/EXAMPLE
Structured Turns	**Turn-taking structures:** Provide a system where students share in a specific order or where a physical object is passed between group members as they each take their turn. Only the person holding the object may speak while the others listen or jot down notes to help them remember their ideas for when it is their turn to share.
Success Signals	**Nonverbal reminders:** Teachers can work with enthusiastic students individually to develop some coaching signals to help them remember and follow classroom norms. **On the down low:** These nonverbal cues can be a subtle way to support the success of students who have a tendency to shout out or miss what others are saying. You can touch your ear while looking at the student to remind them to listen, or hold up a finger as a signal for them to pause and wait their turn.
Creative Outlets	**Harnessing enthusiastic energy:** Provide eager participants with creative ways to harness their energy into productive tasks that are aligned with the goal of the lesson. **Learning recap:** For those students who are anxious to share, find positive ways to channel their energy to support the lesson. You may ask them to capture key points of the lesson and create a drawing or comic strip that summarizes those points. You may ask them to create a Google Slides deck that highlights the key takeaways.

(Continued)

(Continued)

Visual Counters 	**Slow your roll:** Structured turn-taking may not be the right fit for all group discussions. Having visual counters can help enthusiastic learners learn to pace out their participation. **One per turn:** Have students start the group discussion with three counters. Each time they participate in the discussion, they turn in a counter. If a student uses all of their turns toward the start of the discussion, they may experience frustration when they need to wait for all of the other students to take their turn so they can start over again with all three counters. This structure helps students to increase their active listening and wait to have the right opportunity to share throughout the conversation.
Leadership Roles 	**Can you help me?** Providing the enthusiastic learner with a leadership role or responsibility within the classroom may help to foster a sense of responsibility and to encourage self-control. **Possible roles:** Leadership roles may include the following: • A team leader for class projects to help ensure that everyone participates and the group stays on task • A technology director to help set up technology within the classroom or serve as the point person when classmates have tech-related issues • A materials manager who organizes and distributes materials to support overall classroom operations • A learning support coordinator who helps to connect students that need help with those who have strengths in that area

Image Sources: Istock.com/Alexey Yaremenko and Istock.com/appleuzr

CONNECTING WITH INFLUENTIAL LEARNERS

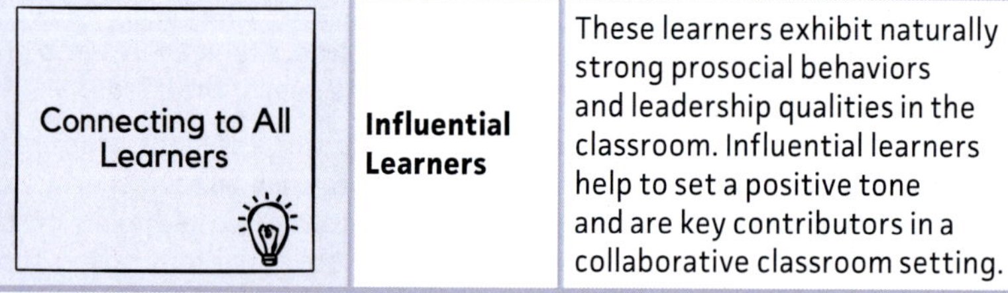

Connecting to All Learners	**Influential Learners**	These learners exhibit naturally strong prosocial behaviors and leadership qualities in the classroom. Influential learners help to set a positive tone and are key contributors in a collaborative classroom setting.

CONNECTING STRATEGY OR SUPPORT	DESCRIPTION/EXAMPLE
Goal Setting	**Still growing:** Even though these influential learners exhibit natural prosocial behaviors and strong leadership skills, it is our responsibility to continue their growth and development. **Set growth targets:** Conduct a conference with the influential learner that includes having them complete a self-assessment of strengths and target growth areas. For example, they may be highly creative and generate detailed project designs but then struggle with time and task management to see the project through. Collaborate on specific goals based on their reflections and your observations.
Peer Mentor	**Supportive partner:** Influential learners can guide less confident students through academic content or social situations, serving as a thought partner and providing encouragement. **Intentional support:** While we would hope that all students within our classrooms are supportive of each other, assigning influential learners as peer mentors can provide intentional support. Those students who are still adjusting to school or who may need extra help in a specific content area benefit from a peer mentor who can check in daily, provide study tips, and offer moral support.
Inclusion Champion	**"What would you like to add?"** Influential learners can be charged with ensuring that all students feel valued and included in classroom activities. This helps to grow their empathy and inclusivity skills. **Inclusion champions:** These students can be trained to observe closely and to include all learners by asking questions such as the following: • What do you think about this? • Do you have any ideas that you would like to add? • Can someone who hasn't spoken yet tell us what you think about the potential solution? • Does anyone have a different opinion or new idea to add?
Stretch Options	**Going beyond:** You should create opportunities for influential learners to continue to stretch and expand their current set of leadership and social skills. **Represent:** These students can be tasked with explaining a class project to the principal or making a request on behalf of the class. They may be able to record a presentation that will be shared with the school board or to share information with students in a lower grade level.
Mediators	**Let's work it out:** With training in basic conflict resolution and mediation skills, influential learners can help to resolve small peer conflicts under the supervision and guidance of an adult. **Multiple gains:** Peer mediators can help to maintain a positive, supportive classroom environment. Their participation as a mediator can help them to further develop their active listening skills, identify neutral problem statements, and lead others through a collaborative problem-solving process.

Image Source: Istock.com/fonikum

CHAPTER SUMMARY

Connecting to all learners is a vital skill that all teachers need to develop over a lifetime. Students differ greatly from year to year and class to class. The more engaged and connected students feel that you are with them, the more powerful their educational experiences. Teachers need to be able to connect to every type of student described in this chapter: culturally and linguistically diverse, exceptional, introspective, enthusiastic, and influential. Strategies to connect with all students must be interwoven with academic learning tasks to help students connect with each other and with their learning.

Reflection Questions

1. What are you already doing in your classrooms to connect your instruction to all learners?
2. What strategies or approaches from this chapter can you implement to create a classroom environment that supports all learners, particularly those who may be marginalized or perceived as different?
3. What shifts, if any, can you make to ensure that all students, regardless of their learning styles or backgrounds, feel valued and capable of succeeding in your classroom?
4. Which strategies from this chapter can you use to help you balance high expectations with the necessary support for students who may struggle with participation or engagement?
5. Which of the strategies suggested in this chapter do you plan to use in your setting, and what information do you plan to gather that will help you adapt what you do?

Conclusions and Next Steps

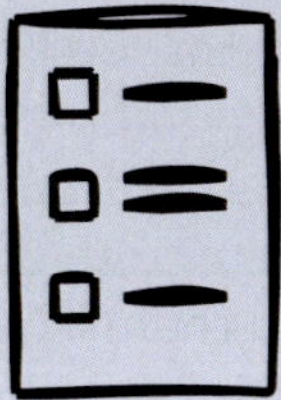

CHAPTER 7

> ***"Be assured that our individual actions, collectively, make a huge difference."***
>
> **—Jane Goodall**

In this chapter we will summarize our journey. We will revisit the key points discussed throughout the book and emphasize the reasons why all of this matters. Beyond that, we are here to support you in planning for your next steps and determining the ways that you can layer ECS into your instruction. Many of you already know the importance of interpersonal interactions and including SEL within instruction. This book will support you in enhancing and sustaining your efforts with purpose and intention. For those that are newer to these ideas, hopefully by now you can see the value of deliberately planning for and providing these opportunities for your students. Once you begin to see how your students engage during these lessons and see their resulting increase in self-confidence, their investment in learning, and their growing capacity for interpersonal interactions, we know that you will be hooked!

At a time when our society is dominated by the use of screens, it is crucial to remember that some of the most memorable and transformative educational experiences take place through direct interpersonal interactions. Lessons that integrate ECS within core content help our students to understand themselves and their strengths better. Intentional planning of experiences across all four domains of ECS empowers us to provide learning opportunities that develop our students' personal connections and allow them to see a vision for their learning, that grow their communication skills, and that prepare them to take an active role in creating a better future for themselves and their communities.

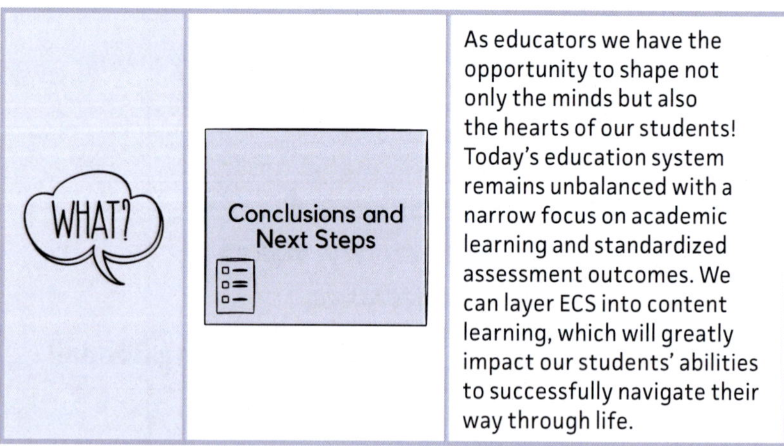

CONCLUSIONS AND NEXT STEPS: WHAT?

What Do You Wish for Your Students? 	**Years from now:** As you picture your current students years into the future, what do you envision and hope for them? We would guess you are not thinking about their standardized achievement outcomes and wishing they could have made larger percentile gains during their time with you. Most likely your vision for them involves their happiness and success as it relates to their relationships, careers, and place in the community. While most of us hold these hopes for our students' futures, many of us teach in systems that do not present enough time and opportunities in a structured and supportive environment for our students to develop the life skills they will need. We can all picture academically talented students that struggle to form relationships with their peers or to effectively share their ideas. The integration of ECS empowers us to better prepare our students with the skills and capacities they will need going forward.
Your Time as a Student 	**Travel back in time:** As we shared toward the beginning of the book, when we pause and think back to our own time in school, most of us do not immediately go to our state test scores or a final grade on a project. Those happiest memories from our school experiences tend to center around teachers that helped us to feel seen, heard, and valued in their classrooms. Others may remember projects that they completed on their own or with friends that were connected to the real world and had relevance beyond a worksheet or test. As an educator this is your opportunity to offer learning experiences that will not only foster personal and academic growth in your students but also have a lasting impact throughout their lives. You can "do your job" or be "*that* teacher"—the one who helps students to see themselves as capable and inspires them to envision their own bright future.
Seeking Balance 	**Skills to back confidence:** Please hear this loud and clear: We are not here to suggest that learning standards should not be front and center in our classrooms. Working toward mastery of grade-level standards is foundational for all students. It would not be useful if we rallied to develop confident individuals who are lacking in knowledge and skills. We are calling for a more balanced approach to the instruction taking place within our classrooms. The focus on academic achievement without consideration of developing ECS and competencies across all four domains, and the increasing amounts of time spent on screens, is not in our students' best interests. This is a call to action. As educators you can use the strategies and frameworks within this book to take a more balanced approach to the opportunities you are providing for the students entrusted to you. Confidence cannot be given but must be gained. Through ECS integration we can help each and every one of our students discover their strengths and continue to grow through meaningful interactions within our core content.

Image Source: Istock.com/spiralmedia

	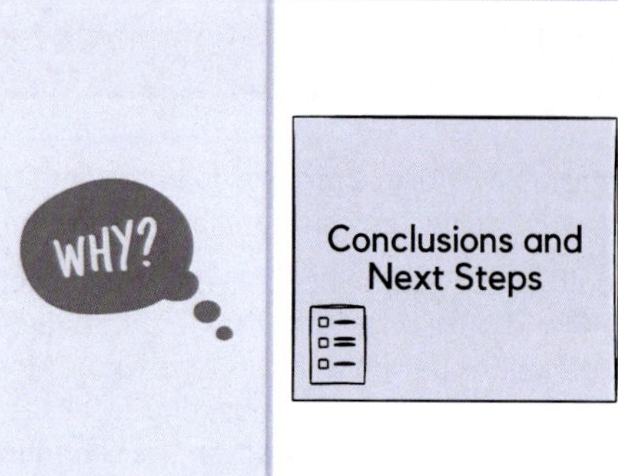	Research shows us that when students receive a more comprehensive education, focused on both academic and personal growth, they become more well-rounded individuals who are better prepared to navigate life's challenges. Long-term studies show that these individuals are more likely to have higher job and life satisfaction.

CONCLUSIONS AND NEXT STEPS: WHY?

Leveraging Mind and Heart 	**Emotion is integral to learning:** When students are stressed or anxious about making a mistake or view themselves as less capable than others, it greatly diminishes their capacity for learning. Delivering lessons directly from publisher-created resources may provide differentiated opportunities for learning the standards, but it will most often not build in consideration for students' feelings or their investment in their own learning. Layering strategies and tools that enhance learning through the inclusion of ECS helps our students to grow as confident individuals with prosocial behaviors and enhances their academic learning, thus providing greater student achievement outcomes. When students have multiple opportunities to learn with and from each other, their engagement increases, as does their depth of understanding and ownership of the content.
How Do I Fit In? 	**Perspective on learning:** As our student population and demographics continue to evolve, how often do we reflect and update our practices and resources to ensure that our instruction is connecting with all of our students? The structures and strategies across all four of the ECS domains help to ensure that the lessons we are providing are inclusive and responsive to all of our students. It helps each student to see themselves in our lessons and to find the relevance in what they are learning. The continued use of these tools also helps to build a supportive, welcoming community of learners who support each other. These spaces help students feel safe to take risks with their learning or with using new languages.

Preparing for the Unknown	
	**Ready for the challenges ahead:** None of us can know with certainty what opportunities and challenges we will encounter in the future. As educators we can enhance our instruction in ways that will help prepare our students to succeed in an ever-changing world. Integration of ECS helps us to nurture strong collaboration and communication skills in our students. It also instills a growth mindset and helps to develop flexible and critical thinking along with a lifelong desire to learn. Providing students with opportunities to explicitly learn about and apply these skills helps to effectively set them up for success in their future academic, personal, and professional endeavors. Chances are your students will not face a standardized assessment as adults, but they will be interacting with others in the real world, so we need to help them grow and develop in academics and across all four ECS domains!

Image Source: Istock.com/Yulia Sutyagina

		Throughout the book we have provided you with multiple strategies that you can use in the delivery of your core content to help your students develop skills and capacities across all four ECS domains. Regardless of the resources you use for core instruction, these strategies can be integrated into your lessons to enhance learning for all students.

CONCLUSIONS AND NEXT STEPS: HOW?

Intentional Planning	
	**Upcoming lessons and students' needs:** You are the expert at knowing both your content and the current needs of your students. Based on your observations and interactions with your students, which of the four ECS domains should you focus on first with your students? • **Chapter 2—"Connections to Self":** Students need to see themselves as capable, independent learners who persevere and think flexibly when facing challenges. • **Chapter 3—"Connections With Others":** Collaboration is observed as a challenge, students hold limited conversations, or not all students have developed connections with peers. • **Chapter 4—"Connections to Learning":** Limited or minimal effort is being made toward learning; students appear to lack motivation or ownership of their learning. • **Chapter 5—"Connections to Community":** Students cannot see the relevance of what they are learning or they struggle to make real-world connections.

(Continued)

(Continued)

Start Small 	**Take that first step:** Many of us are familiar with the quote "The journey of a thousand miles begins with a single step," which is attributed to Chinese philosopher Lao Tzu. This quote applies not only to our students but also to ourselves. It may feel challenging to know how or when to get started including ECS strategies and structures. And yes, we acknowledge that teachers already have many competing demands on them. (Please note the refusal to use the "too many things on our plate" analogy.) That being said, all of the reasons you have read up to this point supporting the need for ECS should make the case as to why this instruction is more than worth the effort. Try one strategy. One structure. Start slow and continue to build ECS into your core instruction, setting realistic goals along the way. Once you see the ways that your students respond and then observe their academic and personal growth, we are convinced you will be motivated to continue to plan for and try more of what we have shared. And yes, let's acknowledge that some of your lessons will not go as planned, which is also the case in academic learning. Reflect, regroup, and try again—your students are counting on you. In some cases, you may be one of the only adults explicitly working to help them grow as young people.
Find Your People 	**Collaborative planning and brainstorming:** A study by the Society of Behavioral Medicine found that working out with a partner or team doubled the time spent working out as compared to an individual attempting to work out on their own (Steinhilber, 2017). Similarly, you may have the best of intentions with adding ECS into your students' learning, but then for any number of reasons not develop the traction you intended. Having one or more colleagues that you can collaborate with will help all of you to set goals and plan how you can start building these opportunities together.

	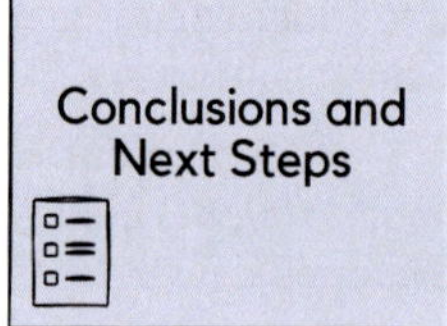	When ECS are embedded into lesson plans, it creates a more dynamic and supportive learning environment, which provides for both the cognitive and emotional development of our students. Another major bonus is that it helps to make learning more fun and rewarding for both students and teachers!

CONCLUSIONS AND NEXT STEPS: BONUS!

Student's Self-View 	**The greatest gift:** Recent research by psychology professors Robin and Orth substantiates what most of us believe: Self-esteem matters (Blouin, 2022). Individuals with higher levels of self-esteem tend to have more success at school or work, have better social relationships, exhibit less antisocial behavior, and exhibit higher levels of both mental and physical health. There is not the same correlation to attaining a specific cut score on an academic achievement test. We have the opportunity to help our students recognize their many strengths and appreciate and celebrate their unique differences while also valuing the perspectives of others. As educators we can overtly believe in each and every one of our students and then take intentional action steps to help them develop this same view of themselves. Too many students compare themselves to peers, typically using academic scores as a measuring stick, which results in many students falsely internalizing that they aren't as good or as capable as their peers. These limiting beliefs readily take hold and can result in students putting forth minimal effort into their learning or social relationships and can prevent them from pursuing opportunities in the future. Building all four domains of ECS into your instruction can help your students develop one of the greatest indicators of overall life success—self-confidence.
Increased Growth and Academic Achievement 	**Maximizing instruction:** Where did the day go? While some days in school can feel incredibly long, and the clock seems to always tick even slower during the final thirty minutes leading up to dismissal, our actual time with our students is limited. Overall, the months in school pass by quickly, and before we know it another school year has come and gone. As we shared early on, a stand-alone SEL lesson or class does not carry enough weight to have students develop, practice, and acquire key ECS skills. You have a unique opportunity to maximize the time you do have with your students. Integrating ECS into your content lessons will both augment students' academic learning and contribute to their personal growth and development.
Active Learning for Continued Growth 	**Beyond the workbook:** When students learn about skills and competencies in a class, often through watching a video and reflecting as a group, they may find value in what has been shared but have difficulty in applying it later within a classroom or real-world context. Developing and growing in important life skills such as effective communication, collaboration, flexible thinking, problem-solving, and valuing insights from others that are different from our own becomes easier with repeated opportunities to practice, interact, and reflect. Like any skill, attaining a level of competency takes practice and thoughtful reflection along the way to identify what is going well and how we can continue to improve.

(Continued)

(Continued)

	For myself (Anne), my golf game comes to mind. I take lessons (thank you, Carol!), watch video clips, read articles, and seek out the latest tech and practice gear to improve my game. While all of that information is important, consistent practice and application are needed for me to end up with fewer strokes on my scorecard. My golf game is still a work in progress! Building ECS across all four domains provides our students with a safe space, guidance, supportive feedback, and the reflection necessary to experience growth.
Developing "Human Skills" 	**Stronger soft skills in a tech-driven world:** In his book *A Whole New Mind,* Pink (2006) discussed the concept of the Master of Fine Arts (MFA) degree becoming the new Master of Business Administration (MBA) degree. He highlighted that the skills such as creativity, empathy, design, innovation, and the ability to connect emotionally with others are becoming increasingly crucial. However, he sees many of the technical tasks and analysis associated with an MBA becoming outsourced or automated. The importance of helping our students develop soft skills or "human skills" becomes even more important in an age when we are increasingly integrating the use of AI into schools and/or the workplace. While there is much value in the strategic and ethical use of AI tools, we need to value and develop the skills and competencies within our students that make us uniquely human. As we shared earlier, these are the qualities that employers are seeking in their new hires.
Growing Our Impact 	**Start a wave:** As an educator you have an opportunity to profoundly impact both the lives of your students and also the broader world. You have the capacity to equip young minds with the skills, competencies, and mindsets necessary to actively engage in societal issues. We can empower our students with critical thinking skills, problem-solving skills, and ethical reasoning that will allow them to analyze and help to address real-world issues. We can provide our students with opportunities to see how their actions can have a tangible impact within their community or beyond. Connecting learning to real-world application, combined with student reflection on their own values related to justice, equity, and compassion, prepares a future generation that will become powerful thinkers, leaders, and changemakers.
Wonder! 	**Contagious enthusiasm for learning:** According to the *Cambridge Dictionary* (Cambridge University Press, n.d.-c), wonder is defined as "a feeling of great surprise and admiration caused by seeing or experiencing something that is strange and new." Think back to recent lessons: Could you feel an actual charge of energy and excitement from your students? Were you feeling it too? Did you and your students wake up looking forward to coming to school? The use of the strategies and frameworks within this book not only helps to develop ECS in your students but also helps to foster curiosity, enhanced engagement, and wonder in your classroom. Students thrive and look forward to these opportunities, and, dare we say it, they even have fun while learning! This energy and enthusiasm is contagious, and you will feel it too.

Taking small steps to enhance instruction with the integration of these skills will create a spark. Don't miss it. Teachers navigate many dimensions throughout the school day, from teaching to management to responsibilities as a staff member, so it can be easy to have your mind on the next thing you have to do. Remain present and set everything else aside as you engage in these moments with your students.

These vibrant opportunities can inspire a lifelong love of learning, discovery, and growth for both students and teachers!

Image Source: Istock.com/fonikum

Thank you for taking your time to read through this book. We hope you are feeling inspired to build ECS into your instruction as a teacher, administrator, grade-level team, school, or district. We hope that you will step back and reflect on the type of education and learning experiences all students deserve. Collectively we have the potential to provide powerful experiences for our students that will help them to grow in academic learning and as young people. Please visit corwin.com to find the resources referenced in the book and to support you in your efforts toward building connections and integrating ECS into your students' learning. As we draw to a close, it is time to come full circle and to return to the quote that launched the book. As Aristotle knew centuries ago, "Educating the mind without educating the heart is no education at all."

Reflection Questions

1. As we circle back to the beginning of the book, how would you define the purpose of education? What is your role in achieving that purpose?
2. Which ECS domain do you think will have the most immediate impact on your students' learning? What is your rationale for selecting that domain?
3. How can the strategies and frameworks from this book connect with your teaching practices to impact your students? What are the next steps you can take to integrate ECS more intentionally into your instructional planning?
4. How can you measure the success of integrating ECS into your lessons? What signs will you look for to determine if your students are gaining these essential skills?
5. What steps can you take to encourage collaboration among colleagues or PLC teams to collectively enhance the development of ECS across your school or district?

References

Abi-Jaoude, E., Naylor, K. T., & Pignatiello, A. (2020). Smartphones, social media use and youth mental health. *Canadian Medical Association Journal*, *192*(6). https://doi.org/10.1503/cmaj.190434

Alhumaid, K. (2019). Four ways technology has negatively changed education. *Journal of Educational and Social Research*, *9*(4), 10–20. https://doi.org/10.2478/jesr-2019-0049

American Psychological Association. (n.d.). *Students experiencing low self-esteem or low perceptions of competence*. https://www.apa.org/ed/schools/primer/self-esteem

Annan, K. (1999). Foreword. In C. Bellamy, *The state of the world's children* (p. 4). UNICEF.

Ascione, L. (2022, August 29). *Students desperately need to see relevance in their learning*. eSchool News. https://www.eschoolnews.com/featured/2022/08/29/students-desperately-need-to-see-relevance-in-their-learning/

Astor, N. (2018). *My two countries*. Forgotten Books. (Original work published 1923)

Bartlett, J. (2022, August 8). *Navigating social identity in the classroom*. University of Illinois Chicago, Center for the Advancement of Teaching Excellence. https://teaching.uic.edu/cate-teaching-guides/inclusive-equity-minded-teaching-practices/navigating-social-identity-in-the-classroom/

Blouin, M. (2022, April 15). *Research review shows self-esteem has long-term benefits*. University of California, Davis. https://www.ucdavis.edu/curiosity/news/research-review-shows-self-esteem-has-long-term-benefits

Blue, J. (2022, February 10). *The role of relevance in learner engagement*. Cambridge University Press and Assessment. https://www.cambridge.org/elt/blog/2022/02/10/role-relevance-learner-engagement/

Braren, S. (2024, January 10). *Social connection and mental health*. Social Creatures. https://www.thesocialcreatures.org/thecreaturetimes/social-connection-loneliness-isolation-mental-cognitive-emotional-health

Caldwell, T. (2016). *Sound of thunder: A novel*. Open Road Integrated Media.

Cambridge University Press. (n.d.-a). Advocacy. *Cambridge dictionary*. https://dictionary.cambridge.org/dictionary/english/advocacy

Cambridge University Press. (n.d.-b). Belonging. *Cambridge dictionary*. https://dictionary.cambridge.org/dictionary/english/belonging

Cambridge University Press. (n.d.-c). Wonder. *Cambridge dictionary*. https://dictionary.cambridge.org/dictionary/english/wonder

Cardon, P. (2024, January 23). The future of work: New study finds AI makes employers value soft skills more. *Fast Company*. https://www.fastcompany.com/91012874/new-study-finds-ai-makes-employers-value-soft-skills-more

Collins, W. (2011). Global community. *Collins dictionary: Complete and unabridged*. https://www.collinsdictionary.com/dictionary/english/global-community

Courtney, T. (2024, May 17). *5 ways to increase elementary students' knowledge of other countries*. Edutopia. https://www.edutopia.org/article/helping-students-develop-awareness-other-countries

Davis, E. (2023, November 9). What students are saying about accountability at school. *The New York Times*. https://www.nytimes.com/2023/11/09/learning/what-students-are-saying-about-accountability-at-school.html

Duckworth, A. (2021, May 3). Why teamwork in class builds competence and confidence (opinion). *Education Week*. https://www.edweek.org/teaching-learning/opinion-why-teamwork-in-class-builds-competence-and-confidence/2021/02

Durlak, J. A., Weissberg, R. P., Dymnicki, A. B., Taylor, R. D., & Schellinger, K. B. (2011). The impact of enhancing students' social and emotional learning: A meta-analysis of school-based universal interventions. *Child Development*, 82(1), 405–432. https://doi.org/10.1111/j.1467-8624.2010.01564.x

Dweck, C. S. (2006). *Mindset: The new psychology of success*. Random House.

Eklund, K., Burns, M. K., Oyen, K., DeMarchena, S., & McCollom, E. M. (2020). Addressing chronic absenteeism in schools: A meta-analysis of evidence-based interventions. *School Psychology Review*, 51(1), 95–111. https://doi.org/10.1080/2372966x.2020.1789436

Farber, K., & Bishop, P. (2018). Service learning in the middle grades: Learning by doing and caring. *RMLE Online*, 41(2), 1–15. https://doi.org/10.1080/19404476.2017.1415600

Fortuna, L. R., Brown, I. C., Lewis Woods, G. G., & Porche, M. V. (2023). The impact of COVID-19 on anxiety disorders in youth. *Child and Adolescent Psychiatric Clinics of North America*, 32(3), 531–542. https://doi.org/10.1016/j.chc.2023.02.002

Gay, G. (2018). *Culturally responsive teaching: Theory, research, and practice*. Teachers College Press.

Gunawardena, M., Bishop, P., & Aviruppola, K. (2024). Personalized learning: The simple, the complicated, the complex and the chaotic. *Teaching and Teacher Education*, 139, Article 104429. https://doi.org/10.1016/j.tate.2023.104429

Gupta, A. (2019). Principles and practices of teaching English language learners. *International Education Studies*, 12(7), 49. https://doi.org/10.5539/ies.v12n7p49

Handel, D., & Hanushek, E. (2022). *U.S. school finance: Resources and outcomes*. National Bureau of Economic Research. https://doi.org/10.3386/w30769

Immordino-Yang, M. H. (2016). *Emotions, learning, and the brain: Exploring the educational implications of affective neuroscience*. W. W. Norton.

Juvonen, J., Lessard, L. M., Rastogi, R., Schacter, H. L., & Smith, D. S. (2019). Promoting social inclusion in educational settings: Challenges and opportunities. *Educational Psychologist*, 54(4), 250–270. https://doi.org/10.1080/00461520.2019.1655645

Kaspar, K. L., & Massey, S. L. (2022). Implementing social-emotional learning in the elementary classroom. *Early Childhood Education Journal*, 51(4), 641–650. https://doi.org/10.1007/s10643-022-01324-3

Kennedy, J. F. (1963). Presidential Papers, White House Central Files, Chronological File, Box 11, July 1963, 16–31.

Kuhlmann, J. (2024, January 29). *Shifting the thinking to learners with authentic voice and choice*. KnowledgeWorks. https://knowledgeworks.org/resources/shifting-thinking-authentic-student-voice-choice/

Langreo, L. (2023). This educator uses coding and SEL to make math more engaging. *Education Week*. https://www.edweek.org/teaching-learning/this-educator-uses-coding-and-sel-to-make-math-more-engaging/2023/11

Lin, J., & Guo, W. (2024). The research on risk factors for adolescents' mental health. *Behavioral Sciences*, 14(4), 263. https://doi.org/10.3390/bs14040263

Litman, J. A., & Jimerson, T. L. (2004). *Curiosity as a feeling of deprivation scale*. PsycTESTS Dataset. https://doi.org/10.1037/t62217-000

Loewenstein, G. (1994). Curiosity. In A. E. Kazdin (Ed.), *Encyclopedia of psychology* (Vol. 2, pp. 414–415). Oxford University Press https://doi.org/10.1037/10517-151

Lyons, S. (2021). The benefits of creating a diverse workforce. *Forbes* https://www.forbes.com/councils/forbescoachescouncil/2019/09/09/the-benefits-of-creating-a-diverse-workforce/

Marshall, M. (2022, October 5). *Benefits of problem-solving in the K–12 classroom*. Institute of Competition Sciences. https://www.competitionsciences.org/2022/10/05/benefits-of-problem-solving-in-the-k-12-classroom/

McCarthy, J. (2023, April 20). *Using differentiation to challenge all students*. Edutopia. https://www.edutopia.org/article/differentiation-challenge-all-students

McDaniel, B. T., & Radesky, J. S. (2018). Technoference: Longitudinal associations between parent technology use, parenting stress, and child behavior problems. *Pediatric Research*, *84*(2), 210–218. https://doi.org/10.1038/s41390-018-0052-6

Merod, A. (2024, April 4). *11% of teachers "very likely" to look for a new job as stress mounts*. K–12 Dive. https://www.k12dive.com/news/teacher-stress-pew-survey/712274/

Merriam-Webster. (n.d.-a). Curiousity. *Merriam-Webster dictionary*. https://www.merriam-webster.com/dictionary/curiosity

Merriam-Webster. (n.d.-b). Resilience. *Merriam-Webster dictionary*. https://www.merriam-webster.com/dictionary/resilience

Merriam-Webster. (n.d.-c). Self-esteem. *Merriam-Webster dictionary*. https://www.merriam-webster.com/dictionary/self-esteem

Merriam-Webster. (n.d.-d). Teamwork. *Merriam-Webster dictionary*. https://www.merriam-webster.com/dictionary/teamwork

Meuers, A. (2023, July 13). *What are the benefits of service-learning?* National Youth Leadership Council. https://nylc.org/what-are-the-benefits-of-service-learning/

Midwest Comprehensive Center. (2018, May). *Student goal setting: An evidence-based practice*. American Institutes for Research. https://files.eric.ed.gov/fulltext/ED589978.pdf

Moyano, N., Quilez-Robres, A., & Cortes Pascual, A. (2020). Self-esteem and motivation for learning in academic achievement: The mediating role of reasoning and verbal fluidity. *Sustainability*, *12*(14), 8768. https://doi.org//10.3390/su12145768

National Association of Colleges and Employers. (2023). *Job outlook 2024*. https://www.naceweb.org/docs/default-source/default-document-library/2023/publication/research-report/2024-nace-job-outlook.pdf

National Education Association. (2022). *Policy statements 2022–2023*. https://www.nea.org/resource-library/nea-policy-statements

National Math + Science Initiative. (2023, July 13). *The importance of creating valuable partnerships with the community*. https://www.nms.org/Resources/Newsroom/Blog/2023/July/The-Importance-of-Creating-Valuable-Partnerships.aspx

National Youth Leadership Council. (n.d.). https://nylc.org/#

Navab, S. (2022). *Educational technology in math classroom: Technology integration influence on math teaching and learning* [Dissertation, California State University]. Scholar Works. https://scholarworks.calstate.edu/concern/projects/8c97kz03g

Pane, J., Steiner, E., Baird, M., Hamilton, L., & Pane, J. (2017). *How does personalized learning affect student achievement?* Rand. https://doi.org/10.7249/rb9994

Paonessa, A. (2023). *Beyond the workbook: A study of service-learning through the lens of culturally and linguistically diverse students* [Dissertation, Concordia University]. ProQuest Dissertations & Theses Global.

Peace One Day. (n.d.). *What will you do to make peace on September 21?* Scholastic. https://www.scholastic.com/peaceoneday/index.html

Pearson. (2022). *Pearson skills outlook: Powerskills*. https://plc.pearson.com/en-GB/insights/pearson-skills-outlook-powerskills

Perera, R. M., & Dilliberti, M. K. (2023, September 21). *What does the research say about how to reduce student misbehaviors in schools?* Brookings Institution. https://www.brookings.edu/articles/what-does-the-research-say-about-how-to-reduce-student-misbehavior-in-schools/

Pink, D. H. (2006). *A whole new mind: Why right-brainers will rule the future*. Better Life Media.

Rubie-Davies, C. M. (2010). Teacher expectations and perceptions of student attributes: Is there a relationship? *British Journal of Educational Psychology*, *80*(1), 121–135. https://doi.org/10.1348/000709909x466334

Ryff, C. D. (2013). Psychological well-being revisited: Advances in the science and practice of eudaimonia. *Psychotherapy and Psychosomatics*, 83(1), 10–28. https://doi.org/10.1159/000353263

Schaps, E., Schaeffer, E. F., & McDonnell, S. N. (2001). What's right and wrong in character education today. *Education Week*. https://www.edweek.org/leadership/opinion-whats-right-and-wrong-in-character-education-today/2001/09

Shoshani, A., & Steinmetz, S. (2013). Positive psychology at school: A school-based intervention to promote adolescents' mental health and well-being. *Journal of Happiness Studies*, 15(6), 1289–1311. https://doi.org/10.1007/s10902-013-9476-1

Steinhilber, B. (2017, September 15). *Why it's easier to get fit in a group*. NBC News. https://www.nbcnews.com/better/health/why-you-should-work-out-crowd-ncna798936

Stott, A. (2018, December 21). *Teaching communication skills*. Edutopia. https://www.edutopia.org/article/teaching-communication-skills/

Strom, A., Lamb-Bell, M., & Raine, F. (2024, May 23). *What is belonging, and why does it matter in schools?* Getting Smart. https://www.gettingsmart.com/2024/05/23/what-is-belonging-and-why-does-it-matter-in-schools/

Sun, J., Anderson, R. C., Lin, T.-J., Morris, J. A., Miller, B. W., Ma, S., Thi Nguyen-Jahiel, K., & Scott, T. (2022). Children's engagement during collaborative learning and direct instruction through the lens of participant structure. *Contemporary Educational Psychology*, 69, Article 102061. https://doi.org/10.1016/j.cedpsych.2022.102061

Taylor, R. D., Oberle, E., Durlak, J. A., & Weissberg, R. P. (2017). Promoting positive youth development through school-based social and emotional learning interventions: A meta-analysis of follow-up effects. *Child Development*, 88(4), 1156–1171. https://doi.org/10.1111/cdev.12864

Thoreson, A. (2023, August 1). *3 health benefits of volunteering*. Mayo Clinic Health System. https://www.mayoclinichealthsystem.org/hometown-health/speaking-of-health/3-health-benefits-of-volunteering

Tomlinson, C. A. (2014). *The differentiated classroom: Responding to the needs of all learners*. ASCD.

Trzesniewski, K. H., Donnellan, M. B., & Robins, R. W. (2003). Stability of self-esteem across the life span. *Journal of Personality and Social Psychology*, 84(1), 205–220. https://doi.org/10.1037/0022-3514.84.1.205

Vygotsky, L. S. (1978). *Thought and language*. Massachusetts Institute of Technology.

Willis, J. (2011, April 14). *Big thinkers: Judy Willis on the science of learning*. Edutopia. https://www.edutopia.org/video/big-thinkers-judy-willis-science-learning/

Yannier, N., Hudson, S. E., Koedinger, K. R., Hirsh-Pasek, K., Golinkoff, R. M., Munakata, Y., Doebel, S., Schwartz, D. L., Deslauriers, L., McCarty, L., Callaghan, K., Theobald, E. J., Freeman, S., Cooper, K. M., & Brownell, S. E. (2021). Active learning: "Hands-on" meets "minds-on." *Science*, 374(6563), 26–30. https://doi.org/10.1126/science.abj9957

Zwiers, J. (2020). *The communication effect: How to enhance learning by building ideas and bridging information gaps*. Corwin.

Zwiers, J. (2024). *Overhauling learning for multilingual students: An approach for achieving pedagogical justice*. Corwin.

Index

Zeitfracht Medien GmbH
Ferdinand-Jühlke-Straße 7
99095 Erfurt, Deutschland
produktsicherheit@kolibri360.de